Miracle-Gro Complete Guide to
Trees & Shrubs

D1316763

Meredith® Books
Des Moines, Iowa

Miracle-Gro Complete Guide to Trees & Shrubs
Editor: Michael McKinley
Contributing Technical Editor: Christopher Starbuck
Copy Chief: Terri Fredrickson
Copy Editor: Kevin Cox
Publishing Operations Manager: Karen Schirm
Senior Editor, Asset and Information Management: Phillip Morgan
Edit and Design Production Coordinator: Mary Lee Gavin
Book Production Managers: Pam Kvitne,
    Marjorie J. Schenkelberg, Mark Weaver
Imaging Center Operator: Trena Rickels
Contributing Copy Editor: Nancy Ginzel
Contributing Proofreaders: Stephanie Petersen, Carolyn Peterson,
    Stan West
Contributing Map Illustrator: Jana Fothergill
Contributing Indexer: Bev Nightenhelser
Photo Coordinator: Susan Ferguson
Other Contributors: Janet Anderson, Debbie Reggenitter, Shelley Stewart,
    Brenda Witherspoon

Additional Editorial Services from Karen Watts/Books
Director: Karen Watts
Contributing Writer/Technical Editor: David Mellor
Designer: Carrie Cook
Photography: Jean Fogle, Georgianna Lane
Illustrator: Alison Lucerne

Meredith® Books
Executive Director, Editorial: Gregory H. Kayko
Executive Director, Design: Matt Strelecki
Managing Editor: Amy Tincher-Durik
Executive Director: Benjamin W. Allen
Senior Associate Design Director: Tom Wegner
Marketing Product Manager: Brent Wiersma

Executive Director, Marketing and New Business: Kevin Kacere
Director, Marketing and Publicity: Amy Nichols
Executive Director, Sales: Ken Zagor
Director, Operations: George A. Susral
Director, Production: Douglas M. Johnston
Business Director: Janice Croat

Senior Vice President: Karla Jeffries
Vice President and General Manager: Douglas J. Guendel

Meredith Publishing Group
President: Jack Griffin
Executive Vice President: Doug Olson

Meredith Publishing Group
President: Jack Griffin
Executive Vice President: Doug Olson

Meredith Corporation
Chairman of the Board: William T. Kerr
President and Chief Executive Officer: Stephen M. Lacy

In Memoriam: E.T. Meredith III (1933–2003)

If you would like more information on other Scotts products, call
800/225-2883 or visit us at: www.scotts.com

Copyright ©2008 The Scotts Miracle-Gro Company.

All rights reserved.
Printed in the United States of America.
Library of Congress Control Number: 2007933530
ISBN: 978-0-696-23459-0

Note to the Readers: Due to differing conditions, tools, and individual skills, Meredith Corporation assumes no responsibility for any damages, injuries suffered, or losses incurred as a result of following the information published in this book. Before beginning any project, review the instructions carefully, and if any doubts or questions remain, consult local experts or authorities. Because codes and regulations vary greatly, you always should check with authorities to ensure that your project complies with all applicable local codes and regulations. Always read and observe all of the safety precautions provided by manufacturers of any tools, equipment, or supplies, and follow all accepted safety procedures.

Photographers
Photographers credited may retain copyright © to the listed photographs.
L=Left, R=Right, C=Center, B=Bottom, T=Top

Contributing Photographer: Jerry Pavia

Cover photograph: Mark Turner, Botanica/Photolibary

Samuel Acosta: 55L2; S. Alexandrovna: 154ML; L. Allain, USDA/NRCS: 145TR, 145BR; Amygdala Imagery: 182BL; A. Andyz: 8B; Linda Armstrong: 122TR; Sam Aronov: 35TL; AtWaG/istockphoto: 199BR; AVTG/istockphoto: 104R; Thomas Barrat: 9T; K. Baskakov: 154BL, 156TL; Stacey Bates: 19BL; James Baty: 146TR; Peter Baxter: 187BL; Claude Beaubien: 154TR; Lance Bellers/istockphoto: 60B; Judith Bicking/istockphoto: 50; Debi Bishop/istockphoto: 194L; John Blanton: 25M; Vera Bogaerts: 44T, 69, 71, 148TR, 182BR; A. Bolbot: 147BL; D. Bomshtein: 97R; Pavel Bortel: 186TL; Mike Brake: 15B; Michael Braun/istockphoto: 176BL; Pat Breen, University of Oregon: 37BL; Inga Brennan/istockphoto: 52B; Kevin Britland: 18TR; Joy Brown: 33BL; 77B; Edward Brubaker/istockphoto: 164TL; Y. Brykaylo/istockphoto: 179BR; Tammy Bryngelson/istockphoto: 43B; Magdalena Bujak: 64TL; George Burba: 215; David Burrows: 31TL; Goran Caknazovic: 202TR; Sarah Calderbank: 45T; Joseph Calev: 38T; Carolyn Carpenter: 45B; Cheryl Casey: 21TR, 193BL; Bronson Chang: 33BR; Yanik Chauvin: 86T; Mindy Chung: 87T; Sergey Chushkin: 191R, 192TL; D. Ciprian-Florin: 184TR; Peter Clark: 74L; George Clerk/istockphoto: 145TL; H. D. Connelly: 32TL; G. Cooper, USDA/NRCS: 131ML, 139BR, 140BL, 192ML; Norma Cornes: 28B; Alan Crawford/istockphoto: 76; Cre8tive Images: 19TL; Amee Cross: 141MR; Jeff Dalton: 164BL; Susan Daniels/istockphoto: 180BR; A. Dewitt: 23TR; Peder Digre: 200TR; R. Dimitry: 95TL; Melissa Dockstragder: 12B; Lee Dowse/istockphoto: 164TR; Anna Dzondzva: 31TR; Inta Eihmane: 87M; S. Elena: 60T; Elena Eliusseeva: 57BR, 99TL; Peter Elvidge: 32BR; Paul Erickson/istockphoto: 174BL; N. Ernova: 85TR; Juan Gabriel Estey/istockphoto: 16B; Rafal Fabrykiewicz/istockphoto: 37MR; Derek Fell: 9B, 26B, 72B, 96B; Joy Fera: 34TR; FloridaStock: 111BR; Jean Fogle: 22T, 23TL, 23BL, 23BR, 28T, 30TL, 31BR, 34TMR, 36BR, 47BL, 48B, 96T, 140TL; Zig Folkman/istockphoto: 62; Douglas Freer: 99BR; Lori Froeb: 161BR; Gaffera/istockphoto: 70R; Markus Gaum: 7BL; Steve Geer/istockphoto: 165R; Andrea Gingervich/istockphoto: 144TR; S. Glebowski: 135BR; Alexandra Gleitz/istockphoto: 118TR; Gina Goforth: 36TR; 132TR; Lynn Graesling/istockphoto: 164BR; Ilya Gridnev: 73T; Igor Grochev: 72TR; Peter Grosch: 113BL; Tom Grundy: 122BL; Robert Gubbins: 84BL; D. Gudowicz: 165TL; U. Hammerich: 125BR; Robert Hands/istockphoto: 77; Susan Harris: 27ML, 27BL,85B,196L; D. Haug, USDA/NRCS: 137BR; Joshua Haviv: 29BL; Carly Rose Hennigan: 123BR; J. Henson, USDA/NRCS: 202BL; Greg Henry: 55TL; D. Herman, USDA/NRCS: 101L, 130TR, 141BL, 161TR; Patrick Hermans: 13B; Uschi Hering: 25TL; HFNG: 18B; Kathy Hicks/istockphoto: 172BR; Anja Hild/istockphoto: 183BR; Nancy Hixson: 200BR; David Hughes/istockphoto: 35B; ICImage/istockphoto: 181BR; iofoto: 24C, 150TR, 182TL; Kalina Iwaszko: 143TR; G. Japol: 49; T. Javarman: 114R; A. Jenson: 32BL; Bobby Johnson: 20BR; Adrian Jones: 85TL; Catherine Jones: 29BR; A. Kammell: 57BL; Andreas Kaspar/istockphoto: 63B; Raymond Kasprzak: 55BL; Gernot Katzer: 191BL; A. Kavram: 53T; KBRPhotos: 53M; Susan Kehoe: 111BL; Nancy Kennedy: 83T, 86BR; Sharon Kennedy: 25B; Phil Kestell: 34B; Anne Kitzman: 55R; Norvin Knight: 141TR; Ann Kosche: 7T; Milan Kryl: 154TL; Emin Kuliyev: 110L; Emilia Kun: 10B; Cheryl Kunde: 24TL; Lado Kutnar/istockphoto: 146ML; B. Kwieciszewski: 209BL; Georgiana Lane: 6B, 47TR, 53B, 61TL, 70L, 74B, 75T, 75B, 105BL, 105TR, 105MR, 105BR, 184L, 184BR, 185TL, 185ML, 185BL, 185TR, 185MR, 185BR, 186BL, 186TR, 186BR, 188 (all), 189 (all), 190 (all); Jill Lang: 13C; Jill Lang/istockphoto: 171BR; R.S. Laurinaviciene: 209BR; Arnold Lebrentz: 147BR; Michael Ledray: 150BR; R.R. Lee: 20BL; A. Lenora: 86BL; Jonathan Lenz/istockphoto: 78B; Michael Levy: 52T; Arturo Limon/istockphoto: 173TR; Matt Livey/istockphoto: 145BL; J. Loader/istockphoto: 18TL; Tina Lorien/istockphoto: 157BR; Diana Lundin: 38BL; Charles Lytton/istockphoto: 170BL; Stephen Mcsweeny: 94; A. Magee: 95B; William Mahnken: 21B; Diane Maire/istockphoto: 68B; S. Manderman: 10T, 41TR; X. Manfred: 14B; Hanna Mariah: 56L; MATS: 8T; V.J. Matthew: 21TM, 46, 107BR, 123BL; Doug Matthews: 91B; Dan Mensinger: 55L4; Christopher Messer/istockphoto: 37TL; Cheryl Meyer: 166TR; V. Mihaylovich: 33TR; R. Mohlenbrock, USDA/NRCS: 98L, 113BR, 144BL; Pamela Moore/istockphoto: 138BR; Patrick Morand: 132L; Gillian Mowbray: 13T; Keith Naylor: 82T; Luba Nel: 57T; Debbie Oetgen: 55L3; Martine Ogee: 92TR; Juan Olvido/istockphoto: 31BL; Stephen Orsillo: 73B;Y. Osadchy/istockphoto: 206ML; Regien Paassen: 32TR; J.Peterson, USDA/NRCS: 113TR, 131TL, 136TL, 140BR, 142BL; Michael Pettigrew/istockphoto: 194BR; Julie Phipps: 27BR; PhotoIntrigue: 151BL; M. Pieraccini: 166BL; Spinoute: 35R; S. Pixelman: 105TL; PKGraphics: 87B; Norman Pogson: 78T; Joy Prescott: 36TL; Puchan: 7BR 15TR, 15T; S. Radosavljevic/istockphoto: 179TR; Stephen Rees: 84BR; Diana Rich: 12T; Christina Richards/istockphoto: 51; C. Rochenthin, USDA/NRCS: 159TR; Ashok Rodriguez/istockphoto: 47TL; Lincoln Rogers: 174TL; I. Roman: 127BR; Jorge Salcedo: 40B; Michael Shake: 127L; Maree Statchel-Williamson: 77TR; Mario Savoia: 17TR; A. Schneider, USDA/NRCS: 122TL; Sally Scott/istockphoto: 157TR, 157MR; Patty Selb: 54T; P. Semenov: 99BL; K. Sergey: 24TR; D. Sharon: 20TR, 25TR, 182TR; Sierpniowa: 143MR; M. Skinner, USDA/NRCS: 131R; S. Shyder/istockphoto: 63T, 72L; Soundsnaps: 58; Kenneth Sponsier: 39TR; Dwight Smith: 21TL; Sue Smith: 48T; Wolfgang Staib: 143L; Ann Steer/istockphoto: 180L; Step2626: 110TR; Andrew Stepanov: 66TL; Linda Steward/istockphoto: 180TR; Nicola Stratford/istockphoto: 19BR; Valda Tappenden/istockphoto: 196TR; Oleg Tarasov: 34L; Ivan Tihelka: 37BR; N. Tiunov: 79T; Tomba/istockphoto: 90R; Marian Trotter/istockphoto: 64B, 65; Baldur Tryggvverson/istockphoto: 81; Maxim Tupikov/istockphoto: 175BR; Maurice van der Velden/istockphoto: 64TR; Liz Van Steenburgh: 15M; C. Vasilyevich: 155BL; E.R. Vasquez: 54B; Robert Venn: 6T, 14T; Z. Vladimirovich: 138BL; P. Vladimirovna: 19MR; Stas Volik: 42TL; Beverly Vycital/istockphoto: 36BL; Sally Wallis: 17TL, 29T, 68T; Bonnie Watton: 27T, 33TL, 34LMR,147TL, 202BR, 207TR; Robert Weber/istockphoto: 193TL; Rolf Weschke/istockphoto: 179L; A. Wheatley: 61B; Roger Whiteway/istockphoto: 42TR, 201BR; Brad Whitsitt: 30B; WizData, Inc.: 24B, 173BL; Yanfeisun: 117R; YinYang/istockphoto: 61TR, 67; YTHAC: 44B; Darell Young: 171L; B. Yurly: 91TL; Elena Zabel: 39BR.

All of us at Meredith® Books are dedicated to providing you with the information and ideas you need to enhance your home and garden. We welcome your comments and suggestions about this book. Write to us at:
    Meredith Corporation
    Meredith Gardening Books
    1716 Locust St.
    Des Moines, IA 50309-3023

Contents

CHAPTER 1

Trees and shrubs in your landscape

▲ Consider the beautiful, established trees in your landscape a priceless gift from the past. And remember to pay it forward by planting trees for the future.

That's a pretty good reason to plant them.

Generally homeowners plant for a variety of reasons, most of all for beauty. The aesthetic appeal of trees and shrubs—the heartening spring blooms, the brilliant fall color, the comforting stateliness of an old oak, the winter cheer of a broad spruce—all of this makes people great fans of trees and shrubs. Whether it's for foliage, form, or flowers, homeowners look to trees and shrubs to punctuate the landscape with perennial beauty that reflects the seasons, offering something wonderful to look forward to year after year.

As much as the house itself, trees and shrubs play a part in the architecture of the home landscape. They frame the scene, giving everything else a visual context. And they act as an anchor, providing a sense of history and long-term value to even the newest of homes. Yet relative to other plantings in the home landscape, trees and shrubs are expensive and require more effort to plant and maintain. So why plant them?

Why plant?

For starters the return on the cost and effort of planting trees and shrubs is greater than that of any other component of your landscape. Established, healthy trees increase the sale value of your property in ways the loveliest garden or the greenest lawn does not. The trees and shrubs you plant and care for have a significant dollar value in relation to the overall value of your property.

▲ Mountain ash, red maple, sugar maple, and paper birch offer welcome shade to this domestic landscape.

► Hydrangeas boost privacy along a picket fence.

Does the amazing burst of bloom on azaleas thrill you? Perhaps you are awed by the glossy green canopy of an ash that shades your home, or by the spare beauty of birches in winter. Maybe your favorite sight is a maple in your yard that announces, with fiery brilliance, the arrival of fall. Your particular taste in trees and shrubs determines what you want to plant and where you want to plant it, but choosing the best plants for your landscape—and caring for them properly—is strictly a practical matter. That's where this book comes in.

▲ Lush apple blossoms are a spring highlight.

How to use this book

Knowing why you should plant trees and shrubs is the first step toward planting them well. Whether you're planting for aesthetic or utilitarian reasons, you need to choose the best trees and shrubs for your purposes. What makes them best is only partly about your personal preferences—the rest is about what the plants need, including a good site and proper care.

The first chapter describes the qualities and characteristics of trees and shrubs, which will have a bearing on your choices. This includes what the trees and shrubs can do for you, such as providing shade or privacy, and the natural features of the plants, such as their foliage or flowers, shape, or seasonal interest.

The second chapter shows you how to assess your property in terms of what you have to work with—soil, space, and light, for instance—and what you want to accomplish. You learn the basics of choosing, transporting, and planting your new trees and shrubs.

The third chapter takes you through the basics of ongoing care for trees and shrubs, including pruning and seasonal protection. You

▲ A mass of coppery beech leaves form a brilliant autumn canopy.

also will learn about starting your own plants from cuttings, layering, and seeds.

The fourth chapter is a troubleshooting primer that shows you how to prevent, identify, and solve problems with pest bugs, disease, pest animals, and cultural issues that are common to many trees and shrubs.

The fifth chapter is an encyclopedia that gives specific information on more than 350 trees and shrubs, including which varieties have the best overall. It's a resource filled with wonderful prospects for planting in your landscape—the only problem being that you may end up wanting them all.

Trees and shrubs at work in your yard

The trees and shrubs in your landscape serve every day in so many ways. They make space more beautiful with foliage, blooms, or berries or more comfortable with shade, while adding curb appeal to your home. A well-thought-out landscape lends dimension and a feeling of permanence to any property. But however lovely a fine tree or shrub can be, or how welcome its shade, its real work goes unseen—and that work represents the plant's lasting value.

Cool and clean the air

If you're lucky enough to live in a place that features established, mature trees and shrubs, you already enjoy the benefit of their cooling and cleaning the air in your yard.

Trees and shrubs release water vapor through their foliage in a process called transpiration, which cools the air nearby by 5°F or more as the water evaporates. So the more trees and shrubs in your landscape, the cooler the overall atmosphere.

At the same time these plants are filtering pollutants from the air that are absorbed through their foliage. The leaves break down and metabolize chemicals, then release them into the air as purified water and oxygen.

And then there's photosynthesis, the process that replaces carbon dioxide in the air with fresh oxygen. The more trees and shrubs that are busy doing this good work in your landscape, the better for your immediate environment.

Wind control

A barrier of trees or shrubs can provide an effective source of wind control that can have a powerful impact on your comfort and enjoyment of your property, and even on

▲ Dense, vertical arborvitae form an effective visual screen and windbreak.

the temperature of your home in winter. Up to 30 percent of winter heat loss in the home is caused by direct, cold wind, so a windbreak barrier of evergreens or dense shrubs where your house faces that wind will help save significantly on home heating bills. Foundation shrubs add further insulation from fierce winter wind and cold. Conversely, shrubs or trees with an open form and light foliage that are strategically planted can help guide

WINDBREAK TREES AND SHRUBS

Arborvitae
Bayberry, northern
Burning bush
Cotoneaster
Escallonia
Grapeholly, Oregon
Hemlock, eastern
Holly, American
Holly, inkberry
Juniper, common
Mountain laurel
Peashrub, Siberian
Pine, white
Privet
Red cedar, eastern
Rhododendron, rosebay
Spruce, Colorado blue
Spruce, Norway
Yew, Japanese

▲ Shade trees and foundation shrubs help cool this house and yard in summer.

Trees and shrubs also help stabilize the soil with root systems that keep soil in place, and foliage and forms that reduce the impacts of wind and rain. Certain shrubs with strongly spreading root systems can solve erosion problems on slopes or other difficult sites in the landscape. Plant plenty of hardy, self-sufficient shrubs in these spots as access to them will be difficult.

Reduce noise

If you live on a busy street in close quarters with neighbors or near community activity areas such as a ballfield or playground, shrubs and trees are your best ally in muffling ambient noise. You'll always have some noise, but a dense row of shrubs or trees with thick foliage can greatly improve the situation. Plant at least two types of trees or shrubs to create a sound screen, and establish at least two rows of plantings to form an effective buffer. And plan for a barrier at least six feet tall because creating a visual barrier to the source of the noise will lessen your perception of the noise itself.

▲ The dappled shade of these mature trees creates a comfortable level of light in the yard.

welcome breezes to spots where they're most needed during hot summer months.

Improve your soil

Like a healthy lawn and other landscape plantings, trees and shrubs play an important role in maintaining good health of the soil. Roots and foliage support a complex underground ecosystem of beneficial microorganisms and insects that keep the soil healthy for the trees and shrubs, of course, but also for all growing things in the area.

Comfortable light

Besides screening for noise a series of trees or shrubs can influence the quality and quantity of light in your outdoor space. A tall, dense privet hedge, for instance, can block sun glare in summer, while a tree with loose and airy foliage, such as a serviceberry, can filter intense light to make your outdoor space more comfortable. Deciduous trees and shrubs offer the best of both worlds—full foliage that offers shade and lessens the intensity of light in the heat of summer, and access to the warmth of the sun in winter when leaves have fallen.

▲ Barberry and cotoneaster help stabilize a sloping landscape.

Compose your landscape

▲ A formal hedge delineates a portion of the landscape while trimmed shrubs add to the view.

Trees and shrubs are the framework of a landscape. If your home is nestled among a wide array of mature trees and shrubs, you can see the framework that already exists, defining your space, accentuating the architecture, and providing important shade, privacy, or aesthetic appeal. If your home is on a new property, the landscape is wide open to your choice of the trees and shrubs that will frame your property. Think of your landscape as a painting you are creating, and you are selecting the components that serve your practical and aesthetic goals. Every tree or shrub you plant in the beginning or add to your landscape over time helps you complete that picture, and should help you make the best, most enjoyable use of every inch of your property.

Frame space

Trees and shrubs can be as effective as a fence to frame your space, whether a dense row of evergreens along the street, a large oak in a far corner of the yard, or a small grove of crabapples at the sunny edge of the property. They can enclose your space or open it, depending on the way the plants are sited on the property. Beyond defining your landscape, trees and shrubs can delineate outdoor rooms, spaces to enjoy in particular ways, from relaxation to recreation to active gardening.

Encourage movement

Once you've determined the ways you'd like to use your landscape—which outdoor rooms you'd like to have—let trees and shrubs play a crucial role in encouraging people to move among the various rooms and also connect the landscape to your home. These plants can form entryways and walkways from space to space, and guide movement in a way that lets you get the most use from your landscape.

Establish views

Trees and shrubs with particular aesthetic appeal can serve as focal points in your landscape. A really distinctive plant can be the star of your backyard show, with other components of your landscape acting as the supporting cast. Imagine beautiful blooming crabapple planted exactly where you can see it from a kitchen window, a stand of handsome evergreens beautifying an otherwise stark winter view, or a stately oak or maple drawing your eye across the expanse of the landscape may suit your taste. Take advantage of the naturally commanding presence of trees and shrubs to establish wonderful views in your landscape.

HERE'S A TIP...

When deciding on a tree or shrub, run through these 10 practical considerations before making a selection:
1. Purpose of tree in your overall landscape
2. Size at maturity (height and width)
3. Rate of growth
4. Evergreen or deciduous
5. Native or nonnative
6. Seasonal interest
7. Overall form
8. Cultural requirements
9. Availability and expense
10. Unappealing characteristics to avoid

▲ The gentle arch of the canopy of a tree frames a lovely garden view.

Define boundaries
An enclosure can be as solid as a dense wall of evergreens or as suggestive as a single tree or shrub. Trees and shrubs in staggered groves contain space while retaining openness.

Block views
Trees and shrubs enhance a sense of privacy and screen unsightly views with their dense branches and foliage.

Develop corridors
The trunks and foliage of trees and shrubs direct traffic and link garden rooms. Passageways can be wide and sweeping, or narrow and intimate. They can be straight and direct, or meandering and full of mystery.

Set focal points
A tree or shrub with an unusual sculptural frame, or seasonal color, draws the eye first. Tall, narrow trees attract attention from a distance. Up close, such columnar trees direct the gaze skyward. Use focal points with care; too many can become confusing.

Enclose intimate rooms
Trees and shrubs make large properties more intimate by dividing space into rooms. The connections between rooms become points of interest, and they encourage movement and exploration.

Expand sense of space
Placing large, overscaled trees up close and smaller plants farther away increases the sense of depth and distance.

Frame views
Looking through a frame of trees sets off a view and magnifies its effect. Enhance the view out a window by framing it with a tree placed to one side.

Establish gateways
The trunks of trees and placement of shrubs establish gateways and portals between different parts of the yard. Examples are areas between the garden room and the corridor, the house and the yard, and the private backyard and the public front yard.

Spread canopies overhead
A canopy protects from hot sun and rain, and provides its own sense of enclosure and intimacy—a garden room without walls.

Extend the indoors out
Trees or large shrubs arching over both house and yard create transitional spaces that extend indoor rooms into the yard.

Express your style

No matter what your personal style, there are many ways to express it in your home landscape. There should be unity between the style of the landscape and the style of your home, of course— a dainty Victorian is unlikely to work with a spare, modern landscape; nor would a rustic country cottage blend well with a formal estate-style landscape. And there are limits that come with the scope of your space; a small lot is unable to sustain trees or shrubs planted on a grand scale, while small-scale plantings would be lost on a larger property.

There are no rules, though, that prevent you from planting what you love, whatever the style of your home or size of your property. The idea is to use trees and shrubs that you enjoy to highlight the qualities of your home and landscape; be practical and work with what you have, but plant to show who you really are. Choosing the right trees and shrubs for your space and style is key, but so is knowing how they work together in an overall landscape design.

Color, texture, shape, and line are the main elements of design—and trees and shrubs offer interesting and dramatic opportunities in creating a design.
● **Color** is the most accessible of all the design elements.

▲ An artful gardener composed this distinctive mix of color, shape, and texture.

▲ Trees and shrubs of different shapes and sizes inhabit gently curving beds that soften edges and draw the eye into the garden.

Who is unaffected by the vibrant red of a burning bush in fall, the lavender blooms on a jacaranda tree, or the lustrous deep green leaves and velvety white blooms of a magnolia? By all means indulge your attraction to color when choosing trees and shrubs for the landscape, but be careful to avoid color conflicts, as you would in any garden planning. Be courageous about color though. A single flame azalea says much less than a group of them. Trees and shrubs with color features beg to be planted in groups for effect if space allows.
● **Texture** is a star quality of many trees and shrubs as well. The texture of leaves, branches, bark, seeds—all are a part of your overall design palette. As with color, the more extraordinary the textural feature, the more you want to highlight the tree or shrub as an accent rather than letting it get lost among other plants. A Pacific madrone, for example, with its stunning, peeling cinnamon bark, simply insists on a site where the texture can be easily admired, without competition from surrounding plants.
● **Shape** further influences the perception and appreciation of an overall landscape. Trees and shrubs

GOING NATIVE

When trees or shrubs are referred to as "native," it means the plants are part of the natural evolution of the landscape in North America. There are many wonderful nonnative trees that have become popular in the home landscape, such as the Japanese pagoda tree or the kousa dogwood among many others. But cultivating a mix of plants in your yard, both native and nonnative, is the best way to support the local wildlife and ecology that depend on plant diversity and native resources for food and habitat.

► The informal style in this country garden is reflected in the graceful evergreen branches, clamorous shrubby roses, and profusion of perennials.

NATIVE SHRUBS FOR INFORMAL USES

Allspice, Carolina
Blueberry, highbush
Buckeye, bottlebrush
Fothergilla
Mountain laurel
Summersweet
Viburnum
Witch hazel, hybrid

▲ Mountain laurel is a favorite native shrub of the Eastern states.

that are pyramidal, columnar, upright, or spreading, for example, complement settings in particular ways. A neat line of tall, narrow Italian cypresses against a wall makes an elegant formal impression, while a weeping willow, with its full shape and pendulous branches, has a relaxed, natural appeal.

● **Line** describes the variety of visual connection points of the landscape composition, from the vertical lines of upright trees to the horizontal lines of level lawn or hardscape, to the curves of planting beds, or to a softly rounded shrub. These lines are created by the form and habit of trees and shrubs and by the plants' placement in the landscape.

Formal or informal?

A fairly standard set of qualities establishes a formal landscape style, including symmetry, paired plantings or other decorative elements, and geometric shapes such as circles, squares, rectangles, and triangles. A formal garden might feature a hedge of low, impeccably clipped boxwood bordering ornate, symmetrical patterns of plants, shrubs, or small trees.

Informal landscapes feature a gentler, less obvious balance, with odd-numbered groupings of plants, irregular patterns within groupings, and an easy way with the occasional specimen planting. While there seems to be little rigor to this approach, careful planning is involved nonetheless. Select and site trees and shrubs in an informal landscape as purposefully as in a formal setting. Some of the loveliest, most natural-seeming landscapes are also the most thoughtfully composed.

Strictly formal and pointedly informal approaches generally fail to mix well within a single landscape. But borrow ideas and inspiration from each to create a landscape that complements your home, makes the most of the features of your property, and expresses your personal style.

▲ The neatly cropped hedges and shrubs send a formal message that matches the architecture of this home.

SHRUBS FOR FORMAL HEDGES

Arborvitae
Barberry
Boxwood
Hemlock, Canadian
Holly
Privet
Rosemary
Yew

What do you want from your trees?

▲ Cedar of Lebanon is among the most elegant of all large trees.

● **Rounded trees** feature a regular shape that can suggest a formal style when planted in a row, or an informal approach when planted as a specimen or in an irregular group. Like others that are broad at the top, rounded trees need space to grow and achieve their ideal form.

● **Spreading trees** have a handsome reach that forms a canopy that provides shade with larger trees. These trees draw the eye out horizontally and work nicely to accentuate the horizontal line of a house or an expanse of lawn.

BEST BIG TREES

Ashes
Bald cypress
Beeches
Birches
Buckeye, yellow
Catalpa, northern
Cedar of Lebanon
Chestnut, American
Cottonwood
Dawn redwood
Elm, American
Fir, douglas
Fir, white
Ginkgo
Hemlock, Canadian
Hickories
Juniper, Chinese
Katsura tree
Larches
Lindens
Magnolia, southern
Maples (red, silver, sugar)
Oaks
Pagoda tree, Japanese
Plane tree, London
Sweet gum
Sycamore
Tulip tree
Walnut, black
Willow, golden weeping
Zelkova, Japanese

When it comes to trees, shape and size have a practical impact. For example, the more natural, informally shaped trees, including those that are rounded, spreading, or weeping, provide the most shade when mature. Columnar trees give a formal impression, as do oval and pyramidal trees. Size is an obvious practical consideration, as a tree that grows to 100 feet over a lifetime may be majestic but unsuitable for a modest-size landscape. Conversely small trees, dwarf forms, or single specimen plantings may be wasted in a large landscape. Understanding the shape and size of trees in relation to your landscape will help you make good plant and site selections.

Shapes of trees

Though there are subgroups and subtleties of shape that go beyond the basic classifications below, these will help you begin to assess what shapes appeal to you and which will be most useful—from both practical and aesthetic standpoints. Also note that many standard shaped trees are available in weeping or columnar varieties, which gives you even more options in your landscape.

● **Open irregular trees** grow up and out and have an uneven, asymmetrical form.

● **Oval trees** have a narrower rounded form and are also quite effective in even rows or informal groups.

FAVORITE WEEPING TREES

Beech, European weeping
Cherry, weeping Higan
Cherry, weeping Yoshino
Hemlock, Canadian weeping
Katsura tree, weeping
Maple, cutleaf Japanese
Snowbell, Japanese weeping
Spruce, Serbian weeping
Willow, weeping

▲ The weeping willow is a familiar favorite.

▲ The beech tree is one of the great large trees in the American landscape.

- **Weeping trees** are showstoppers with their graceful, pendulous branches sweeping down toward the ground. They are particularly effective as specimen plantings.

- **Columnar trees** are upright and narrow and best planted in a row to give the impression of a green wall. Columnar trees are quite distinctive and are often used in a formal landscape.

Size matters

When you daydream about the mature trees you'd like to see growing in your yard someday, they're usually big and grand, like an oak or an elm. But fact is that not every property can handle even one large tree, much less several. And while a large property can easily accommodate big trees, small trees are often unsuited to the space.

Take into account the size of a tree at maturity—both height and spread—when you are planning your landscape. Large and small trees need an appropriate amount of space to grow to full size without crowding other plantings, obstructing views, or coming too close to the house or other structures, including overhead power lines or driveways.

Small trees, which reach 15 to 30 feet at maturity, generally can be planted as close as 5 to 10 feet from a home or other structures. They present little threat to overhead power lines.

Medium trees, which are 30 to 50 feet at maturity, should be planted at least 20 feet from a house and have a clearance of 10 feet of unplanted area around the planting site.

Large trees, which are 50 feet or taller at full size, need to be planted at least 35 feet from a house, to give them plenty of open space to grow up and out, as well as to establish a healthy root system below the ground. A large tree should have a clearance of 15 feet of unplanted area from the planting site.

▲ The medium-size saucer magnolia brightens the landscape in early spring.

- **Vase-shape** trees take an opposite form to pyramidal trees, with branches growing up from a midpoint of the trunk into a V-shape that opens up to the sky.

- **Pyramidal trees** come to somewhat of a point at the top, and taper down evenly toward the ground. Many evergreens and certain deciduous trees take the pyramidal form, which tends to lift the eye upward.

BEST SMALL TREES

Almond, flowering
Apple
Buckeye, red
Chaste tree
Cherry, flowering
Crabapple, flowering
Crape myrtle
Dogwood, flowering
Fringe trees
Goldenchain tree
Harry Lauder's walking stick
Hawthorns
Magnolias (star, sweet bay)
Maples (amur, Japanese, paperbark)
Olive, European
Peach
Pear, common
Redbud, eastern
Serviceberries
Smoketree
Snowbell, Japanese
Stewartias

▲ In autumn, the color change of a single small tree creates a big impact.

Shade and privacy

▲ River birch trees grow into a quick screen with great visual appeal.

The two most functional purposes of trees in the landscape are shade and privacy. Shade trees offer more than merely pleasant respite from the heat of the sun; when strategically planted they can contribute to cooling a home from 5 to 10 degrees. And trees planted for privacy can block unsightly views, muffle noise, and help block intense light or wind. Planting trees wisely can measurably increase both the enjoyment and the value of your home.

A shade tree is one with enough size and spread at maturity to block direct sunlight. Obviously large trees provide the most shade, but small trees can work for small spaces. A small- to moderate-size tree with a spreading canopy can supply more than enough shade for a backyard patio, while a large shade tree can cool a significant portion of a house or yard. You need only to decide where you need shade and how much space you have to work with to find an appropriate shade tree for your landscape.

A shade tree can be a spectacular specimen planting, such as a Southern magnolia, or a dependable tree, such as a beech or an oak. Most shade trees are deciduous, which is doubly helpful because when the leaves are gone, the sun is able to warm the same area in winter that the trees cooled in summer.

If you're planting for shade, know where the sun hits your home at various parts of the day and over the course of the warmer seasons to plant most effectively. And if you're really anxious to enjoy the benefits of a shade tree, consider planting a mature tree. While it's more expensive, you can save yourself 10 years of waiting to enjoy its cool bounty.

Plant for privacy

Most of the same trees you can plant for windbreak or screen provide privacy as well. They can block views of your home or property from the outside as well as hide unsightly views and muffle neighborhood noise from the inside.

Look carefully at your property from all of the outside views as well as from the yard and from inside the house. You can address the areas you would like to make more private in various ways. Rows or hedges of evergreens and dense shrubs provide year-round, continuous privacy, but certain trees can offer a similar benefit when planted strategically. For example, although poplars are deciduous, their columnar form allows them to be planted close together to form an effective privacy screen, even after the leaves drop in autumn.

▲ A hedge of dense arborvitae makes a great screen for noise and privacy.

FAST-GROWING TREES

Alder, European black
Ash, green
Bald cypress
Birches
Box elder
Catalpa, Northern
Cottonwood
Cypress, leyland
Dawn redwood
Goldenraintree
Honeylocust, thornless
Maple (red, silver)
Pine, eastern white
Poplars
Quaking aspen
Spruce, Norway
Sweet gum
Sycamore
Tulip tree
Willows
Zelkova, Japanese

BEST TREES FOR PRIVACY

Arborvitae
Cedar, eastern red
Cypress, leyland
Dawn redwood
Fir, douglas
Fir, white
Hemlock, Canadian
Junipers
Pines
Poplar, Lombardy
Spruces

▲ The black locust grows quickly into an effective shade tree in the home landscape.

Consider how much privacy you really need. If you require something less than an estate-style wall of dense and impenetrable evergreens, staggered rows of plantings might give you the privacy you want without the feeling of being strictly closed in. Individual trees strategically planted at various intervals around a property can combine to be as effective a privacy screen as a dense row of evergreens. Even the trunks and limbs of a stand of river birches might offer all the screen you need, even in winter.

BEST SHADE TREES

Ashes
Beeches
Buckeyes
Catalpa, northern
Cedar of Lebanon
Dogwood, flowering
Eucalyptus
Honeylocust, thornless
Horsechestnut, common
Katsura tree
Maples (red, sugar)
Oaks (Northern red, white)
Plane tree, London
Sweet gum
Tulip tree
Yellowwood
Zelkova, Japanese

▲ When this old oak leafs out, it will shade the entire front yard.

▲ This young tulip tree will grow relatively quickly into a specimen that will provide shade for generations to come.

▲ A single weeping Canadian hemlock can block an unwanted view.

Exciting foliage

The shape and size of the foliage determines a tree's density and ability to provide shade or screening. The texture can be smooth, glossy, leathery, or ridged and rough. And the leaves or needles can stay on the tree throughout the year, making it an evergreen, or drop every autumn and emerge anew in spring, making it a deciduous tree.

Finally leaves can be green, yellow, or red, or they can be variegated, with pronounced stripes or irregular streaks of color. Some trees have foliage that has it all, such as the box

▲ Sycamore maple (*Acer pseudoplatanus*) features handsome spring and summer foliage.

▲ The flowers and cones of a Lawson's false cypress prove fascinating.

Gardeners tend to be most enthusiastic about autumn foliage, as fall is when many trees put on their color extravaganza. But the color, shape, and texture of new foliage, summer foliage, and evergreen foliage in winter round out the whole beautiful picture of trees and their leaves and needles.

In the most basic of categories, trees can bear leaves that are known as simple—which are whole, undivided, and unlobed. There are also trees with compound leaves and lobed leaves as well as trees that feature broad-leafed foliage and narrow-leafed foliage, including scalelike leaves and needles.

SHOWY SUMMER FOLIAGE

Beech, European
Box elder
Cherry, flowering (purple-leafed)
False cypress
Linden, silver
Maples (Japanese, Norway)
Plum, flowering (purple-leafed)
Redbud, eastern
Silk tree
Sweet gum
Sycamore

▶ Simple

▶ Lobed

▶ Compound

▶ Scalelike

▶ Needlelike

▲ Broadleaf

elder 'Flamingo', which sports variegated leaves of green and creamy white licked with pinkish red around the edges.

Consider the color, texture, and shape of foliage across the seasons when

▲ A Japanese maple dazzles throughout the growing season, but especially in autumn.

▲ White ash foliage is one of the highlights of autumn.

▲ The katsura tree features signature honey-colored fall color.

selecting trees for your landscape. Your favorite may still be that red maple that makes cars slow to a stop as they drive by your yard in autumn. But you may also discover the quaking aspen, with its delicately shimmering leaves, or the sassafras, with its deliciously aromatic foliage. There's a wide world of foliage that's as beautiful as the most elegant blooms—and lasts throughout the growing season.

FLASHY FALL FOLIAGE

Ashes
Bald cypress
Beech, American
Birch, paper
Black gum
Cherry, flowering
Crape myrtle
Dogwood, flowering
Franklin tree
Fringe tree, white
Ginkgo
Hawthorn, cockspur
Katsura tree
Larch, European
Linden, littleleaf
Maples (amur, Japanese, red, sugar)
Oaks (scarlet, white)
Pawpaw
Pear, callery
Persimmon
Pistachio, Chinese
Quaking aspen
Sassafras
Serviceberries (Allegheny, apple)
Sourwood
Stewartia, Japanese
Sweet gum
Tallow tree, Chinese
Tulip tree
Zelkova, Japanese

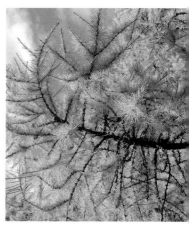

▲ The needles of the European larch turn a glowing gold before dropping to reveal the tree's stark, architectural form.

▲ Dogwood fall foliage stands out.

▲ A sweet gum tree delivers a wallop of fall color.

Beautiful blooms

▲ The late-spring blooms of the goldenchain tree display vivid color.

▲ Eastern redbud is one of the first trees to flower in spring.

Trees with distinctive blooms can also be shade trees or serve other important functions in the landscape. But that matters little to some, who live for the moment they see their redbud flower, their silk tree burst into bloom, or their goldenchain tree drip with pendulous flowers. If you're in the bloom-loving camp, go for more than the brief single-season payoff. Discover trees that bloom across the growing season so you can plant for a series of wonderful sights that occur throughout the year, rather than all at once.

Think of a chorus when you plant flowering trees, each chiming in at its own time. There are early-blooming favorites like serviceberries or redbuds; flowering cherries, crabapples, and dogwoods, which bloom a little later; and magnolias or dove trees,

EARLY SPRING BLOOMERS

Maple, red
Redbud, eastern
Sassafras
Serviceberries

MIDSPRING BLOOMERS

Cherry, flowering
Dogwood, flowering
Empress tree
Pear, callery
Plum, cherry

LATE-SPRING BLOOMERS

Dove tree
Fringe tree
Goldenchain tree
Horsechestnut
Magnolia, bigleaf
Silverbell, Carolina
Yellowwood

▲ The flowering dogwood is one of the outstanding harbingers of spring.

▲ The plum tree bursts into bloom before leafing out in mid spring.

▲ The flowering star magnolia puts on a spring show.

▲ The horsechestnut is a large tree with massive blooms.

▲ The silk tree's feathery pink blooms are a delight of summer.

which bloom late in spring. Summer sees hawthorn, snowbell, and Southern catalpa flowers on center stage, while late summer and fall feature chaste tree and franklin tree blooms. And the bottlebrush blooms from spring through fall across the entire growing season. There's no end to the display of color and luxurious, often fragrant blooms you can bring to your home landscape.

Be sure to take into account a tree's growth habit as well as its size and spread at maturity. Planting shorter, more compact trees in front of larger, broader trees allows each to enjoy its moment in the limelight, whenever that may be.

SUMMER BLOOMERS

Catalpa, Southern
Eucalyptus, red-flowering
Goldenraintree
Hawthorns
Locust, black
Silk tree
Smoke tree
Stewartia, Japanese

LATE-SUMMER BLOOMERS

Chaste tree
Crape myrtle
Franklin tree
Pagoda tree, Japanese
Sourwood

▲ The false spirea features one of the summer's most distinctive displays.

▲ The densely flowering crape myrtle offers something to look forward to in late summer.

Evergreen appeal

Evergreens play a unique role in the landscape, keeping color alive through the dark months of winter but also providing habitat for wildlife and valuable protection for your home and property from wind and weather. They also offer a powerful contrast to the form and foliage of other trees and plantings throughout the growing season. A background of tall evergreens makes other plantings visually pop.

Evergreens, with their distinctive shapes and textures, add their own stamp to the landscape. **Needled evergreens,** such as hemlocks or yews, bear cones and are generally pyramidal in form. They grow slowly but dependably and require very little care. **Broadleaf evergreens,** such as hollies or Southern magnolias, have leaves that last through winter but drop as a new set

▲ Evergreens offer an infinitely varied palette of colors, shapes, and textures.

▲ The pepper tree is a favorite broadleaf evergreen in the South.

EVERGREEN VERSUS DECIDUOUS CONIFERS

Evergreens that bear cones are called conifers. Yet not all conifers are evergreens, though there's much overlap in their use in the landscape. Deciduous conifers feature evergreen-type needles that turn an attractive color in fall, then drop, leaving behind a dramatic silhouette in winter. Soft, new foliage returns in spring, as with all deciduous trees. Deciduous conifers include the bald cypress, dawn redwood, and larches.

BROADLEAF EVERGREENS

Camphor tree
Cherry laurel
Eucalyptus
Holly, American
Magnolia, southern
Olive, European
Pepper tree

▲ A weeping cypress adds elegance to the landscape year-round.

FAVORITE NEEDLE EVERGREENS

Arborvitae, American
Cedar, Japanese
Cedars
Cypresses
False cypress
Fir, douglas
Firs
Hemlocks
Pines
Redwood, coast
Spruces
Umbrella pine, Japanese
Yews

appears on the tree in spring.

Evergreen shapes and habits are varied—from traditional, pyramidal Christmas tree forms, to pendulous and spreading forms, to dramatically columnar or dwarf forms. Very often where there's an evergreen, there's a weeping or a dwarf variety of that evergreen that can be used as a wonderful specimen in the landscape.

▲ An evergreen can be trimmed to form a shade tree.

HERE'S A TIP...

There are many shades of evergreen. Mix and match the colors and textures of evergreens—say the sharp, dark green leaves of a holly with the whorled needles of the Japanese umbrella pine and the silvery blue foliage of the Colorado spruce. There's often a strong and varied selection available within even a single kind of evergreen, including golden cultivars, weeping varieties, or dwarfs.

▶ This blue spruce in a stone wall bed is an exciting surprise.

Late-season interest

▲ Bright red magnolia seeds are part of the tree's year-round good looks.

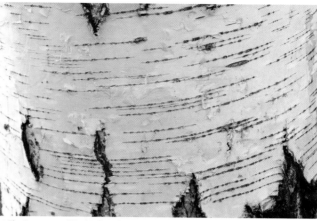

▲ The European white birch makes a beautiful landscape specimen with bright bark.

Sometimes the best a tree has to offer appears long after the leaves have fallen and the temperatures have dropped in winter. Even in that spare seasonal landscape, bright berries, gorgeous textured bark, lingering foliage, and dramatic shapes put on a stunning show. Plant with these elements of seasonal interest in mind so you have something to look forward to in winter.

Colorful fruit

As blooms do, fruit appears on different trees at different times throughout the growing season. Some edible fruit, such as that of the serviceberry, appears in summer and tends to be

▲ The bark of a Mindanao gum or eucalyptus boasts interesting colors.

TREES WITH ATTRACTIVE BARK

Beech, American
Birches
Cherry, sargent
Chokecherry, amur
Cork tree, amur
Crape myrtle
Dogwood, kousa
Elm, Chinese
Eucalpytus
Maple, paperbark
Quaking aspen
Sassafras
Sycamore

TREES WITH WINTER FRUIT

Black gum
Box elder
Crabapple, flowering
Dogwood, flowering
Goldenraintree
Hawthorns
Holly, American
Magnolias
Maple, amur
Pepper tree
Persimmons
Sourwood

▶ The fruit of the persimmon hang on long after the leaves have fallen.

▲ The bare form of a mature oak is humbling in winter.

▲ Dangling catkins delight on the whimsical form of a leafless Harry Lauder's walking stick.

▲ A grouping of crape myrtles boasts fine form and elegant bark.

TREES WITH INTERESTING STRUCTURE IN WINTER

Beech (American, weeping European)
Cherry, weeping
Cork tree, amur
Crabapple, weeping
Crape myrtle
Dawn redwood
Harry Lauder's walking stick
Hornbeam, European
Larch, European
Maple, Japanese
Oaks

harvested by humans and wildlife as quickly as it ripens on the branch. Other fruits, such as dogwood berries, ripen later, and still others, such as hollies and hawthorns, save their best and brightest berries until winter. Most of the late-season fruit is for the birds, as they say, and for those who appreciate the bursts of color in winter.

Distinctive bark

Winter is the best time to appreciate the distinctive character of a tree's bark. From peeling bark to mottled bark to bark with fascinating grooves and ridges, or even to scented bark, as with the sassafras tree—there's much to admire in the winter scene without foliage and flowers to distract us. When a tree description mentions its interesting bark, pay attention. This tree may become your favorite plant in the winter landscape.

Sculptural form

When certain trees lose their leaves, they become the most commanding presence in the yard. Suddenly their elegantly extended limbs and branches or weeping form become newly visible, silhouetted against the winter landscape or frosted with snow. Consider planting even one of these favorites as a specimen to be enjoyed all year long.

▲ Each Japanese maple has its own distinctly sculptural form.

What do you want from your shrubs?

▲ Shrubs are the ideal anchor and accent in a mixed border.

Shrubs offer creative opportunities for experimenting in the landscape. They range in size from large, broad types that can reach 20 feet in height to low-growing, spreading shrubs that barely reach 6 inches. In foliage, flowers, fruit, and form, shrubs offer almost every possible color, texture, and shape. And unlike many trees shrubs beg to be planted in groups—their size allows it and grouping magnifies the effect of a single plant. Shrubs are affordable and available through many sources, so planting a sophisticated mix of shrubs is well within any gardener's reach.

Shrubs can serve as borders, privacy screens, focal points in a garden or at the entrance to a home, and as foundation plantings that disguise or enhance the ground-level view of a house. They can be planted in symmetric patterns to suggest a formal style, or in asymmetric combinations that can bring the landscape to life.

Shapes of shrubs

Select shrubs with the shape and size of the mature plants in mind. Avoid loading a bed with too many young shrubs that will crowd each other out as they grow. Shrubs tend to be vertical or horizontal in basic form, with vertical types generally accentuating a composition and drawing the eye up, while horizontal types fill out the composition and draw the eye out. Take into account how tall, spreading shrubs might work with shorter, rounded forms or low-growing, groundcover types in an overall design. Think about these basic shapes of shrubs as you plan for their use in your landscape.

▲ An artful mix of evergreen shapes and colors make a tidy foundation bed.

● **Pyramidal shrubs** come to a point at the top and taper down evenly toward the ground. These tend to anchor beds or mixed groups and are also useful for screening.

● **Columnar shrubs** are upright and narrow and make the strongest vertical, visual impact, either as a foundation planting or an accent in a bed.

● **Vase-shape shrubs** grow up and slightly outward in an open habit. These are most often multistemmed, though they can be pruned to tree form.

● **Rounded shrubs** have an orderly, formal appeal, whether naturally rounded or trimmed to that effect.

● **Horizontal-layered shrubs** feature a handsome, broad, horizontal form and layers of branches that reach outward.

● **Arching or fountain-shape shrubs** suggest exactly that—a fountain of branches and foliage and flowers bubbling up and out. These make fine specimen plants in a garden bed or shrub border.

● **Weeping shrubs** are more horizontal than arching, with a pronounced sweep of the branches toward the ground. These make fine specimens.

● **Mounded shrubs** are low-growing, with a rounded, horizontal form. These are useful for accent and filling out a design.

● **Prostrate shrubs** are the lowest-growing form, with a spreading, ground-hugging reach.

▲ The theme is round in this border of evergreen and deciduous shrubs, ornamental grass, and perennials.

EVERGREEN AND DECIDUOUS

Mix evergreen and deciduous shrubs in your landscape design. They provide winter interest and complement one another as the colorful foliage and flowers on deciduous shrubs unfold over the growing season. Plan for deciduous and flowering shrubs that peak at different times to make the most of this combined effect.

BROADLEAF EVERGREEN SHRUBS

Azalea
Boxwood, common
Coyote brush
Escallonia
Grapeholly, Oregon
Heavenly bamboo
Holly
Indian hawthorn
Leucothoe, drooping
Mahonia, leatherleaf
Rock rose
Veronica, shrubby

HERE'S A TIP...
Because shrubs have such distinct, almost geometrical forms, there's an easy way to think about how you might work with them in your landscape design. Take a photo of each of the areas of your landscape where you'd like to plant shrubs. Make several large prints of each photo, then use markers to rough out different combinations of shapes and sizes of shrubs that might suit your planting area. You'll quickly see where height or spread works (or not) and places where smaller forms will make a distinctive impression.

▲ The vanhoutte spirea is a classic fountain-shape shrub.

FAVORITE WEEPING SHRUBS

Bottlebrush, weeping
Cotoneaster, rockspray
Holly, English weeping
Peashrub, Siberian
Spirea, bridalwreath

▲ Weeping Siberian peashrub and pink heather pleasantly complement each other.

EDIBLE FRUIT

One of the delicious benefits of planting certain shrubs in the home landscape is the abundant, edible fruit they produce. Elderberries or blueberries ripening on the bush are an absolute highlight of summer, for example. Other shrubs with edible fruit include natal plum, flowering quince, rugosa roses, and American cranberrybush viburnum.

Highbush blueberries ripen on the stem.

▲ The layered reach of the doublefile viburnum plays up its form and flowers.

Borders, foundations, and privacy

Shrubs are among the most versatile plants you can put to work in your landscape. They can be used singly or sparingly among other plants in the yard and garden, or used in groups for aesthetic or practical reasons. They shape and define space, frame particular areas, create accents or focal points, hide or enhance certain views, and even form green walls for privacy or other reasons.

Shrub borders

Shrub borders are groups of shrubs planted together at the edges of the landscape—along property lines, against fences or walls, tucked into corners, or lining an embankment. Plant shrub borders densely where mature plants overlap by a third to suggest depth and fullness. Size, shape, color, and texture all work together to create a balanced but varied impression. An effective shrub border features a range of shrubs of different shapes and sizes, usually anchored by a large shrub or a small group of larger shrubs. Consider all the features of shrub plants—form, foliage, flowers, fruit, winter interest—to create a successful and diverse shrub border.

Foundation shrubs

Foundation plantings originally hid the underporch areas of Victorian homes. They quickly became popular for their ability to add dimension and balance to the front of any home. Today shrubs in foundation plantings help frame entryways, soften the edges and angles of a structure, and, as ever, hide unwanted views.

Successful foundation plantings take into account scale and proportion. A tall, multistory home, for example, accommodates larger shrubs, while smaller shrubs suit single-story dwellings. Horizontal shrubs in a foundation planting engage the eye straight on or draw it downward, echoing the line of the natural landscape. This works well to temper a tall or narrow space. Vertical shrubs draw the eye upward and can help frame

▲ This informal yew hedge makes an effective property border.

SHRUBS FOR HEDGES

Azalea
Barberry, Japanese
Boxwood, common
Cherry laurel
Forsythia, border
Hollies
Mountain laurel
Privet
Rose of Sharon
Sweet olive
Yews

SHRUBS FOR MASSING

Certain shrubs lend themselves to massing, which is a dense grouping of a single kind of shrub in a border or bed. Massing is usually meant to impress with a profusion of blooms or distinctive foliage or fruit. Rhododendrons and azaleas excel at massing, as do many roses and fine-textured shrubs such as rosemary or lavender. Even groundcover shrubs can make a dramatic impression when massed. Five or more of the same distinctive shrub, planted in close quarters, can quite successfully present a massing effect.

▲ Closely planted rhododendrons and azaleas mass beautifully in this shrub border.

SHRUBS IN A MIXED BORDER

Mixed borders contain small trees, shrubs, perennials, and annuals and tend to be more of a focal point in the home landscape than an all-shrub border. Because they feature perennial and annual plants, mixed borders require regular maintenance throughout the growing season, while a shrub border, once established, requires very little special care outside of seasonal pruning to tidy up the forms.

▲ A mixed border shows off a lively collection of deciduous and evergreen shrubs, perennials, and annuals, as well as a starring attraction, such as this white flowering dogwood at the center of this planting.

a space or transition between other forms.

Screens and privacy plantings

Shrubs planted closely together can form effective visual screens for privacy or to buffer noise or unsightly views. When planted thickly and pruned as hedges, their combined dense form is as good as a wall. Hedges are higher-maintenance than shrubs in general due to the pruning and shaping, but the particular plants that adapt to forming hedges—those that grow densely and can handle the shearing—really rise to the occasion.

▲ A successful shrub border requires little ongoing maintenance once established.

GROUNDCOVER SHRUBS

Blueberry, lowbush
Cinquefoil, bush
Cotoneaster, bearberry
Euonymus, wintercreeper
Heather, Scotch
St. johnswort, shrubby
Sumac, fragrant

▲ Foundation shrubs screen and balance other vertical elements in the landscape.

Fantastic foliage

▲ Oakleaf hydrangea foliage turns a handsome burgundy in fall.

SHRUBS WITH RED OR BRONZE FOLIAGE

Abelia, glossy
Andromeda, Japanese 'Christmas Cheer'
Barberry, Japanese
Elder, American 'Black Beauty'
Photinia, redtip
Smoketree 'Royal Purple'

▲ The purple-leafed smoketree is a fine specimen in almost any landscape.

▲ Fothergilla offers spectacular red foliage in fall as well as captivating off-white blooms in spring.

As do trees, shrubs can present plenty of spectacular fall color, but it's the wide range of foliage, color, and texture throughout the growing season that makes shrubs so versatile and useful in a landscape design. Because shrubs cover more space in the landscape, the impact of the foliage can be dramatic.

Groups of shrubs present broad strokes of color, from shades of blue and gray to bronze and red to an array of yellows. Blocks of green are neutral and generally complement anything planted nearby. Blues and grays are cool and restive, while reds and orange enliven things. And yellow-greens, used sparingly, can give a vibrant glow to any landscape.

The trick is to create a composition that features layers of related colors punctuated by shots of contrasting color—for example, true greens integrated with blue-greens, with perhaps a shot of variegated yellow-green or scarlet. Introduce variations in the texture of foliage or the shapes of the shrubs to

SHRUBS WITH EXCELLENT FALL COLOR

Beautyberry, Chinese
Burning bush
Chokeberry, red
Cotoneaster, bearberry
Enkianthus, redvein
Fothergilla
Hydrangea, oakleaf
Mountain ash, European
Summersweet
Viburnum
Witch hazel, hybrid
Yellowroot

▲ Burning bush never disappoints when it shows off in the autumn sun.

▲ Locate bushy lavender on a pathway where it releases its delicious fragrance when you brush against it.

▲ Sea buckthorn flaunts its distinctive berries and signature gray-green foliage.

add dimensions of interest—both up close and from a distance.

Brilliant fall foliage thrills the eye and is often the high point of the year in a garden.

When weather turns cool, the sudden burst of color from a burning bush or an oakleaf hydrangea can be brief but is so intense that it becomes a fond memory of the season.

SHRUBS WITH SCENTED FOLIAGE

Allspice, Carolina
Juniper
Lavender, English
Myrtle
Rosemary

SHRUBS WITH BLUE-GRAY FOLIAGE

Arborvitae, oriental
  'Blue Cone'
Boxwood, common
  'Newport Blue'
Buffaloberry, silver
Daphne, burkwood
Holly, inkberry
Lavender, English
Mirror plant 'Variegata'
Olive, Russian
Rosemary
Sea buckthorn
Silverberry, Russian
Spruce, blue 'Globe'
Yew, English 'Cheshuntensis'
Zenobia, dusty

SHRUBS WITH YELLOW-GREEN FOLIAGE

Arborvitae, oriental
  'Aurea Nana'
Aucuba, Japanese
Boxwood, common
  'Elegantissima'
Euonymus, wintercreeper
  'Emerald 'n' Gold'
Juniper, common
  'Depressa Aurea'
Pittosporum, Japanese,
  'Wheeler's Dwarf'
Privet, golden vicary
Spirea, bumald 'Goldflame'
Umbrella pine, Japanese
  'Aurea' and 'Ossorio Gold'
Yew, English

▲ Japanese aucuba plays off the deep green foliage and bright blooms of hydrangea.

▲ This blue spruce colony accents the landscape with its distinctive coloring.

Beautiful blooms

Shrubs that feature outstanding blooms are hard to resist. The flowers are generally right at eye level, giving you everything they have in a limitless range of colors. Warm-color blooms range from scarlet reds to oranges and yellows and golds. Cooler colors include deep purples, blues, and all shades of white. Flowering shrubs bloom from early spring through summer, offering lots of potential for color throughout the growing season.

But as much as you may love a shrub for its flowers, choose it first for its form and foliage, which you'll see all year. Mix warm- and cool-color blooms carefully to avoid an awkward clash. And take into account all the types of blooms, from the big, complex flowers of many roses or rhododendrons to the dainty blooms of a deutzia.

▲ Purple rhododendron and flame azalea light up a woodland border.

SPRING-BLOOMING SHRUBS

Andromeda, Japanese
Azalea
Beautyberry, Chinese
Beautybush
Blueberry, highbush
Brooms
Buttonbush
Camellia, Japanese
Currant, alpine
Daphne, burkwood
Daphne, rose
Deutzia
Fothergilla
Kerria, Japanese
Lilacs
Quince, common flowering
Rhododendron
Spirea

▲ The pendulous blooms of the Japanese andromeda are a spring highlight in a shady part of the yard.

▲ The delicate pink blooms of a weigela brighten the landscape with color in the middle of the growing season.

▲ Butterfly bush blooms are a beacon to winged wildlife in the garden.

▲ Sweet-smelling acacia blooms never fail to put a smile on the face.

▲ Summer-blooming landscape roses spill over a stone wall.

HERE'S A TIP...

Buy your most eye-catching, colorful flowering shrubs, such as rhododendrons, azaleas, or roses, while they're blooming so you can see the true color of the flowers, which can vary from plant to plant even within a specific cultivar. No matter how gorgeous the bloom looks in the photo on the plant tag, it's anybody's guess what the real color of the blossoms will be until they're open and on display. You may worry that you've all but missed the blooming season by buying your plant so late, but you will have a healthy, established shrub—blooming in exactly the color you hoped for—to look forward to next year.

SUMMER-BLOOMING SHRUBS

Abelia, glossy
Allspice, Carolina
Bunchberry
Butterfly bush
Chaste tree
Cinquefoil, bush
Crape myrtle
Fuchsia, common
Heather
Heather, Scotch
Hydrangea
Lavender
Mountain laurel
Rock rose
Rose of Sharon
Roses
Viburnum
Weigela

SHRUBS WITH FRAGRANT BLOOMS

Abelia, glossy
Acacia, sweet
Allspice, Carolina
Azalea
Butterfly bush
Buttonbush
California lilac
Chaste tree
Crape myrtle
Daphne, burkwood
Deutzia, slender
Fothergilla
Gardenia
Honeysuckle
Lavender, English
Lilac
Magnolia
Mexican orange
Mockorange, sweet
Pittosporum, Japanese
Summersweet
Viburnum
Winter hazel, buttercup
Zenobia, dusty

▲ Many gardeners mark the bloom time of their hydrangeas as the mid point of the growing season.

▲ The gardenia bloom releases a heady scent.

Late-season interest

The world of shrubs is rich with choices that offer visual and textural appeal long after the growing season is over. Fruit and berries in colors ranging from bright red to orange, yellow, blue, and purple adorn many shrubs well into winter. Shrub interest along with the colorful bark and architectural structure of nearby trees simply command a winter landscape. Anyone who ignores a landscape until springtime is missing a wonderful opportunity to see some of the most exciting features shrubs have to offer.

▲ The lingering fruit of a Japanese barberry sparkles despite a winter freeze.

▲ Firethorn berries sizzle colorfully long after the growing season's end.

SHRUBS WITH FLASHY WINTER FRUIT

Barberry, Japanese
Bayberry, northern
Beautyberry, Chinese
Cotoneaster
Firethorn
Grapeholly, Oregon
Heavenly bamboo
Holly
Sea buckthorn
Snowberry
Sumac, staghorn
Viburnum
Winterberry

▲ The berries of this cranberrybush viburnum will remain on the plant into the winter and help sustain birds.

▲ The fruit of the beautyberry develop their bright purple color in fall.

SHRUBS FOR WINTER WILDLIFE

Arborvitae
Barberry, Japanese
Boxwood, common
Holly
Juniper
Privet
Viburnum
Yew

▲ Juniper berries and foliage add color to the winter landscape.

WINTER BLOOMS

Witch hazel blooms on bare branches are among the first signs of spring.

Some flowering shrubs are sentinels of spring, breaking into bloom long before other plants in the landscape show any signs of life. Witch hazel, winter daphne, and winter honeysuckle will bloom earliest, usually in late winter. The bright yellow blooms of forsythia and beloved catkins of pussy willow give gardeners enough hope to have faith until spring truly arrives.

Buttercup winter hazel, forsythia, lilac, and flowering quince are great shrubs for forcing into bloom indoors. A few weeks before the shrub's usual flowering time, cut stems up to 3 feet long and stand them in a tall container of water in a cool room until the buds swell. Then move the container into a warmer room and place it in bright but indirect sunlight. Flowers will develop within days.

▼ The hankow willow has a one-of-a-kind twisted form.

▲ The bare red stems of the red-osier dogwood captivate in winter.

SHRUBS WITH EXTRAORDINARY BARK AND FORM

Broom, warminster
Deutzia, fuzzy
Dogwood, red-osier
Euonymus, wintercreeper
Harry Lauder's walking stick
Honeysuckle, winter
Hydrangea, oakleaf
Kerria, Japanese
Mock orange, sweet
Spirea, Japanese
Willow, hankow

All-star trees and shrubs

▲ The intensely colored foliage of highbush blueberry adds to the autumn display.

▲ River birch boasts peeling bark that enhances its textural appeal.

What makes a great tree or shrub? Versatility and utility in the landscape, easy to grow, easy to care for, and most of all, multi-season appeal. Almost all the evergreens—pines, spruces, junipers, firs—fall in this category, of course, which is why they're so valued in every landscape. Consider these all-star trees and shrubs that provide great bang-for-your-buck value in the home landscape.

The **highbush blueberry** shrub has just about every quality you could hope for—a handsome, natural form, sweet spring blooms, amazing edible berries, and reddish fall foliage that ranks with the maples in seasonal beauty. Birds and other wildlife are crazy about the berries, but they also appreciate the dense, multi stemmed shrub as a winter habitat. Plant several bushes then make yourself a pie.

River birch trees are lovely and extremely useful in the home landscape. A fast-grower, it can provide quick shade, especially planted in a group. It has distinctive, pale peeling bark that reveals a cinnamon brown underneath. The leaves don't turn color before dropping in the fall, but they rustle pleasantly in the breeze throughout the growing season.

Crape myrtle, a Southern favorite, features gorgeous blooms of pink, white, lavender, or magenta that can last from spring all through summer. Leaves turn a rich orange or red in autumn. When they drop, the small tree's exquisite mottled bark and multistemmed form command the winter landscape. A wonderful specimen tree, this plant looks good alone or planted in a row.

Douglas fir is a top-notch evergreen with its classic pyramidal shape and truly beautiful blue-green needled foliage, which is enhanced by large cones that stay on the tree well into winter. This tree will please the eye as a single specimen planting or can be

▲ Douglas fir stands up to winter.

arranged in a row as a screen.

Both the dwarf and large forms of the **fothergilla** shrub are very special in the home landscape. Its neatly rounded, natural habit gives it great appeal mixed with other shrubs and landscape plantings. But it's the extraordinary honey-scented white blooms that appear in spring, and the long-lasting splash of bright orange to red foliage in fall, that make this shrub a winner.

The **franklin tree** is famous for its fragrant bark and glorious, camellialike,

▲ Crape myrtle has it all: Incredible blooms, elegant form, and gorgeous bark.

▲ Fothergilla 'Mt. Airy' displays unusual flowers in spring and bright foliage color come fall.

▲ The red maple is a headliner of the fall foliage spectacle.

▲ A 'Winter King' hawthorn offers strong form and colorful fruit.

▲ A franklin tree has delightful blooms.

▲ The Norway spruce provides year-round good looks.

late-summer blooming flowers. It's a modest-size tree that perfectly suits any size landscape, complementing surrounding plantings like a well-mannered host. It has a fine, open form and handsome, fissured bark that's revealed after the leaves turn a vivid orange-red before dropping in autumn. The franklin tree makes an excellent specimen or accent planting.

The **'Winter King' hawthorn** is a fast-growing, small tree with a broad vase shape and lustrous green foliage that turns orange or bronze before dropping in autumn, revealing lovely silvery gray bark that appeals all winter long. It also boasts delicate clusters of white blooms that appear in spring time, followed by brilliant red, long-lasting berries favored by birds and wildlife. Unlike other hawthorns, the 'Winter King' has few thorns, making it an appealing specimen planting, particularly beautiful among evergreens.

The **red maple** is all about the red. It features red flowers in early spring, red fruit in summer, foliage that turns yellow to fiery red in fall, and red stems that provide interest in winter. It has a handsome upright, rounded habit and grows rather quickly. If you can have only one maple, this is the one.

The **Norway spruce** is a graceful, commanding evergreen with a distinctive upright, pyramidal form and pendulous branches. This tree is a favorite of neighborhood wildlife, which love it for the cones and the friendly, protective habitat it provides. It generally grows to 60 feet or more, so a little Norway spruce goes a long way!

The **tulip tree** is a grand tree. It has a handsome oval to rounded form and can grow to 100 feet at maturity, making it the tallest deciduous tree in North America. It also grows quickly, so it's a great prospect for a shade tree in a large landscape. Distinctive tulip-shape blooms appear near the top of the tree in late spring, and the foliage turns a bright yellow in autumn. Plant more than one if space permits; the tulip tree is truly impressive in a grouping.

▲ The bloom of a tulip tree reminds you of it's name.

Planting your trees and shrubs

▲ Landscape plants thrive in the mild winters and summers of the Pacific Northwest.

▲ Coastal California features warm dry summers and mild winters that are similar to a Mediterranean climate.

Climate, soil, and light are most important in determining which trees and shrubs are right for your landscape. As with any plants in the landscape, you have to know and respect the requirements of your trees and shrubs to see them thrive. If a plant is known to grow best only to a certain hardiness zone, or in loamy soil, or in full sunlight, avoid cheating those requirements, no matter how much you want to see that plant growing in your landscape. Trees and shrubs are too costly an investment to risk in this way.

Besides learning about a plant's requirements through books and other resources, take a look at what grows well in your area. Although a tree you fancy is described in a catalog as appropriate for your hardiness zone, it may dislike your local climate or even your yard's microclimate. Assess what's available at a local nursery or garden center and ask about particular trees or shrubs you're considering. Also note plants you see thriving in your neighbors' yards. These are the most useful clues as to what will grow well in your home landscape.

Climate zones

The U.S. Department of Agriculture has published a map of plant hardiness zones

▲ Cold, harsh winters and hot summers characterize the climate in the Midwest.

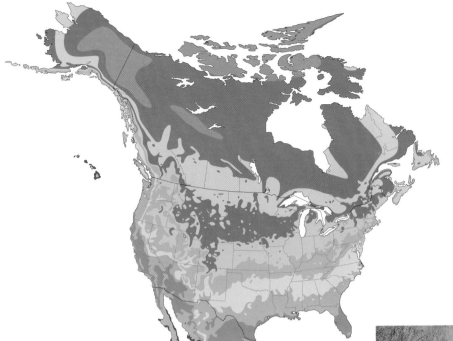

Range of Average Annual Minimum Temperatures for Each Zone

Zone 1: Below -50 F (below -45.6 C)
Zone 2: -50 to -40 F (-45.5 to -40 C)
Zone 3: -40 to -30 F (-39.9 to -34.5 C)
Zone 4: -30 to -20 F (-34.4 to -28.9 C)
Zone 5: -20 to -10 F (-28.8 to -23.4 C)
Zone 6: -10 to 0 F (-23.3 to -17.8 C)
Zone 7: 0 to 10 F (-17.7 to -12.3 C)
Zone 8: 10 to 20 F (-12.2 to -6.7 C)
Zone 9: 20 to 30 F (-6.6 to -1.2 C)
Zone 10: 30 to 40 F (-1.1 to 4.4 C)
Zone 11: Above 40 F (above 4.5 C)

▲ Extreme dry heat limits what will grow easily in the desert Southwest.

▲ Long cold winters and humid summers are the standard in the Northeast.

▲ Almost-constant humidity, mild winters, and long hot summers are the distinguishing characteristics of the climate in the Southeast.

(see above) that indicates the range of average annual minimum temperatures for each region of the United States. This map can help you choose plants that will survive a typical winter in your region. Zone 1 is the coldest area on the zone map, while Zone 11 is the warmest.

Plants are classified by the coldest temperature and hardiness zone they can endure. For example plants hardy to Zone 6 survive where winter temperatures drop to -10°F. Plants that are hardy to Zone 8 would die long before it became that cold. Plants that fall within a range of hardiness zones—say, Zones 4 to 6—are known to be able to survive winter in the coldest area of that zone range and summer in the warmest area.

Avoid trees or shrubs that are designated as hardy on the border of your hardiness zone; trying to grow beyond a plant's normal zone comfort level creates challenges to its success from the first day. Stick to the trees and shrubs that are known to grow vigorously and happily in your hardiness zone.

Basic climatic regions

● **Pacific Northwest:** This region is characterized by mild winters, mild summers, and generally moist conditions, except for two months in late summer. Conifers grow extremely well in this mild-but-humid climate.
● **Coastal California:** This region is known for mild winters and warm, dry summers that are similar to those in the Mediterranean.
● **Southwest:** This region is characterized by extreme heat and high humidity in nondesert areas. Drought-tolerant plants are useful in this region.
● **Midwest/Plains:** This region is known for cold winters, hot summers, and generally windy, often dry conditions.
● **Northeast:** This region has cold winters and mild but humid summers.
● **Southeast:** Mild winters and long, hot, humid summers characterize this region. The landscape ranges from swampy lowland to drier upland forest areas.

Selecting a site

▲ The Japanese maple is a beautiful tree suitable for planting in a shady spot.

The success of trees and shrubs on a particular site depends on soil conditions, weather patterns, sun and wind exposure, proximity to buildings, and more. Consider every plant's requirements when choosing a planting site for it.

Site considerations

Most landscape plants grow best in loose, workable soil that drains well and contains some organic matter. Many soils are less than ideal. For example, you may want to create a privacy screen in a poorly drained area using evergreen trees, only to find that they will fail in wet soil. However, some plants require less than ideal soil to thrive. Certain desirable shade trees and shrubs that suit your area may grow well in heavy, clay soil, while others will do best in light, sandy soil.

Slopes pose a particular challenge beyond the quality of the soil. Enhance your chances for success when growing trees and shrubs on a slope by covering the planting area around these plants with a mulch or groundcover to prevent soil erosion. Sloped ground makes watering difficult and causes nutrients to run off into ground- or surface water. The best approach is to create level terraces for planting. Choose varieties of shrubs, such as prostrate or low-growing and sprawling ones, that will form groundcovering masses.

Exposure

The compass direction that a particular landscape plant faces is known as its exposure.

CHALLENGES OF PLACEMENT

As you plan to add trees and shrubs to your yard, consider these potentially challenging situations:

Street plantings in areas with winter snow and ice are easily injured by salt applied to roads. Place valuable landscape plants at least 20 feet from the road.

Trees or shrubs planted too close to driveways, sidewalks, and homes may damage the structures as a result of root growth.

Place foundation plants in front of the drip line of eaves. The plants will receive water when it rains but will avoid damage by snow or ice sliding off the roof.

Before you dig any planting holes for trees and shrubs, contact your local utility companies and ask them to identify the location of any cables buried on your property. Overhead wires should also be considered where tall trees are being planted.

▲ Chinese holly (above) and Japanese pittosporum (right) thrive in shade.

For example a tree or shrub located on the south side of a dwelling has a southern exposure. Plants with a northern exposure may face an open sky but receive no direct sunlight. Plants that require full sun do best with a southern or western exposure.

There are various degrees of sun and shade. An area in partial shade receives less than six hours of sunlight per day. Half shade occurs on the east and west sides of a house. On the west side cool morning shade is followed by afternoon sun, which can be intensely hot. Deep or dense

THE AIR FACTOR

Air circulation is important to the health of your trees and shrubs. Give your plants enough room to breathe where they won't be stifled in close quarters due to humidity or lack of air circulation. Pay attention to air pollutants that may exist in your landscape. If you live on a busy road or in an urban area, certain plants will fail to thrive. Look for trees and shrubs that are known to be tolerant of these conditions.

▲ Healthy trees are most likely to tolerate air pollution in urban settings.

▲ The red-osier dogwood will thrive in the shade.

TREES FOR SHADY SITES

Dogwood, flowering
Fringe tree, white
Hemlock, Canadian
Holly, American
Maple, Japanese
Redbud, eastern
Serviceberry, Allegheny
Silverbell, Carolina
Sourwood

▲ Dense and mounded shrubs have been cultivated as a groundcover on a sloping site.

▲ Japanese kerria is a cheerful bloomer, surprisingly well-suited to shade.

shade exists in areas untouched by sun.

It helps to track the sun and shade patterns across your landscape through the seasons prior to planting trees or shrubs. For example, in late June the sun rises the farthest north, is high overhead at noon, and sets in the northwest sky. In late March and in late September, it rises in the east, sets in the west, and is lower at noon. By late December the sun's course is a low arc in the southern sky. The greatest heat strikes western walls and windows in early winter. For

SHRUBS FOR SHADY SITES

Aucuba, Japanese
Cherry laurel
Euonymous, wintercreeper
Gardenia
Heavenly bamboo
Holly, Chinese
Hydrangea (smooth, oakleaf)
Kerria, Japanese
Leucothoe, drooping
Pittosporum, Japanese

summer shade, plant trees on the west side and keep the south side open to winter sun.

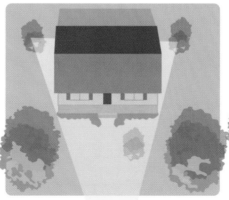

▲ Note the patterns of light and shade created by the sun as it moves across your landscape during the morning, middle of the day, and late afternoon .

Improving your soil

▲ Sandy soil is fine for California lilac 'Blue Concha'.

▲ The black locust is a classic tree for sandy soil.

After moving into a home in a new or an established neighborhood, gardeners are frequently disappointed to discover that the soil causes landscape plants to struggle for survival. That's why it's so important to understand your soil before selecting or planting trees and shrubs for your landscape.

Know your soil

There are three main ingredients of soil—sand, silt, and clay. Any given soil contains varying proportions of these ingredients, as well as differing chemical compositions, which can affect the way plants grow.

Sandy soil will crumble easily in your hand. Silty soil feels slightly greasy, while clay soil clumps together when you squeeze it. Clay loam, often confused with topsoil, consists of roughly equal parts of sand and silt in clay.

The density of the soil is as important as the type. Soil that is too sandy drains too quickly so that a tree or shrub is unable to retain the proper amount of moisture. Dense clay soil is so sticky it chokes the roots, as does compacted soil.

Soil also features differing levels of acid or alkaline, to which trees and shrubs show distinct preferences or sensitivities. Acid and alkaline refer to the pH level of the soil, which is measured on a 14-point scale. Midway, around 7, is considered neutral, while lower numbers are acidic and higher numbers are alkaline. Most trees and shrubs prefer neutral or slightly acid soil, while others, such as hollies, azaleas, and rhododendrons, prefer a distinctly acid soil. Chlorosis, common in the Midwest, is due to high soil pH caused by mulching practices and irrigating with alkaline water.

Soil testing

A soil test will give you exact information about pH, nutrient deficiencies, and the presence of organic matter or harmful salts in your soil. This test will help you determine what amendments might boost the health of your soil before planting new trees and shrubs. You can purchase a simple, do-it-yourself test kit at your local garden center, but you'll get the most accurate results if you work with a professional soil-testing lab. Your local county extension office may conduct residential soil tests or can recommend a private lab.

To get reliable test results, gather samples from several spots around the area to be planted. Using a core sampler or a clean trowel or shovel, collect samples from at least 3 inches deep into the soil. Take the sample from bare soil in a planting area, or take a sample from below the layer of thatch on your lawn. Each sample should be about an inch wide and from 4 to 12 inches long. Mix the samples together in a clean bucket, measure about a pint of this soil mixture into the soil test container, and send it to the lab.

Amend your soil

Your soil test results will show what you have—

WHAT'S YOUR SOIL TEXTURE?

To get a general idea of the texture of your soil, collect several spoon-sized samples from the top 6 inches of soil from different spots around your yard. Let the samples dry thoroughly, then grind them together with a rolling pin.

Next fill a quart jar two-thirds full of water; stir in a teaspoon of dishwashing liquid, add the soil, cover, shake vigorously, then set in a place where the jar will be undisturbed. The soil will eventually separate into layers of sand, silt, and clay.

After an hour, the sand will have settled to the bottom of the jar. Mark this level on the side of the jar. After two hours, the silt will have settled on top of the sand; mark this level too. In two days, the clay will have settled and the remaining water will be clear. Mark the top of the clay layer level on the jar.

The proportions of sand, silt, and clay in the jar approximate the proportions in your soil. If one component makes up more than half the total amount of the soil, that is your dominant soil texture.

Clay

Silt

Sand

and what you need—in your soil. It will also suggest which amendments will be helpful in improving the health of your soil. Soil amendments are different from fertilizers; fertilizers temporarily add nutrients to the soil that are then consumed by plants and need to be reapplied at least once a year. Soil amendments change the soil's pH, improve its ability to hold and distribute water and nutrients, and help to protect the soil from compaction.

● **To change pH:** Lime is the most common amendment added to soil to raise pH, while sulfur is most commonly used to lower pH. Both come in varying forms, strengths, and speeds of effectiveness. Consult your soil analysis report for recommendations of application rates.

● **To improve drainage or increase water retention:** Organic matter is the solution to most drainage problems, including clay soil that drains too slowly and sandy soil that drains too quickly. The most common forms of organic matter are compost and sphagnum peat moss. Compost is simply decomposed plant material, which you can make yourself or purchase at your local

◄ The sycamore is a tree that thrives in a consistently wet site. So plant a group of them if space permits.

TREES FOR WET SITES

Alder, European black
Bald cypress
Birches
Black gum
Maple (red, silver)
Sweet gum
Sycamore
Willows

garden center. It is made of decayed organic materials such as straw, grass clippings, newspaper, leaves, certain food wastes, spent plants, hay, chipped brush, and farm manure. This mixture helps with drainage and provides a slowly released boost of nutrients to the soil. Peat moss absorbs water, but offers no nutrition to the soil. It is acidic, however, so is suitable for acid-loving plants like rhododendrons and azaleas or blueberry bushes.

● **To reduce sodium:** Gypsum relieves compaction in clay soils and helps to leach out

▲ A rototiller helps to turn the soil deeply and mix amendments to best effect.

excess sodium. Plants damaged by the effects of winter salt spray may benefit from the application of gypsum to the soil.

● **To improve poor soil:** If your soil is generally nutrient poor, mix in a rich topsoil such as Miracle-Gro® Garden Soil for Trees & Shrubs.

To add amendments to a planting bed, remove all debris, stones, and large roots in the soil. Rake or rototill to upend the soil to 6 inches deep, then mix in

the appropriate amount of amendment thoroughly. When amending the soil surrounding an individual tree or shrub to be planted, mix amendments in with the backfill soil before returning it to the hole after planting.

You won't see a dramatic change in the first year after adding amendments to a deficient soil. However, over three to five years of regular incorporation, you will see significant improvement in soil conditions and plant growth.

▲ Nandina thrives in moist soil.

SHRUBS FOR WET SITES

Allspice, Carolina
Bayberry, Northern
Chokeberry, red
Dogwood, red-osier
Holly, inkberry
Summersweet
Winterberry

Choosing the best plants

It takes more than a green thumb to create a successful landscape. Selecting and purchasing high-quality plants and ensuring they're the right plants for specific locations are essential to cultivating an attractive and productive home landscape.

Resist the impulse to buy unneeded plants simply because they are inexpensive or appealing. Plant selection should follow a design that you have created for your yard.

Consider the eventual mature size of each plant. Squeezing in extra plants leads to overcrowding and potential problems with insects and disease. Trees and shrubs are more likely to decline and die prematurely if spaced too closely together or planted too close to the street or structures. Buy dwarf forms of desired plants when they are available to use in a small space. Carefully measure and mark the area that each plant will occupy. It's relatively easy to divide and move herbaceous perennials; trees and shrubs are another matter.

Always select plants adapted to your specific landscape and general region. Look around your neighborhood and note the trees and shrubs that appear to be thriving there. Consider adding those plants or improved varieties of them to your landscape. Check with local nurseries, gardening experts, and cooperative extension publications to determine a plant's pest susceptibility and invasiveness. If you live in an urban area, choose plants that can tolerate challenging site conditions such as compacted soil and air pollution.

It makes sense to look for trouble-free plants for your landscape. Native plants are widely promoted as an important part of a beautiful, low-maintenance garden. When possible select plants that are indigenous to your region. Native plants are great where appropriate

▲ Take the time to shop carefully for plants that are full and have healthy foliage.

and available, but consider nonnatives as well. There's a place for both in the home landscape.

Shrubs and trees that have been actively growing in a nursery for more than four years are more expensive, difficult to transplant, and slower to establish than younger woody plants. And large, older plants suffer greater transplant shock when dug up, transported, and planted than younger plants, making the greater investment in labor and money riskier. But the greater investment in larger plants may be worthwhile if your objective is to fill a bare space as quickly as possible.

What to look for

Take your time when selecting plants. Bring a checklist to remind you what species and types will best fit your plan. Here are characteristics of high-quality, desirable plants:
● Plants are true to type; they have the correct leaf color, size, and shape. They also have the correct tag; note that mislabeling is common.
● The top growth and root mass of container plants is balanced. Branch tips show healthy-looking new growth.
● The root system is white to light beige in color. Roots are growing throughout the container or root ball.
● Tall tree species have a single trunk, or leader, that is thickest at the base. The trunk is strong though the tree may benefit from

▲ Trees and shrubs grown at a well-tended nursery or tree farm will bring their robust good health to your home landscape.

staking until established.
- Some smaller tree species, such as crape myrtle, have multiple trunks.
- On older trees branches are spaced along the trunk.
- Choose roses with dark, glossy leaves, new growth, and flower buds when shopping for container plants.
- When purchasing a tree look for one that has a gradual taper to the trunk and well-spaced branches.

What to avoid

Plants in greenhouses and nurseries may appear healthy at first glance but might reveal problems upon closer scrutiny. Inspect the crown, bark, leaf undersides, and root system (gently remove plants from containers to see their roots). Watch for the following:
- Off-color and undersize foliage indicates stressful conditions, such as lack of water or nutrients, or root damage.
- Dead or dying branch tips indicate poor growing conditions, root injury, or even insect or disease problems.
- Scraped, dented, or missing bark reveals physical injury from support wires, tools, etc., which can retard plant growth.
- Plants that are wilted, have weeds growing around the main stem, or are waterlogged indicate poor care.
- Dead (brown), overgrown, or circling roots (especially roots that grow around the crown of the tree, which can girdle and kill the plant) indicate the plant has been in a container too long.
- Plants with obvious signs or symptoms of pests or diseases indicate poor care. For example spongy black bark at the base of the plant indicates crown and root rots. Small raised bumps on tree and shrub bark may be symptoms of scale insects, which suck sap and debilitate plants.
- Blooming roses are no more desirable than plants without blooms. Snip off flowers at planting time to help channel the plant's energy into rooting rather than blooming.

Bare-root plants

Deciduous trees, shrubs, grapevines, brambles, roses, and fruit trees are often sold as bare-root plants. Bare-root plants are less expensive than container-grown plants and are available through garden centers and mail order companies. They are grown in rows in nurseries, dug up during the dormant season when relatively young (two to five years), and made available for planting from late winter through early spring. The soil clinging to the roots is washed or shaken off prior to packaging and shipment. Roots are then wrapped in moistened shredded newspaper, sphagnum peat moss, or other organic materials that can hold water. The roots should not be allowed to dry out.

The major disadvantage of bare-root plants is that you must be able to plant during unpredictable weather, which may be cold, wet, and windy. Minimize this problem by digging and amending the planting area the previous fall. If you are unable to plant when your order arrives, bury the root systems in a shallow trench of moist garden soil. This technique, called heeling in, keeps plants alive but dormant until conditions are more favorable for planting.

Some gardeners soak the roots of large bare-root trees, shrubs, and roses in a container of water for up to 24 hours prior to planting to hydrate the root system. Soak the roots of smaller plants for at least four hours for best results. Avoid soaking roots for longer periods to prevent suffocating them.

Quick to establish

Novice gardeners may mistakenly believe that bare-root plants are less desirable than container or balled-and-burlapped (B&B) plants because they appear to lack substance. They are sold in

◄ Look for tight, healthy buds on flowering shrubs at the nursery.

a dormant state without a mass of soil, and display no leaves or flowers. But a healthy, well-grown bare-root plant is easy to plant and may establish a root system faster than a potted or B&B plant. The roots of the latter types must grow out of the soil they've become accustomed to and adjust to soil with different texture and structure. This may impede root development. Plants may decline and die if the new soil is of poor quality. Bare-root plants, by contrast, can quickly exploit their new soil environment to grow roots.

Desirable qualities

Characteristics of a healthy bare-root plant include:
- Buds are tight and dormant rather than leafing out or blooming.
- The trunk and stems are free of cankers (dark or sunken areas in the bark).
- The crown (juncture of shoots and roots) is firm and solid to the touch.
- Roots are white or light brown and firm rather than black or slimy.
- The plant's identification tag and growing information are attached to it.

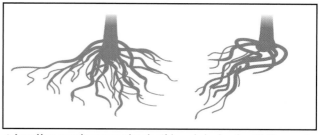

▲ A good bare-root plant prospect has plentiful, evenly developed, moist, fibrous roots.

▲ Don't select anything but the healthiest, most evenly colored and most vigorous prospects to plant in your home landscape.

Balled-and-burlapped plants

Balled-and-burlapped (B&B) trees and shrubs are grown in rows in nurseries and are periodically root-pruned. Root-pruning keeps the root systems fibrous and compact, promotes new root growth, and makes eventual digging and transporting more efficient. Plants are dug using machinery that creates a spherical root ball. This shape is the most stable and helps the plant retain a large number of roots with a small amount of soil. Even so most of the root system is left behind in the nursery. The root ball is dug when the soil is wet; otherwise the root ball may break apart and severely damage the root system. Most balled-and-burlapped plants sold by nurseries and garden centers are large deciduous trees and large evergreen trees.

The root ball is wrapped in burlap to hold it together after it is dug. A wire cage is often used to hold the root ball and burlap in place. Balled-and-burlapped trees and shrubs establish relatively quickly and can be planted successfully in spring and fall. Summer plantings are also feasible as long as the plants are watered regularly.

TIPS FOR B&B PLANTS

Always pick up B&B plants from underneath the root ball. Otherwise the weight of the soil may cause it to pull away from the roots and trunk, damaging the plant.

The root system should feel solid. A loose root ball indicates broken roots and careless handling. Check the root system by gently moving the trunk back and forth. The whole root ball should move with the trunk. A trunk that moves independently of the root ball is a sign of broken roots and a poor plant.

Keep the root ball uniformly moist prior to planting.

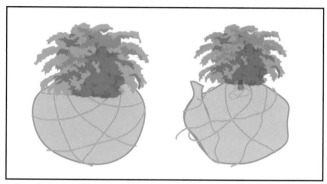

▲ A good balled-and-burlapped prospect is healthy, well-hydrated, and tightly bound with string or twine.

PLUSES AND MINUSES OF B&B PLANTS

On the plus side:
B&B plants are usually large and will fill the allotted area more quickly than either bare-root or container-grown plants.

B&B stock can be planted anytime the ground is unfrozen.

On the minus side:
B&B trees and shrubs have drastically reduced root systems and have difficulty taking up enough water to support the top growth. They must be watered frequently, especially during extended hot, dry weather.

The root ball is heavy. A cubic foot of soil and roots can weigh more than 100 pounds.

◀ The roots of balled-and-burlapped plants should be kept moist until planting.

Container-grown plants

Containers are a convenient way to purchase, transport, and plant nursery stock and herbaceous perennials. All flowering annuals and vegetable and herb plants are grown and sold in some type of plastic or fiber container. Container plants can be purchased and planted anytime the soil is unfrozen.

▲ A healthy nursery specimen, planted properly, will establish quickly in the landscape.

▲ Don't pick the first plant to catch your eye; compare every one for balanced growth and overall good health.

Watch for root problems

One drawback to container plants is that they are often rootbound. The root system may outgrow the container if the plant remains in it too long. If possible, before you purchase the plant, gently remove it from the container to examine the root system. Healthy roots have white growing tips. Roots should be visible throughout the planting mix. They will not be matted at the edges or at the bottom of the root ball. Overgrown roots, reaching tightly around the crown and trunk of a woody ornamental plant, can injure and eventually kill the plant. These strangling or girdling roots may be obvious. If not look for them by gently scraping aside the top few inches of growing medium.

Before planting container stock tease apart the roots and spread them into the planting hole. This breaks some of the roots and stimulates new root growth. When prepared this way container-grown trees and shrubs perform well in the landscape even though they have become slightly rootbound in their containers.

Avoid purchasing container-grown plants if the root mass is dark brown, smells odd, or tightly circles the bottom of the pot. Container plants may become waterlogged if they sit in puddles or poorly drained areas in the nursery or garden center. This can lead to root rot and poor growth when they are planted in a landscape.

Keep plants well watered

Container-grown plants may require more frequent watering after planting than bare-root plants or balled-and-burlapped plants. Container plants are grown in a loose medium that drains well but dries out more quickly than garden

▲ Look for tight blooms on flowering shrubs like roses, but also look for blooms that reveal the true color of the flowers.

soil. Even healthy-looking container plants typically undergo significant water stress. The plants tend to develop a compact root system with a large number of fine roots. After planting they may require water every other day, if rainfall is lacking, to keep the concentrated roots alive and to encourage new roots to grow into your yard's soil.

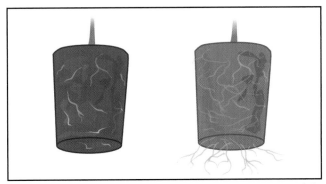

▲ A good container plant has healthy white roots that are not overgrown, crowded, or growing out the bottom of the container.

BUYING ROSES

There are three basic options when buying rose plants for your landscape or garden.

Bare-root roses. These are dormant plants whose soil has been removed from the roots to reduce the weight for shipping. They are sold by mail order suppliers and at some garden centers. Look for three or more strong canes or a Grade 1 label. Most bare-root and potted roses are grafted or budded plants. When a small piece (the bud) of the desired rose variety is removed from a cane and attached to a root system from another rose, these two parts heal together to become a rose plant.

Potted roses. Look for plants with three or more canes in 2-gallon containers. Choose plants that have already leafed, appear strong and healthy, and have new growth and buds.

Own-root roses. The term refers to roses that have been rooted from cuttings, divisions, layering, or tissue culturing, using a piece of cane to produce roots of its own. Unlike a budded or grafted plant, an own-root plant that freezes to the ground usually survives and resprouts from below the soil surface.

Transporting and storing before planting

Preparing your new trees or shrubs for planting begins with the way you transport them home from the nursery. All the care you give the plants before putting them in the ground increases their chances of succeeding, so the way in which you transport them is critical.

Transporting

If possible use an enclosed truck or van to transport your plant from the nursery, as this will protect it from wind damage or sun exposure. If you must use an open truck, tip the tree as much as you can to keep it out of the direct force of the wind as you travel, taking care to set it in a way that protects branches from being damaged. Cover it with a tented tarp or a breathable mesh material to guard against wind damage and to keep the roots from drying out in the sun. Secure the plant from shifting around with rope or bungee cords.

Root balls should be kept moist during transit. Water the roots before placing the tree into the vehicle, and lift the tree by the root ball or container—never the trunk—to put it into the vehicle. If you are transporting more than one tree, set them together snugly to keep them from moving around during transport; secure rope or bungee cords around them to keep them from falling over.

Storing

It is best to plant trees as soon as possible, but if you must store them before planting, your top priority is to protect the tree from drying out. Store the tree out of the sun and wind, which can dry out the roots quickly. Daily or even more frequent watering is essential. If the tree must be stored for a few days, cover the root ball with a material that retains moisture, such as burlap, canvas, or peat moss. If storing the tree for a week or more, heel in the tree—that is, temporarily plant it in loose soil—to keep it hydrated.

When to plant

In most areas early spring is the best time to plant deciduous trees, as they are still dormant. In the North early spring planting is best, once the danger of frost has past and before new buds and growth appear. Fall or winter planting should be done in areas where summer weather

▶ Keep trees out of the sun and wind, if possible, as they wait to be planted. Water the roots well, keeping them consistently moist until planting.

Planting mature trees has become a popular way to instantly make a landscape look established. The downside is the cost—the price of the mature tree and the transporting charges often make this process prohibitively expensive for most homeowners. Depending on the species a mature tree can cost anywhere from $200 to $2,000 or more, and another few hundred for transporting and planting the tree. But if you're intent on immediate satisfaction, planting a mature tree is the way to go.

The most important thing you can do when buying a mature tree is to purchase it from a reputable nursery that can help you choose the tree, properly transport it to your home, plant it, and give advice on caring for it. Look for healthy trees—good foliage and roots and overall shape. Consider the area where you'll be planting and determine whether the height and shape of the fully mature tree suits your landscape requirements.

Planting a mature tree usually requires professional help. A good rule of thumb is that if a tree requires professional transport to get it to its destination, it requires professional planting, too. Professionals have the best equipment for digging and preparing the site for planting. They use a large hydraulic tree spade (as above) to remove an oversize plug of soil to make a hole for the new tree. This spade is also used to lower the tree into the hole. Mature trees with deep root systems, such as oaks, require a generous-size hole that will accommodate their roots. Evergreens, which have shallower root systems, are transplanted more easily.

An added bonus of working with the pros is that if you pay to have the nursery plant your tree, it usually guarantees the health of the tree for at least a year. If your nursery fails to offer a guarantee, find another nursery.

Your newly transplanted mature tree will need to be solidly staked and carefully backfilled. Water well but skip fertilizing until the following season; this tree needs to spend its energy healing rather than generating new growth.

is extremely hot or dry and winter weather is mild, such as the South and the West.

Bare-root trees should be planted only in the early spring. Plant balled-and-burlapped trees in the early spring before the new buds or in early summer after the new growth has slowed. Container trees can be planted nearly anytime during the year, but the latest planting should be

before any risk of frost in the fall so the roots have time to become established before the ground freezes.

Evergreens are best planted in the early fall, when the hot days of summer are past but there's still time before the cold of winter for the roots to become established. Make sure you get them in the ground well before there's any chance of a hard frost.

Planting step-by-step

▲ Prepare the rootball of a container-grown plant before planting it.

▲ Loosen any wrap and remove binding of a balled-and-burlapped plant.

▶ Dig a generous-size hole, setting the backfill on a tarp and mixing the soil with compost before returning it into the hole.

In addition to the health and quality of the new plants themselves, proper planting is crucial to the future success of your new trees and shrubs. Most trees and shrubs that fail to thrive do so as a result of bad preparation and careless planting. If you choose the right site for the tree, prepare well for planting, plant correctly, and take care of it, all that's left is to watch your tree grow. Here are the step-by-step basics for planting a tree or shrub:

WHAT YOU NEED

Basic supplies and tools include: a garden spade or roundhead shovel; a plastic tarp; a handheld cultivator or spading fork; a sharp knife or garden shears; manure, compost, or enriched soil such as Miracle-Gro Organic Choice Garden Soil or Miracle-Gro Garden Soil for Trees & Shrubs; and a garden hose or large-capacity watering bucket.

1. Dig the hole

Using a spade or shovel, dig a hole about three times the width of the root ball and deep enough to hold the entire root ball, with the base of the trunk even with the surrounding ground. Remove the soil to a tarp set next to your hole. Break up any compacted soil on the sides of the hole using a spading fork or hand cultivator to help the roots penetrate the soil, but leave the bottom undisturbed to provide stable ground on which the tree will rest. A balled-and-burlapped tree should be unwrapped so you can see the roots of the tree to determine the correct depth of the hole. Bare-root or seedling trees should be planted in a hole that is three times wider than the unfurled root system to allow enough room for the roots to freely establish themselves in the surrounding soil.

2. Prep the tree for planting

Container-grown plants should be prepared by removing all container materials, including strings, wire, and tags. If a gentle shake fails to dislodge the plant from the container, cut down the side of the container in order to remove the tree. Handle the tree by the root ball only—never try to pull the tree out of the container by the trunk. If the roots are tightly wrapped around the root ball, take a sharp knife and make four or five vertical slits about 1½ inches deep into the roots. Spread the roots out gently into the hole when planting.

Balled-and-burlapped trees should be set in the hole with the burlap still wrapped around the root ball. Once the tree is placed in the hole, unwrap the tree, and remove the ties and the burlap. Loosen tangled roots either with your hands or by making four or five vertical slits into the roots with a sharp knife.

Seedlings or bare-root trees should be removed from the packaging and placed in the soil immediately. Spread the roots out into the hole and gently push them into the soil to keep them from drying out.

IMPROVE YOUR SOIL

When you dig a hole to plant a tree or shrub, you have a unique opportunity to improve the quality of the soil and give your new planting a better chance to thrive. After you remove the soil from the hole to the plastic tarp, use a shovel to mix in another 30 percent of manure, compost, or enriched soil to the backfilled soil. This will help the soil provide essential nutrients and drain well, which are key to the new plant's survival during that crucial first season in its new home.

▶ One of the most common mistakes people make when planting trees and shrubs is not digging a deep or wide enough hole for the new plant. A hole needs to be at least three times as wide as the root ball and deep enough to contain the entire root ball; if you scrimp on the size of your hole, you're not giving the roots room and freedom they need to become established.

Planting step-by-step *(continued)*

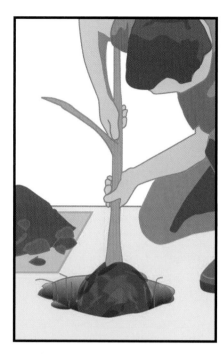

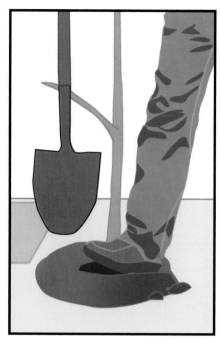

► Set the tree in the hole, remove ties and burlap, and loosen roots before backfilling.

◄ Tamp the soil lightly after backfilling, leaving a basin shape in the middle to help retain water.

▲ The wrapping materials on balled-and-burlapped trees and shrubs shouldn't be removed until the plant has been set in the hole; these materials protect the root ball until the moment you're ready to begin backfilling.

3. Set the tree

Set a balled-and-burlapped tree in the hole and straighten it before filling in with dirt. Backfill the hole and gently tamp the soil about one-third of the way up. Continue to backfill, gently tamping the soil as you go. Build up the soil to create a rim around the edges of the hole, forming a basin that will help the soil retain water while the tree becomes established in the ground.

Set seedlings or bare-root trees in the hole so that the point where the roots meet the tree rests about 2 inches higher than the surrounding soil. This way the roots and backfilled soil will settle to the same height as the surrounding ground. Spread the roots and carefully begin to backfill the hole. About halfway through, gently water and then finish filling in the hole. Tamp the soil lightly as you go to keep the tree in place.

▲ Spread the roots of a bare-root plant over a mound of undisturbed soil in your hole. The mound gives the tree a firm foundation and the roots will grow around and beyond it. Lay a stick across the hole to help ensure the crown of the plant will be even with the surface of the soil.

TREE SHELTERS

An alternative to staking a small tree is using a tree shelter. Available at nurseries and garden centers, tree shelters are photodegradable tubes that are placed over young trees to protect them from wind, extreme temperatures, and damage from mowing or hungry deer or other animals. Staked solidly to the ground, a tree shelter also promotes a straight trunk.

▲ Water thoroughly.

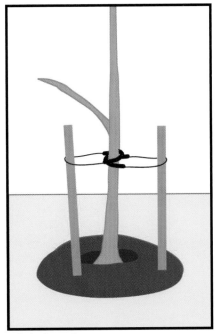

▲ Stake the tree for extra support.

▲ Apply mulch around the basin of soil.

4. Water

Water thoroughly, slowly filling the basin to let the soil absorb the water. Water deeply, until all the air bubbles have stopped coming to the surface; this lets you know that the water has reached the entire root ball. Continue to water thoroughly once a week until the roots have had time to become established—usually in about six weeks.

5. Stake the tree

Stake a tree to stabilize it until the roots are strong enough to secure it in the ground. Some trees can go unstaked, but young trees exposed to wind, top-heavy trees, and evergreens should be staked to keep them in place while the roots settle in. Proper staking will allow the tree some movement so the roots can establish and grow as they would with the natural movement of an unstaked tree. Use 3-inch-wide rubber strapping or webbing, wrapped around the lower part of the tree, at least 3 feet from the ground. The size of the tree determines how many stakes you'll need. A small tree, 3 inches or less in diameter, can be secured with one stake positioned facing the wind. A larger tree may require two or three stakes to do the job. Remove the stakes after one year so the tree can learn to grow and withstand the elements on its own.

6. Mulch

Mulch will help keep the new tree hydrated, maintain the soil at a fairly even temperature, and prevent competing grass and weeds from stealing water and nutrients from the tree. Spread a 2- to 4-inch layer of organic or wood-chip mulch around the tree, making sure to leave a 6-inch ring of mulch-free soil around the trunk. The mulch should be loosely spread to ensure that enough water and air go through the soil and to the roots.

▲ Taking time to properly prepare and to settle your plant in its new home pays off by increasing its chances of surviving the critical first year.

Caring for your trees and shrubs

▲ Water and fertilize low-growing evergreen shrubs well until established; eventually they will be among the most low-maintenance plants in your landscape.

The ongoing care of your trees and shrubs has long-term effects on their health and success. Besides seasonal efforts such as mulching, winter protection, and pruning, basic maintenance consists primarily of watering and feeding your plants.

Watering

Supplying water to developing root systems is the single most important thing you can do for new plants. Many woody shrubs and small fruit trees have relatively shallow root systems. Natural rainfall alone will probably fail to give your new plants adequate water at the right time. New plants require frequent watering to promote root growth. Here are some guidelines to follow to determine when and how much to water:

Water all plants thoroughly after planting. The appropriate amount of water depends on the type of soil, the size of the planting area, and the weather.

Plants growing in sandy soil require more frequent watering. Soil high in clay absorbs, releases, and drains water slowly. Adding organic matter to soil helps it better hold water for plant growth and drain away excess water.

Water before you notice wilting foliage. New plants may require watering once week for several months if rainfall is lacking. Water to keep the rootball moist but avoid drowning the plant.

Water plants deeply and thoroughly. Dig down 4 to 6 inches with a screwdriver or finger to test for moisture.

Water in the morning if possible. Avoid wetting foliage if watering late in the day. Plants need time to dry off before nightfall to avoid disease.

Water spring-planted shrubs and trees throughout the growing season and into the fall. Water fall plantings until the ground freezes (if it does) and then periodically during winter thaws.

Once garden and landscape plants are established, water them deeply and less frequently to encourage a more extensive root system and improved plant growth.

Avoid excessive watering where soil drainage is inadequate. Roots die off when the soil's pore spaces are filled with water instead of air for more than 24 hours.

Feeding

Trees and shrubs generally don't require fertilizing in the first year, as plenty of

TREES AND SHRUBS FOR CONTAINERS
Aucuba, Japanese
Boxwood, common
Buckeye, bottlebrush
Cherry, Japanese flowering
Citrus (dwarf varieties)
Crabapple, flowering
Daphne, burkwood
Dogwood, flowering
Goldenchain tree
Heavenly bamboo
Junipers
Maples (amur, Japanese)
Palm, sago
Redbud, eastern
Rosemary
Rose
Silverbell, Carolina
Sweet olive

▲ Trees and shrubs in a hot, arid climate need supplemental watering until established.

CARING FOR CONTAINER PLANTS

Planting in containers is a great way to enjoy the authentic tree-and-shrub feeling in a small space, such as a patio or a deck. Growing these plants in pots gives you flexibility on placement, allowing you to move them to follow the sun or to protect them from harsh weather. Many small trees and shrubs are suitable for container planting, but you have to keep a few care guidelines in mind.

Choose a container that is large enough to accommodate the plant's mature root system. Plant in a lightweight, enriched soil mix, and plan to water and feed these plants much more frequently than those in the ground. Plants in pots lose water and nutrients rapidly through the drainage holes that are necessary at the bottom of the pots. Water generously, as often as necessary to prevent the soil from drying out and leaves from wilting; water daily during hot, dry weather.

Feed regularly with a liquid fertilizer such as Miracle-Gro to replenish nutrients to the soil. And consider adding water-absorbing crystals to your potting soil, which can improve the retention of water in the container. A spoonful of crystals can have a significant benefit for potted trees and shrubs.

Plants in pots are more susceptible to winter damage because they don't benefit from the protection of the soil that plants in the ground have. If you intend to keep your potted trees and shrubs outdoors year-round, choose plants that are at least one zone hardier than where you live. Or plan to move containers into a protected area such as an unheated garage during winter.

sources, depending on the conditions. Water deeply (12 to 18 inches) but as infrequently as possible to encourage deep rooting. Water early in the day and avoid wetting foliage and fostering disease.

You can water roses in a number of ways, from hoses and sprinklers to drip irrigation. Drip systems, employing either emitters or soaker hoses, work the most efficiently.

If you are planting roses on sloping ground, terrace the area with landscape timbers, bricks, or stones to impede runoff and help each plant receive enough water. But roses suffer in low-growing or poorly draining areas that remain wet or soggy. Avoid the latter situation by improving the soil with plenty of organic matter.

Roses need food in order to grow, bloom, and be healthy. They have greater nutritional needs than many other plants, and supplemental feeding is essential if you want top performance. Choose a complete, balanced formula made for roses and apply it once a month during the growing season. Apply slow-release food less often, depending on the formulation. Follow the product directions when feeding roses.

▲ Small trees and shrubs growing in containers help make up for the lack of a patio garden.

Stop feeding roses about two months before the first frost or at least a month before cold weather sets in. Feeding encourages new growth, which would have insufficient time to adjust to the weather change and would likely be damaged by cold. All roses need a resting period over winter, whether you live in a frost-free region or a frigid one; feeding should be suspended until plants resume growing in spring.

nutrients are stored in the plant already. And extra fertilizing too soon after planting will encourage leafy growth at the expense of developing roots.

So begin fertilizing in the late spring the first season after planting. For young trees a liquid quick-release fertilizer such as Miracle-Gro at 15 percent strength is plenty. For mature trees use a continuous-release granular plant food such as Miracle-Gro Shake 'n Feed Plant Food. Even a well-established, fully mature tree appreciates an annual boost of fertilizer. Feed trees and shrubs a minimum of once a year, though twice a year in the South can be beneficial. Test your soil every few years to ensure vital nutrients remain in good balance.

Watering and feeding roses

Although some varieties of roses can survive with less than optimal watering, adequate moisture helps increase a plant's potential for healthy growth, gorgeous flowers, and lush foliage. Supplemental watering is needless when sufficient rainfall occurs. During the growing season most roses need 1 inch of water per week from rainfall or other

▲ A young Colorado spruce will reward you for your attentive early care with good health and longevity.

▲ Feed and water your roses to maximize their blooming potential.

Mulching and seasonal protection

▲ Mulch even mature trees to ensure they get and retain the moisture they need throughout the growing season.

- **Grass clippings, shredded leaves, and pine straw.** These organic mulches break down quickly into organic matter.
- **Gravel and rock.** This type of mulch is laid on top of breathable landscape fabric. Avoid using black plastic sheeting under gravel, as the plastic prevents air and water movement to the roots of plants.
- **Newspaper.** All pages except glossy paper can be used. Most newspaper inks are soy-based and contain no dangerous heavy metals. Overlap the newspaper sections, in layers up to six or eight sheets deep, and cover them with wood chips, grass clippings, or compost.

How to mulch

Whichever mulch you use under trees and shrubs, apply it properly. For young trees, smaller trees, and shrubs, mulch should extend at least 3 feet in diameter around the plant. For medium or larger trees, mulch an area 8 to 12 feet in

Beyond the basic feeding and watering required for the ongoing maintenance of your trees and shrubs, it's important to take a seasonal approach to long-term care. Mulching at least twice a year can go far in protecting your plants from summer drought and harsh winter conditions. Mulching also prevents unintentional run-ins with lawn mowers, string trimmers, footballs, bicycles, etc. Take special care to protect your plants from seasonal conditions such as harsh winter weather and hungry animals.

Mulching

Mulch is a layer of organic or inorganic material used to blanket the soil. It provides multiple benefits by helping to preserve soil moisture,

keeping weeds down, controling erosion, insulating plants from rapid temperature fluctuations, and preventing mud and disease organisms from splashing onto plants during watering. Organic mulches gradually break down and contribute organic matter and nutrients to the soil.

Types of mulch

- **Shredded wood, bark, bark or wood chips.** These are used extensively around foundation plants; cedar and cypress mulches last the longest. Large bark chips last longer than smaller bark chips. Avoid buying bulk mulch that smells of alcohol or is steaming and hot to the touch.

▲ Mulch benefits every plant in the garden bed, retaining moisture, inhibiting weeds, and establishing an area protected by damage from foot traffic or lawn equipment.

◀ Cypress mulch

▶ Pine needle mulch

◀ Garden bark mulch

▶ Wood chip mulch

◀ Rock mulch

diameter, depending on the size of the tree. This is meant to cover the drip line, which is the reach of the plant's branches.

Keep the mulch 6 inches away from the plant's trunk to avoid creating a haven for rodents or disease organisms. Mulch at least once at the beginning of the growing season, then replenish the mulch before winter to protect the roots from the harsh effects of freezing and thawing soil.

Winter protection

Young trees and shrubs are especially susceptible to winter injury caused by deicing salts, extended freezing temperatures, alternating freezes and thaws, and browsing animals. Plants that are only marginally hardy in your area are more prone to these problems. Frost cracks caused by wide temperature swings through the day, may occur on the southwest side of thin-bark trees, such as apple and peach. Prevent the problem by painting the trunk of these trees with white latex paint, or wrapping them with a light-color material.

Minimize potential problems by taking good care of your new plants. Avoid pruning or fertilizing in late summer; both practices stimulate late growth at a time when perennial plants enter natural dormancy. Water woody ornamentals throughout fall and winter if rainfall is inadequate and snow cover is absent.

Evergreen plants can dry out and suffer winter burn when the soil freezes— preventing water uptake— while leaves continue to lose moisture. Antitranspirants are available to coat evergreen leaves and reduce water loss by the foliage. These products degrade rapidly

▲ Surround vulnerable trees with mesh to protect them from ravaging animals.

and must be reapplied several times each year to be effective.

Protect trees and shrubs from harsh winter winds by creating a protective wind barrier. Set stakes around the tree and wrap that established perimeter with burlap.

Many animals feed on and damage trees and shrubs during the growing season and especially in winter. Surround trees and shrubs with hardware cloth, a tree guard, or appropriate fencing to prevent deer, rabbits, and voles from feeding. Some repellents dissuade deer and rabbits; use snap traps to reduce the vole population. See pages 94 and 95 for more information on protecting your trees from pest animals.

Tree and shrub maintenance

▲ Regular pruning helps trees and shrubs become lasting assets on your property.

After regularly feeding, watering, and mulching, pruning is the single most important ongoing maintenance care you can provide your trees and shrubs. Pruning keeps your plants looking good and benefits them as well.

Why prune?

When considering whether to prune, take a look at what pruning can accomplish.

Maintain size and shape

You planted that tree or shrub with its mature size and shape in mind, but somewhere along the way, it has gotten overgrown and scraggly-looking. Pruning from when the plant is young helps keep the size and shape you want. Once things get out of hand, pruning is the only way to get things back under control. But the longer you wait to begin pruning, the longer it will take to reach your ultimate goal in size and shape of the tree or shrub.

Some trees and shrubs are planted because they will become big and fulfill a specific need in the landscape. Others are planted without those intentions yet seem to outgrow your ability to take care of them. Fruit trees, for example, are best kept to a size where you can easily reach the fruit for harvesting.

Keep it healthy and attractive

The healthier the plant the more attractive it will be. Pruning not only keeps the desired size and shape of the tree or shrub, it can prevent infestations of insects or diseases that overtake ailing branches. Removing dead and diseased branches and limbs eliminates access for diseases and insects. A healthy tree or shrub is also better able to withstand the weight of snow or the effects of heavy storms as the limbs are stronger and able to handle the additional stress.

Increase fruit and flower production

Pruning certain plants helps produce more flowers as cutting back old wood allows additional blooms to develop on the emerging new wood. The same is true for plants that flower on old wood; pruning at the right time of year ensures that the buds will survive and produce more flowers. Fruit trees especially should be pruned with flower production in mind. Proper, timely pruning keeps the blooms intact, and the more blooms, the more fruit.

▲ Your trees and shrubs will look their best when you follow a year-round calendar of maintenance.

Stimulate new growth

New growth is important to the continuing health and good looks of a tree or shrub. Not only does pruning encourage new growth, it keeps it growing in the direction you desire. Branch and limb problems, such as crossing or rubbing branches, can damage a tree and ultimately make it weaker. Removing those branches allows the tree to keep growing stronger and produces a more

◀ A citrus tree in the home landscape should be kept at a manageable height for easy harvesting.

▲ Modest day-to-day grooming maintains the good looks and health of your trees and shrubs.

▲ Pruning and other annual maintenance help a mature apple tree continue vigorous growth and production.

attractively shaped tree. Pruning also helps eliminate branch and limb crowding. Removing some limbs opens the interior of the plant to more air and light, reducing the occurrence of diseases such as powdery mildew and leaf spot. For some plants severe cutting back will actually rejuvenate the plant, promoting new and healthy growth and allowing you to structure the plant into your desired shape and size.

Show off bark and branches

Pruning can also expose colorful bark and branches. The bark of birch trees adds interesting color and texture to the landscape, for example, but only if you can see it.

Prune to make the most of attractive bark in winter.

Remove dead and diseased branches and limbs

One of the most important reasons to prune is to remove damaged limbs, as they can harm other limbs and branches and allow insects and diseases access to the plant. Keeping the tree free from damaged limbs also helps prevent later problems from frost, wind, snow, or storms.

Pruning safety and equipment

▲ Good safety habits and well-cared for equipment are important to successful pruning.

It's a fact that pruning can be hazardous. While a tree limb falling on you is sure to hurt, a cut from a thorny rose bush hurts as well. Common sense and the proper use of the right equipment will help keep you safe while pruning.

Safety

Wear protective gear whenever you prune no matter how small the job may seem. Accidents can happen, and the more you protect yourself from the start, the less likely you'll be hurt. Always wear safety goggles, long-sleeved shirts, long pants, heavy gloves, and sturdy footwear. You also may want to wear a hard hat when pruning trees, especially if you are removing larger limbs.

Equipment safety is also important when pruning. Working with ladders and power equipment poses its own risks, so take precautions when using this equipment. Make sure to properly maintain any power equipment and to follow manufacturers' safety guidelines. Inspect all power equipment before use to ensure it is in good condition. Wear eye protection and ear protection against loud noise. Place ladders securely against a surface and on even ground. Never stand on the top step or two of a ladder.

Be aware of your environment when pruning. Power lines can be extremely dangerous to prune around, and those areas should be left to professionals. Ladders and power lines make a bad mix, so be sure when you carry or place a ladder that it is away from any power lines. Be alert to weather conditions when pruning. Never use a ladder or power equipment in the rain, and stop working at the first sign of thunder, even if there is no rain. Lightning can be deadly if you're pruning under a tree.

Equipment

Even the most inexperienced pruner needs some basic equipment in the shed when the need to prune arises. The minimum you should keep handy includes a sharp, small-bladed knife, a pair of heavy gloves, eye protection and at least some of the following tools.

● **Pruners.** Hand pruners are a must because they are the tools you will use the most. You can use them to cut

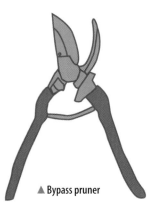

▲ Anvil pruner

▲ Bypass pruner

stems up to ½ inch in diameter, and for many different types of pruning jobs. Hand pruners come in two varieties—anvil or bypass. An anvil-type pruner has a sharp blade that cuts the stem against a flat anvil. The stems may be crushed when using this type of pruner so keep the blade sharp to minimize trauma to the wood, or use a bypass-type pruner.

The bypass-type pruner has a sharp blade that cuts against a curved anvil, providing a cleaner cut. You can also purchase a pole pruner, which has the same cutting mechanism as either an anvil or bypass pruner but with a long pole attached to get into those hard-to-reach areas of full hedges and shrubs.

● **Loppers.** Long-handled loppers handle bigger jobs than pruners do. They cut stems up to 1½ inches in

▲ Lopper

diameter and can reach into smaller trees and large shrubs with ease. The long-handled loppers give you good leverage when cutting larger stems to make the cut cleaner and more easily. They usually extend your reach an additional 16 to 36 inches (depending on the size you buy) and come in either the anvil or bypass style of cutting mechanism. Buy a ratcheted or gear model for even easier cutting. Try them out before you buy them to ensure there is enough space between the handles to avoid pinching your fingers.

● **Hedge shears.** You can buy either handheld or power hedge shears to keep your hedges looking their best. Manual shears look like

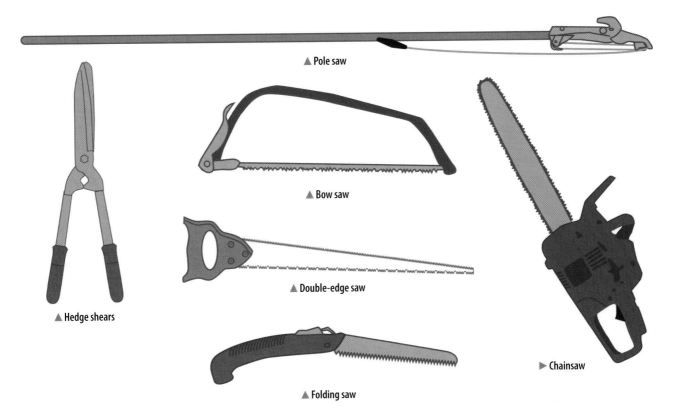

▲ Pole saw

▲ Bow saw

▲ Double-edge saw

▲ Hedge shears

▲ Folding saw

▶ Chainsaw

long-handled scissors but with long cutting blades. You can either hold them and use them like scissors in one hand, or use both hands for more control. Electric-, battery-, or gas-powered hedge shears are preferable for bigger hedge-pruning jobs. Not only will they move more quickly through the stems and limbs, they allow you to achieve a more definitive shape and easily top off a hedge. Be careful to avoid cutting through the cord with an electric-powered shear, and consider wearing ear protection against the noise.

● **Saws.** Manual pruning saws cut through limbs up to 4 or 5 inches in diameter and come in many sizes. The size of the pruning job should determine what size saw is appropriate. Small, folding, Japanese-type saws are great for smaller jobs and for areas of a tree or shrub where growth is dense. These produce clean, smooth cuts and can easily be toted around in your pocket from job to job. Make sure to buy a folding saw with a locking mechanism that will ensure the blade stays open while you're cutting. Bow saws are

inexpensive, have replaceable blades, and work well for larger limbs. But their shape may prohibit use in tighter areas. Curved-blade pruning saws work on larger limbs as well and can fit in tighter spaces than a bow saw can. Never use a carpenter's saw to prune because it is made to cut dry rather than green wood.

● **Chainsaws.** Use a chainsaw to cut large limbs. Whether battery-operated, or powered by gas or electricity, the chainsaw is the big gun in the pruner's arsenal. The biggest concern with the chainsaw is

safety—it can be dangerous. Wear protective goggles, long pants, gloves, ear protection, and even a hard hat. Follow all manufacturers' directions for use and safety, and be sure to keep both hands on the handle when using it. Buy a chainsaw with an automatic brake that will stop cutting in an emergency.

Taking care of equipment

One of the most important chores of pruning is often overlooked. Taking proper care of your equipment will help you achieve safe pruning and good, clean cuts and will make your investment in pruning tools well worth the money. Always clean your equipment after use. Use a couple of drops of lubricant oil on the blades to prevent rust. Oil the moving parts occasionally to keep them in working order. Keep the blades sharp, and replace or sharpen saw blades as needed. Always store your pruning tools in a dry, protected place, and well out of the reach of children.

PRUNING SAFETY CHECKLIST

Make sure equipment is sharpened and/or running properly before setting up to prune. Be alert and use common sense while you work.
● Wear snug-fitting clothing, protective glasses, and a hard hat—and ear protection and sturdy leather boots if using power equipment.
● Before beginning work, check for the presence of electrical or other overhead lines, as well as dead or hanging branches.
● Determine in advance where pruning debris will fall. Protect plants or objects below, and make sure no one will be hit when debris drops.
● Assign a helper to assist from below, for aid with equipment and as a general lookout for safety.
● Secure stepladder or extension ladder properly before ascending. Be sure one hand is on the ladder and one hand firmly holds the saw.
● Stop the job if it seems an awkward reach or in any way unsteady, or if you lack the proper equipment. Call a professional to do any work that you cannot reasonably do yourself.

Pruning basics

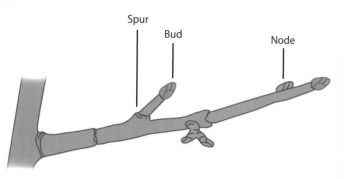

Spur

Bud

Node

▲ Winter is the best time to observe the pruning needs of deciduous trees.

U nderstanding the how, why, and when of pruning is easier if you first look at a few basic components of a woody plant. The **buds** of a woody plant grow where the leaves (or stems) or flowers (or fruit) begin. They are new, dormant shoots that are often covered with scales, from which the leaves or flowers will emerge. A **node** is the place where the bud is attached to the stem. **Spurs** are condensed stems where flowers or fruit develop. These parts of the woody plant are what you are concerned with when pruning most any tree or shrub. Other areas of trees or shrubs relevant to pruning will be discussed in later pages.

When to prune

When to prune is one of the most asked questions about pruning. The answer is that it depends on the kind of plant you need to prune. Here is a basic summary of plants and their best times to prune.

Spring is the time to prune plants that flower in the summer and bloom on new growth. Broadleaf evergreens, which are unflowering, as

► Shear hedges as necessary throughout the summer to keep a tidy form.

Roses such as 'Paul's Scarlet Climber' can be deadheaded throughout their growing season to stimulate further blooming.

Hire a professional when there is a big job to do, especially pruning a large, mature tree. Pros are far better equipped to handle challenging conditions for which the average person has neither the proper tools nor the skill. Trimming high limbs, cutting very large limbs, or pruning near power lines— these are all situations in which you should definitely hire an arborist. Besides handling difficult pruning tasks, they can evaluate your trees for insects or diseases.

An arborist can take care of problematic or damaged branches.

To find a reputable, certified arborist in your area, contact the International Society of Arboriculture at 217/355-9411 or isa-arbor.com. Its members have been tested and certified with at least 3 years' experience. You can also contact the Tree Care Industry Association, which is a trade association of tree care professionals. Call 800/733-2622 or go to www.tcia.org.

Ask any arborist you are considering hiring to show you proof of liability insurance and worker's compensation, in the event of any accident that might happen on your property. Ask for current local references too. Get an estimate and a contract for the cost and scope of the work—which should always include the removal of debris.

well as evergreen or deciduous hedges can also be pruned in the spring. Plants that flower in the spring can be pruned right after flowering in the late spring or early summer.

Summer is the best time to shear hedges or to prune summer-blooming plants; do this right after flowering. Mature roses can also be pruned in the summer after the blooms are gone.

It's unwise to prune in fall, unless the plant is already dormant in colder climates.

Roses should be trimmed before winter weather arrives.

Prune deciduous trees and nonblooming deciduous shrubs in winter. Late winter or very early spring are good times to prune fruit trees.

How often to prune

The frequency of pruning depends on how fast the tree or shrub grows, the shape you wish to keep, the plant's age, the weather, and the planting site. Fast-growing plants probably require more

frequent pruning to keep them healthy, while slow-growing plants may need pruning less often because they keep their shape longer. The weather and planting site take part in the growth process as well. Favorable weather and a good planting spot mean a healthier plant, and therefore more pruning. Younger plants, especially trees, will require pruning more often to train them into the desired shape. As a tree matures, the growth pattern is established and less frequent pruning is needed. Your reason for pruning also

Broadleaf evergreens such as holly can be pruned in spring.

Pruning basics *(continued)*

dictates how often you need to do it. If you're pruning to keep an unruly bush out of the way of the front door, you may need to cut it back a few times during the growing season to keep the way clear. If you're removing damaged limbs, pruning after storms or harsh weather will need to be done as necessary. Formal hedges take a lot of time to keep up, so be prepared to prune regularly to keep the clean lines.

How much to prune

How much to prune a particular plant is determined by the type and health of the plant, and the reason for pruning. Some plants need more trimming than others. Shearing a hedge, for example, can remove only the unruly stems from the desired shape or create a certain shape with additional cutting. Some plants need to be cut back or renovated, which requires much more severe pruning. The basic rule of thumb is to remove only one-fourth of the plant at one time (unless you know the plant can take heavy pruning). If a plant needs severe pruning, spread the process over a period of years to achieve the desired results, and avoid removing

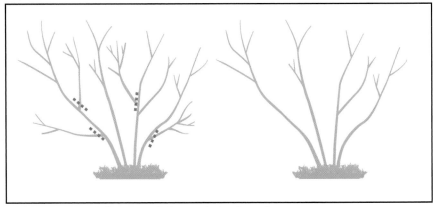

▲ A thinning cut strategically removes a limb or stem back to the trunk.

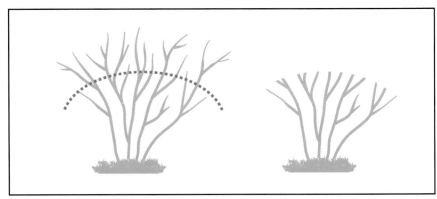

▲ A heading cut generally encourages growth that fills out the top of a plant.

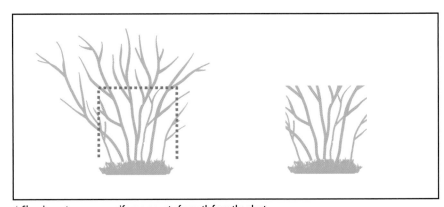

▲ Shearing cuts remove a uniform amount of growth from the plant.

▲ Pruning back roses stimulates vigorous new growth.

too much of the plant at once and damaging it.

Cuts

There are three basic types of cuts that you make when pruning. Knowing how the cut will affect the plant is essential to determine the best way to prune it.

Thinning cuts are simply that—removing limbs or stems all the way to the main branch or trunk. Thinning allows more light and air into the plant, making the remaining branches healthier. Thinning

the plant will keep it growing in its natural habit but will encourage the remaining branches to grow even more vigorously.

Heading cuts are cuts made in no specific place on the stem but remove the main bud on the stem. Avoid leaving stubs. Cut back to just above the lateral bud. These cuts allow for new stems to grow and fill out the plant more completely. These types of cuts can cause overcrowding, which can be unhealthy for the plant. Depriving the inner limbs of

air and light from excessive growth can damage plants.

Shearing cuts are used to remove a uniform amount from all over the plant. Rather than selecting individual branches and stems to prune, you prune them all. This maintains a desired shape, such as a formal hedge, that will need to be pruned regularly to keep it neat. Most trees and shrubs fail to tolerate shearing, so be sure to shear only those plants that can take it.

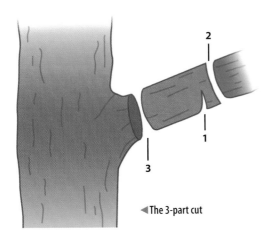

▲The 3-part cut

How to make the cuts is determined by what type of plant you are pruning. Selective pruning (as opposed to shearing cuts) are determined by the growth habit of the plant. Plants with alternate branches should be pruned ¼ inch above a bud that faces away from the tree. Slant the cut away from the bud. Plants with opposing branches should be cut halfway in between the buds. You can use either a flat cut or a slanted cut.

The 3-part cut

When pruning large limbs from a tree, use a 3-part cut method for best results. The ultimate goal is to prune the limb to a bit above the collar of the branch. The collar is the enlarged area where the base of the branch meets the trunk. The first cut should be made from the bottom of the branch up. Cut about halfway through the branch, 6 to 8 inches away from the collar. The second cut is made from the top down. This cut should be made a few inches farther out on the branch than the first cut, and cut right through the branch. Make the third and final cut at the base of the collar of the branch. This technique will protect the bark from peeling off the trunk when removing the large limb.

▲ Prune a dormant apple tree in winter.

PRUNING CALENDAR

Winter
Prune shrubs with berries or trees. In late winter to early spring, prune deciduous trees, fruit trees, and deciduous shrubs that do not bloom in the spring. Only prune when the temperature is consistently above 20° F.

Early Spring
Prune trees and shrubs that bloom in summer, as these generally bloom on new growth. Also prune non blooming broadleaf evergreens, as well as evergreen and deciduous hedges. Prune hybrid tea, floribunda, grandiflora, and miniature roses, and remove winter dieback on climbing and rambling roses.

Late Spring or Early Summer
Prune shrubs that bloom in spring, just after the blossoms fade. Pinch or trim one-half of the new growth (or candles) on pines and other needled evergreens.

Summer
Shear deciduous or evergreen hedges as necessary. Prune mature climbing roses and rambling roses after blooming. Prune dogwoods, maples, walnuts, and yellowwoods, if necessary. Prune shrubs and trees that bloom in summer after the flowers fade.

Late Fall
Trim long rose canes, which will be damaged by winter wind and weather.

▲ Prune deciduous shrubs in winter when you can identify the best thinning cuts.

Pruning deciduous trees

▲ A well-maintained and trained young oak (above) will become the old oak of the future (left).

▲ This mountain ash sapling will quickly take to training.

Trees will look better, be healthier, and add value to your property when they are properly pruned. From the time a tree is planted until it is finally mature, investing the time to care for it with pruning is well worth the effort. Prune deciduous trees in winter when the tree is dormant and you can see the overall structure of the branches without the leaves.

Young trees

● **Establish a central leader:** Developing a central leader makes the tree look like a tree instead of an overgrown shrub and will provide the best support for the rest of the branches. Use thinning cuts to remove smaller branches from the trunk you have selected to develop. If there are multiple branches growing from the ground, choose the sturdiest, most centered vertical branch as the central leader. Begin this task in the second year after the tree has been planted. Waiting any later could mean much more extensive pruning on a young tree, and it may fail to survive the stress.

● **Develop branch structure:** Pruning for the rest of the tree should begin in the third year after the tree has been planted. Choosing scaffold branches, pruning temporary branches, and remowving branches with narrow crotch angles should be done at this stage.

● **Scaffold branches:** These are the main branches of the top of the tree that make up the basic skeleton of the tree's crown. The best branches to keep as scaffold branches are ones that are a bit thinner than the trunk, grow at an angle of at least 45 degrees from the trunk, are spaced evenly vertically and radially, and are far enough from the ground to allow yard activity under the tree. This task could take a few years to accomplish as the tree begins to take its final shape and the branches become more fully developed.

● **Temporary branches:** These are branches that cover a portion of the trunk, are lower to the ground, and begin to cover more of the trunk as the tree matures.

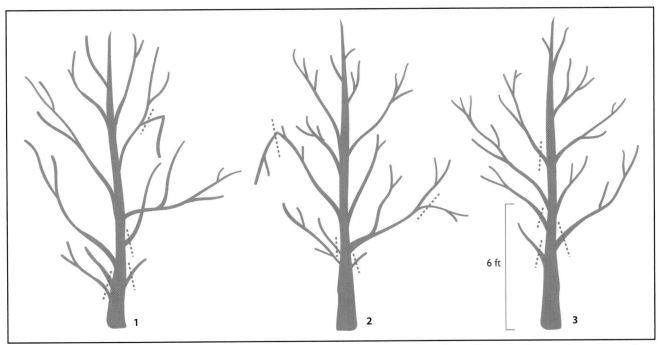

▲ 1. Remove damaged or crossed branches and temporary lower limbs on a newly planted tree. 2. In year 3, remove damaged branches and prune to shorten or remove lower branches. 3. In year 5 or 6, thin lightly and prune low branches to a clearance of 6 feet.

GENERAL PRUNING TASKS FOR TRAINING A YOUNG TREE

● Remove broken branches to eliminate threat of pests or disease.
● Remove suckers, which are upright growths from the roots. Remove watersprouts, which are weak growths on the limbs.
● Train a central leader or main stem for certain species. Remove competing leaders to establish a solid form and structure for the tree.
● Prune branches that form a narrow angle with the trunk to establish branches with strong, wide, open angles. (Trees with strictly upright forms don't require this task.)
● Remove crossed or rubbing branches.

Remove these branches over time if necessary—avoid pruning too much at once. Some trees fail to develop temporary branches or the branches were pruned off at the nursery before you purchased the tree.
● **Prune weak crotch connections:** This is necessary to ensure the overall health of the tree. These are branches that angle narrowly against the trunk. The bark of these branches becomes damaged because it can't grow correctly in the narrow angle, and the branches are susceptible to breakage during storms and heavy winter snow. Remove these branches as they develop.

There are additional routine pruning tasks that should be done while the tree is young and still developing. Remove any branches that cross or rub another branch as this damages both branches and makes the tree susceptible to disease and pest problems. Prune off any broken or damaged branches as you notice them. Be sure to check for damaged branches after heavy snow, wind, or strong storms.

▶ This 'Autumn Blaze' maple is still a gangly teenager, but is already showing off its true colors.

Pruning deciduous trees *(continued)*

Mature trees

Mature trees need little pruning if the tree was trained correctly when young. Prune to preserve the overall shape of the tree, which should not

▲ Remove suckers and watersprouts as soon as they appear.

be difficult if it has been trained properly. Use thinning cuts to trim smaller branches and remove any dead or damaged branches immediately.

● **Maintain the central leader:** If a secondary leader has begun to grow, you will have to take action. On mature trees the larger the secondary leader, the longer it will take to remove it. If it is large remove only one-third of the secondary leader at one time. It may take several seasons to accomplish the task, but the tree will be better off when you take the time to do it correctly. Use a heading cut to remove the secondary leader at each pruning.

Keep the crown branches healthy by removing any damaged limbs as soon as possible. This allows the tree to heal faster and prevents access to the tree for insects and diseases. Crossing or rubbing branches should also be removed for the health of

the tree. If the branch is large, remove only one-third of it at a time (pruning once a year) until you have reached the final collar cut. Use the 3-cut technique to remove the largest part of the branch. This task may also take a few seasons to accomplish.

Remove suckers and watersprouts from the mature tree. Suckers are small branches that grow at the base of the tree. These usually grow from the roots and should be removed immediately. Watersprouts are similar to suckers but grow vertically from the branches in the crown. Remove these immediately as they sap energy from the branches you want growing.

● **Care for the crown:** Crown work, such as thinning and raising, can be done on a mature tree. To thin use thinning cuts to remove smaller branches in the crown, allowing more light and air into the tree and improving its health. Raising the crown of a tree involves removing branches at the

▲ A clean collar cut calluses quickly and causes no damage to the trunk. Cut at an angle, not flush with the trunk.

bottom of the crown in order to widen the space between the ground and the crown bottom. For instance you may want to raise the crown on a shade tree to place lawn furniture underneath. Also it makes sense to raise a crown if you have difficulty doing yard work under the canopy

▲ Prune vertical watersprouts, broken or crossed branches, and stray lower limbs on a mature tree for a neat but full form.

▲ Cuts inside the collar promote trauma and disease for the trunk.

THE KINDEST CUT

Pruning only helps your trees if you do it with great care. First, be sure your pruning tools are sharp and clean, in order to make smooth cuts and encourage quick healing. Most of your cuts should be thinning cuts, which remove the branch back to where it's attached to a limb or the trunk, just outside the branch collar. Never cut inside the branch collar, as this is an invitation to disease. Use the 3-part cut to remove larger limbs. And don't dress or wrap the wounds from your pruning; if you prune carefully with the proper tools, the tree will heal on its own.

▶ Long-term pruning care for mature trees addresses crossed or damaged limbs or branches and water sprouts.

of a large tree. These adjustments should only be handled by a professional arborist.

● **Never top off:** One pruning situation you should always avoid is topping off a tree. This involves basically shearing off the top of a tree to maintain a certain height, which destroys the branches to a certain point. The first problem with topping is that you remove too much of some of the branches during cutting rather than the recommended one-third of a branch at a time. The tree may fail to recover from this type of shock, and the branches can become havens for insects and diseases. The second problem with topping is that it removes many leaves in the process, which can lead to sunscalding and may permanently damage the tree. Allow no one to top off your tree and banish any idea about doing it yourself.

◀ Call an arborist for tough pruning tasks, such as trimming this damaged pine after a storm.

Pruning shrubs

▲ This mature red-osier dogwood will take well to being cut all the way back to renew the plant.

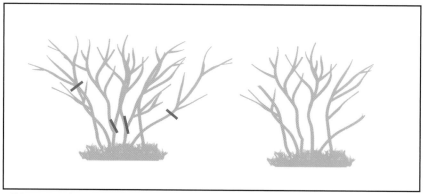

▲ Thinning cuts of up to a third of the plant will renew a shrub, promoting healthy growth and retaining its natural shape.

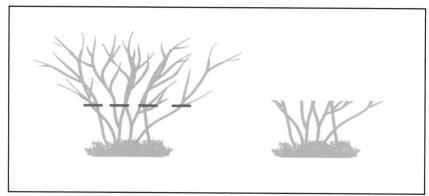

▲ Rejuvenation pruning on certain mature shrubs cuts back stems to within 6 inches of the ground.

Begin pruning a shrub when it is young and you'll have a much healthier, better-looking plant as it matures. Pruning flowering shrubs increases flower production, and general pruning of shrubs helps promote thicker growth. Unpruned shrubs are often twiggy, with a lot of foliage on top but bare branches at the bottom. A little pruning can go a long way toward the enjoyment of your shrub.

▲ New growth will develop in springtime on a pruned firethorn *(Pyracantha)*.

Shaping and sizing

Pruning to maintain the desired size and shape of your shrub should begin when the plant is young. Once you achieve the preferred overall shape, you can also control the size of the shrub with pruning. The basic shape of the plant can be anything from upright to rounded, but it should be shaped to follow its natural growth habit. You will be unable to prune a shrub with a broad, spreading growth habit into a narrow, upright plant. Use thinning cuts when pruning for shape and to control the size of the shrub. Remove suckers, watersprouts, and weak or damaged stems. Use loppers to remove the largest of the limbs to where they meet at a lateral branch.

Renewing and rejuvenating

Prune to renew or rejuvenate a shrub when the plant becomes older and less vigorous or when a shrub has been left to grow unchecked and has become wild-looking. Prune also to increase flower and fruit production if the plant has been a mediocre producer.

Renewal pruning is the removal of older stems to promote new growth. The plan is to remove all the old wood over a period of three to four years, which will renew the plant with all new growth by the end of that time. To do this remove only one-third of the old stems during yearly pruning. Eventually you end up with an almost entirely new plant. Renewal pruning encourages new growth on otherwise leggy old shrubs that have become bare at the bottom. Some plants, such as lilacs and honeysuckle, do very well with renewal pruning in that the shrub looks more attractive and flowers more profusely afterward.

Use rejuvenation pruning on older, overgrown plants to completely cut back the stems of a shrub to stubs. Some shrubs, such as red-osier and yellow-twig dogwoods, handle this type of pruning quite well. Others may die if pruned this severely. If you have doubts about whether your shrub can tolerate this pruning, try renewal pruning first to see if it will produce new shoots after being cut back. Use a saw or lopper to remove the stems to within 6 inches of the ground. Prune in early spring so the shrub's new growth has a chance to mature in summer. Forsythia, however, should be pruned after the blooms have faded in spring. It may take a few months for the entire shrub to produce new growth, so wait patiently.

Avoid confusing topping off or heading back a shrub with either renewal or rejuvenation pruning. Topping off or heading back cuts remove the top of the shrub, encouraging new growth at the cuts but doing nothing to make the lower part of the shrub fuller and more vigorous.

Flowering shrubs

Prune spring-blooming shrubs in late spring, after the flowers have faded. The flowers grow from buds that begin to appear on the shrub during the summer for

▲ Prune hydrangeas as soon as their flowers fade but before new flower buds set for the following season.

blooming the next spring. If you prune in winter, you remove the developing buds and will see little or no flowering the following spring. Pruning after the blooms fade encourages new growth on which more buds can grow for best flowering the next year. Cut the stem about ¼ inch above a bud or twig. If you cut too close to the bud, it may become damaged from the cut, but if you cut farther away, you'll end up with a dead twig end.

Prune summer-blooming shrubs in late winter or early spring, before the flowers bloom. This allows time for

new growth, from which new buds can develop and bloom in summer. These shrubs flower on new growth, so the cuts allow time to produce that new growth. Pruning later in spring or in fall will result in wounds that may cause dieback of the plant. Again cut the stem ¼ inch above a bud or twig for best results.

Notice which way a bud is pointing when you prune. You can direct the growth of the new shoots by cutting above a bud pointing in a certain direction. If a bud points upward, the new growth from a pruning cut

above that bud will grow upward. If it points downward or sideways, likewise the new growth will point downward or sideways at that pruning point. Taking this into consideration allows you to determine where pruning should happen according to what you want to accomplish. If you need to fill in a certain area of a shrub, prune stems according to how they will grow to help fill in those spots. If you want to avoid tangles of stems on the inside portion of the shrub, trim so that the new growth will face toward the outside of the plant.

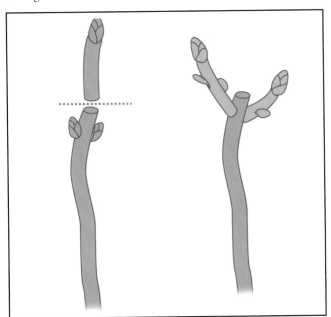

▲ For spring-blooming shrubs, prune after flowers have faded to stimulate new growth on which next year's flowers will appear.

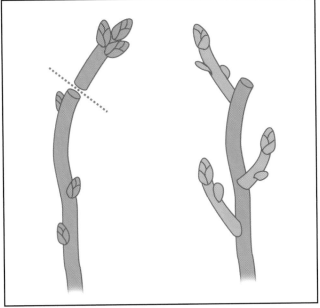

▲ For summer-blooming shrubs, prune before new growth begins in springtime; each cut will produce new stems on which flowers will appear.

Pruning hedges

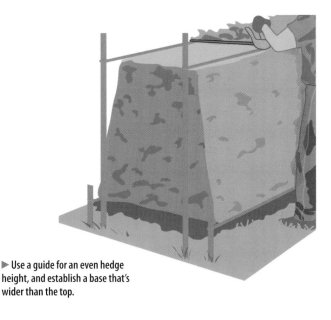

▶ Use a guide for an even hedge height, and establish a base that's wider than the top.

▲ Hedge pruning is an ongoing task of summer.

▲ Blooming broom makes a spectacular naturally shaped hedge.

Maintaining the shape of a hedge is only one reason to prune. Pruning to a specific shape can actually help protect the plants from snow damage and improve the overall health of the plant. Some hedges will require more pruning than others, but all will benefit from at least some pruning during the year.

Shaping

Begin shaping a shrub when the plant is young. If it is allowed to grow too large, severe pruning can damage the plant or even kill it when you're trying to achieve a specific shape. Begin pruning within a month after the hedge has been planted. You should prune about one-third to one-half of the new growth, which will promote growth of new shoots on the young plant. If a plant is allowed to reach its mature height without pruning, the inner branches will be weaker, and all new growth will be at the ends of the outside branches.

The best shape for a hedge is one that is narrower at the top than at the bottom. This shape allows more light and air to get into the base of the hedge, encouraging better health and more vigorous production of foliage. It also

▲ Traditional hedge shapes (from left to right) include wedge, pointed, rounded, and informal or natural.

strengthens the limbs to better handle a load of heavy snow in winter. Prune informal hedges with loppers or pruning shears, removing individual branches to maintain a looser-shaped hedge. Prune them several times during the growing season, trimming about half the length of new growth at each pruning.

Shearing

Formal hedges require shearing to maintain their shape. You can begin when a hedge is two to three years old, shearing it along the top to give it a uniform appearance. Trim up the sides of the hedge, making sure to keep the bottom portion wider than the top. This task is easiest when you use hedge shears, especially electric-, battery-, or gas-powered shears for fastest cutting. Hand shears can be useful on shorter hedges, as it may be hard to maneuver power shears around the plants. Shear a hedge whenever 2 to 3 inches of new growth appears. Shear almost to the bottom of the new growth, which will allow the hedge to grow uniformly. Begin shearing in spring so the leaves will grow to cover the cuts. Stop shearing in late summer to avoid cut stems that would suffer from an early cold spell.

Renovating

Renovate a hedge when it has become bare at the bottom or when it looks overgrown and unkempt. For severe renovation cut the plants to within 2 to 3 inches of the ground and basically start over with the hedge. You may have planted a hedge as a privacy screen, so be prepared to be without it for a few years as the hedge grows back. With less severe renovation you could cut back the hedge to about 5 feet high, leaving you with some privacy until the hedge reaches the desired height. You can also rejuvenate a hedge as you would a single shrub by cutting back one-third of the oldest limbs every year to produce a renewed hedge in three years.

Use pruners or hedge shears to remove smaller branches from the hedge as you begin to renovate. Use a saw or lopper to remove the largest limbs. If you cut the hedge all the way back, make sure to use equipment large enough to cut through the branches without crushing them in the process.

▲ A cherry laurel hedge calls for an annual shearing to keep it growing lush.

Pruning evergreens

Because evergreens grow in many ways, you must know the type of evergreen you have to prune it properly. The basics of pruning evergreens are the same as with other types of plants. Removing dead or damaged wood is important, as is keeping the plant healthy by letting more light and air reach the inside branches.

▲ Prune needled evergreens when new growth slows in summer.

Needled evergreens

Evergreen trees with thin needles, also known as narrow-leafed evergreens, include junipers, pines, yews, arborvitae, spruce, and firs. Needled evergreens usually grow into a basic shape on their own and stay that way, but sometimes you may need to give them a little help to keep them looking their best.

Start training young evergreens by ensuring there is a central leader in the tree. Remove competing leaders if they develop to give the tree the most stable growth habit possible. Shaping a young evergreen usually requires only thinning cuts to keep the overall form of the tree. A mature evergreen may need shearing to shape it up, but shear it only to trim it to its natural shape. If a tree has been pruned and trained properly when young, shearing probably will be unnecessary as the growth has been encouraged and controlled from the beginning.

All needled evergreens should have dead or damaged branches removed as soon as you notice them. Brown spots in trees may be corrected by identifying the underlying problem and either treating it (if the limbs and needles will recover) or removing the browned stems. New growth will eventually fill in the spot, but you may have to suffer through some time with a lopsided tree.

The time to prune needled evergreens is less rigid than it is for some other trees. Pruning can be done almost anytime, but try to do it in late spring or early summer when the new growth stops. These trees should be pruned while the new needle growth is still soft, so avoid waiting too long into the season to prune.

The technique for removing growth from evergreens depends on how the new growth appears. Some trees, such as pines, have candles of new growth at the ends of the branches. To maintain a more compact size, pinch off or cut these candles halfway up the length of each of them. If you need to even out a tree whose new growth is in the form of candles, remove the full candles from the side of the tree that is well shaped, and leave the full candles on the

▲ Prune select branches to gently shape an evergreen and to allow balanced exposure to sunlight.

▶ This collection of evergreens calls for a variety of pruning techniques, from shearing to the subtlest hand-pruned shaping.

side that needs filling in. As the growth evens out, continue to prune the candles halfway up to maintain the shape. Use shears to cut back other evergreens, such as arborvitae or junipers, to keep the plant growing into the desired shape and to maintain its size.

Thin an evergreen by cutting the branches and shoots that grow the wrong way on the tree. Sometimes you'll see a branch growing upward when the rest of the branches grow horizontally. That's the branch that needs to be removed to maintain the tree's natural shape. Remove by cutting the branch to the collar. A folding saw is probably the best tool for this job as it will be able to fit into the dense branches of the tree. Give trees such as the yew regular thinning cuts to allow air and light into the center of the tree.

Broadleaf evergreens

Most broadleaf evergreen trees require little or no pruning. Removing damaged limbs is always important, so be sure to do this task. Broadleaf evergreen shrubs, however, should be pruned much the same as deciduous shrubs. Prune blooming shrubs after flowering and cut or thin to maintain the desired size and shape. Remove the flowers when they fade from these shrubs, such as rhododendron and azaleas, by carefully pinching off the spent flowers with your fingers. This technique avoids damaging the new shoots that emerge below the old flowers in the way that pruners would. Keep shears away from a broadleaf evergreen. They cut through the large foliage and make the whole shrub look unsightly until the next season.

◀ Shaping young evergreens encourages them to mature into well-formed trees that require little maintenance.

▶ Evergreens that take to shearing and severe shaping offer opportunities for experimentation.

Pruning roses

▲ A rose hedge requires annual spring pruning to maintain its neat shape.

the risk of further damage to the plant. Get rid of any suckers growing from the ground as they sap energy from the rest of the plant.

During blooming season remove flower stems after the petals fall. This is called deadheading and encourages the development of new flowers. If you are cutting blooms for use in flower arrangements, cut the stem ¼ inch above the second five-leaflet mass below the bloom.

The timing for pruning established roses depends on where you live and what type of rose you have. Generally most pruning is done in late winter or early spring right before the new growth begins. In colder climates wait until the snow melts and use the blooming of forsythia (if you see them) as a guide to get started. Prune off all dead stems—these will be black or brown while healthy stems are green—to the ground. Cut o ff smaller, weaker stems to create a full, healthy plant. In warmer climates these same tasks can be done in winter, as long as there is no chance of a frost that would harm the newly cut stems.

The type of rose you have also makes a difference in when you prune because variety determines whether it blooms on new or old wood. If you are unsure, wait to prune for a year to determine if the flowers grow on the old or new canes. If the blooms form on the tips of a stem, it blooms on new wood. If they bloom from farther down the stem, it most likely blooms on old wood. Prune roses that grow on new wood in the early spring. Roses that bloom on old canes should be pruned after flowering.

▲ Take a rose cutting ¼ inch above the next outfacing five-leaflet cluster below the blossom.

vaselike shape. If you need to fill in more toward the center of the plant, cut right above a bud that faces inward.

The type of tool you should use depends on the size of the stem you are removing. Use hand shears on smaller stems and loppers on larger stems. Avoid using anvil-type pruners as they can crush the stem and leave

▲ A clean cut at a 45-degree angle close to an out-facing bud will help stimulate and direct new growth.

Different varieties of roses require different types of pruning at different times of year. With so many variables associated with this job, the information below will make it easier to figure out what to do when.

When to prune

Certain pruning tasks can be performed at almost any time of the year. These jobs should be done on all roses, so be sure to complete them. Remove damaged, diseased, dead, thin, weak, or crossing stems. This will not only clean up the plant's appearance but will diminish

How to prune

Cut the stems at a 45-degree angle about ¼ inch from a bud. Cutting too close to the bud can damage it, and cutting too far away from the bud can leave a dead stub. Cut above a bud facing the outside of the plant, which will direct the new growth in that direction, creating a nice

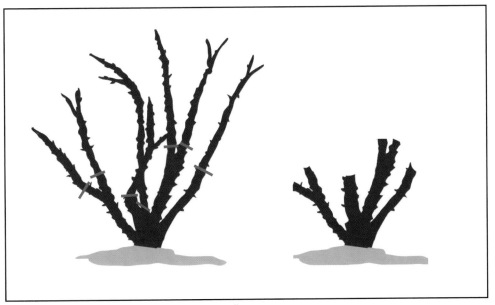

▲ Prune a dormant hybrid tea rose to five to seven 18-inch tall canes.

▲ Any dead or damaged parts of canes should be pruned in spring to bolster the plant's new, healthy growth.

a place for diseases to easily enter the plant. Always wear heavy-duty gloves to avoid being pricked by thorns.

How much to cut is determined by whether you are doing light or heavy pruning. Most roses require only light pruning, but rejuvenating the plant is considered heavy pruning.

To perform light pruning, remove all but six to eight healthy stems to form the base of the plant. These should be cut back from one-third to one-half of the stem, usually leaving 18 to 36 inches of stem. This will produce more new blooms but smaller flowers than on heavily pruned bushes. Heavy pruning, or rejuvenating, should be done only on roses that bloom on new growth. This entails removing all but three to five stems and cutting them down to where only three stems remain. This will rejuvenate a weak plant and produce larger blooms, but fewer of them, for a while.

◀ Deadhead spent flowers to make room for new blooms.

Training trees and shrubs

Some small, soft-wooded trees and shrubs lend themselves to training to a certain shape or against a structural form. The time and effort it takes to train plants goes beyond what is necessary for ordinary care and maintenance, but the results can be very rewarding.

Espalier

Espalier is a technique for training a tree or shrub to grow in a two-dimensional form, looking and behaving like a vine growing up a wall, fence, or trellis in a symmetrical pattern. There are several types of espalier; familiar forms include the horizontal, where branches grow straight out from a central trunk; the palmette features branches that fan outward; and the double cordon, which has two tiers of horizontal branches growing from a central trunk. Just about any deciduous or evergreen tree or shrub with flexible branches is a suitable prospect to train this way.

To create the double cordon, affix three horizontal wires to the wall, spaced about 18 inches apart, with the bottom wire 18 inches from the ground. The wires should be placed about 6 to 12 inches away from the wall so that the plant will get enough air circulation. The plant is initially pruned so that the central leader is cut down to 18 inches, the same height as the bottom wire. As the new shoots grow from that cut, choose one shoot to grow directly up to the second wire, then choose two others that will eventually grow horizontally along the bottom wire. Using flexible ties, tie the vertical branch to the second wire and the horizontal branches to the bottom wire.

In the winter, tie the side branches to the bottom wire to establish the first horizontal row. Prune the branches to about 18 inches long, cutting to a downward facing bud. This will encourage new shoots, and as these new

▲ Flowering fruit trees are excellent prospects for espalier.

GOOD PLANTS FOR ESPALIER

Apple (dwarf)
Cedar, atlas
Cotoneaster
Crabapple, flowering
Firethorn
Forsythia, border
Fuschia, common
Gardenia
Pear
Quince, flowering
Sweet olive
Viburnum
Yew

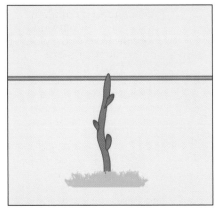

▲ To train to espalier, clip a new plant to 18 inches, just above the bottom of your first horizontal training wire.

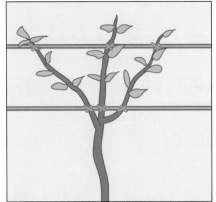

▲ Select three shoots that grow from the cut to train; one straight up and the others in both directions secured along the bottom wire.

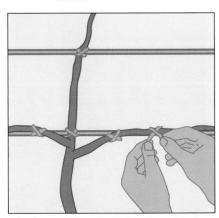

▲ In winter, pull down the side branches and tie them horizontally along the bottom wire.

shoots grow, tie them to the wires as you have the others to start filling in the espalier. Eventually, there will be three lines of horizontal branches spread out along the wire form. This process takes time and meticulous pruning, but it's very rewarding and creates a terrific, eye-catching specimen.

Training to an arbor

The same kinds of trees and shrubs that make good espalier prospects—those with soft, flexible branches—can be trained to an arbor. Plant the young tree or shrub 12 inches from one or both sides of the arbor. Affix the central leader and two strong stems to the arbor with flexible ties. Continue to tie new growth to the arbor as it makes its way up the structure. Prune according to the age and seasonal specifications of the plant to encourage new growth along the arbor. When established, prune to maintain shape and encourage dense foliage, flower, or fruit.

Training roses

Train roses, especially climbers, to create a beautiful impression in the landscape. Roses with a natural climbing habit are easiest to train, although almost any rose can be trained. The key to training roses is having the right support. Choose a sturdy arbor or pergola and use soft, flexible ties to attach the roses to the

▲ In late winter or early spring, prune back the prior season's growth to the framework of the arbor.

▲ Train evergreen or flowering shrubs to grow on an arbor.

support so that eventually the plant will grow and arch up over the support. Both sprawling and climbing roses can be trained this way.

When training climbing roses to grow up a wall, plant the same type of roses together for the best effect. Plant them 5 to 6 feet apart to allow

▲ Climbing roses are ideal for training on an arbor, pergola, or fence.

▼ A beautiful allée of trees can be replicated with time and patience.

enough room for them to spread outward. As they grow, interlocking canes will produce a full look. Use sturdy, flexible ties to attach the canes to the wall.

Regular, long-caned roses can also be trained against a wall or fence, as long as the canes are flexible enough to tie them gently into place. As you would with climbing roses, use flexible ties to hold the branches horizontally as they grow, which will produce more of the lateral branches upon which flowers appear. Prune any canes that grow outward from the front of the plant and encourage growth laterally by pruning to upward-facing buds.

Tree roses don't need training, but they always need to be staked. Staking is essential to keep the fragile trunk from bending or breaking and to keep the tree growing in an upright habit. When planting a new tree rose, replace the nursery's wooden stake with a metal stake so it won't rot over time.

Relocating trees and shrubs

▲ Most young trees can handle relocation if you take care to stake and maintain it as when it was first planted.

Sometimes you need to move a tree due to overcrowding, bad site selection, or perhaps because you failed to realize what beautiful flowers you would be unable to see from the back window when you planted that tree so far from the house. Transplanting causes a certain amount of trauma to any plant, but most young trees and shrubs can handle it if it's done carefully. Mature trees dislike relocating due to the size and complexity of their established root system, so hire a professional arborist to relocate them.

Transplanting

Trees should be relocated when the growing season is over, usually in the fall. Prepare the new site for the tree or shrub before you do anything to remove it from the original site. The longer the tree is out of the ground, the more trauma to the plant, so have everything prepared in advance.

To prepare the new site, you should first rake and remove all the yard debris from around the area, including twigs, leaves, and clippings. Follow the step-by-step instructions on pages 49 and 50 in Chapter 2 to properly prepare the new site for planting and to plant the tree or shrub correctly.

Preparing an established tree for transplanting involves cutting its root system to a manageable size for transporting but leaving enough intact so its roots can become easily established in the new location.

Using a spade, cut through the roots 12 inches out from the trunk for every inch of trunk width. For instance, a 3-inch-wide tree would require this cutting area to be 36 inches in diameter. Dig under the roots at least 12 to 18 inches deep to create the root ball. Gently jiggle and tilt the tree back and forth to loosen the root ball. Once it is free from the ground, place it carefully on a large tarp or piece of burlap for transporting.

If the tree is too large to be dragged along on the fabric, tie the tarp or burlap loosely around the trunk and lift the tree to transport in a wheelbarrow or wagon to the new location. If the tree must sit for any length of time before transplanting, wrap the root ball in burlap and keep it moist until replanting.

Water, mulch, and stake (as necessary) according to the planting instructions on page 51. Do not fertilize, as it will stimulate new growth at a time when the plant's energy needs to be spent at the roots. Take special care to protect the transplanted tree or shrub from harsh winter weather.

SAVING AN UPROOTED TREE

When a tree becomes uprooted from severe wind or storm damage, it is possible to save it by replanting and staking, though this is not a sure thing. Trees that are 5 years old or less and smaller trees, up to 25 feet high, have the best chance of surviving the trauma of uprooting. Consult an arborist as quickly as possible about larger or mature trees that have been uprooted; a professional may be able to help you save the tree— or he may advise you that the tree can't be saved and can help with its proper disposal.

Partially uprooted trees with 10 to 50 percent of the roots exposed can be replanted and staked as you would stake a new tree. The tree should be replanted right away and prune away all broken limbs as soon as it's upright and replanted. Use the 2- or 3-stake method to ensure that the tree will have enough support as it recovers from the damage. Use fabric or mesh-webbing to protect the trunk from the wire or rope and keep the staking in place for about 2 years. Keep the roots covered and moist as the root system becomes reestablished.

It's possible to save trees or shrubs uprooted by storms if no more than half the roots were exposed and action is taken quickly to reestablish it back in the soil.

Propagating

If you really want to get into your landscape, consider propagating your own plants instead of buying them. You'll get the exact characteristics of a plant that you already know you like without guessing what a new one will look like. And if you enjoy watching things grow from tiny to big, little beats planting a tree from seed.

Cuttings

Growing new plants from cuttings can be done with either softwood or hardwood plants and involves removing a small stem from the tree and placing it in a rooting medium. After a couple of months, the roots should be formed enough to replant the cutting in the landscape.

Begin by removing a portion of the stem or stem tip. Cut the piece from the stem with a sharp knife. Place the cutting in a damp paper towel to keep it moist until planting it in a rooting medium, such as lightweight soilless potting soil, perlite, or vermiculite. Dipping cut ends in rooting hormone powder promotes success.

Remove any leaves or needles from the lower few inches of the cutting. Plant the cutting in a pot or tray of the planting medium and cover with a plastic canopy to help retain moisture. Place the cuttings in a spot with indirect sunlight. Watch for mildew that might appear in this humid environment, in which case, remove the canopy for a day or so to dry out.

After a month or two, you can tell if it has rooted by giving a gentle tug test. Carefully tug at the cutting to see if it resists the pull. If there is resistance roots have begun to develop. If the cutting shows little or no resistance, it has yet to root. When it develops viable roots, you can plant it as you would any new plant.

The timing for propagating by cutting depends on the type of tree you're going to grow. Hardwood evergreen cuttings, for example, should be taken in the fall to late winter. Deciduous hardwood plants should be cut in late fall to early winter. Semihardwood cuttings from holly, azalea, camellia, and rhododendron should be taken in summer. Correct timing helps the development of buds, increasing the plant's chances of surviving after being planted.

▲ With proper care and siting, someone could be enjoying the shade from this home grown oak seedling in 20 years.

◄ Root boxwood from semihardwood cuttings taken in late summer. The cuttings should snap right off the plant when bent sharply.

EASY SHRUBS TO GROW FROM CUTTINGS

Barberry, Japanese
Boxwood, common
Burning bush
Cotoneaster
Firethorn
Gardenia
Holly
Leucothoe, drooping
Rhododendron
Yew

Propagating
(continued)

Layering

Layering is a propagating technique used for many plants whose cuttings fail to root. It involves bending a stem from a plant into the ground and allowing that portion of the stem to take root.

Choose a bushy or spreading shrub to layer. In spring or summer bend a lower stem from the parent plant until it comes in contact with the underlying loose soil. Scrape away a small portion of bark (about halfway around the stem) from the area in contact with the soil, using a sharp knife. Apply a rooting hormone to the wound and push it into the soil. Place a heavy object, such as a brick, onto the portion of the stem in the dirt to keep it in place. Check for rooting at the wound site, and when it has become well rooted, cut it from the parent plant and transplant it into the landscape.

A spreading juniper may be propagated by layering, but the process is a bit different. Dig a small trench along the underside of the juniper. Pull down a stem to the loose soil, then wound the bark about halfway around the stem and place it into the soil. Bend a wire into a U-shape and use it to anchor the stem into the ground. In a few months, you'll have a newly rooted juniper plant that can be cut from the parent plant and transplanted.

Growing from seed

If you like to see the fruits of your labor from start to finish and have plenty of time to wait for the final results, plant a tree from seed. All those trees in nature have grown from seeds, so give it a try. These are the basics of growing from seed, but there can be differences in how long the process takes, depending on what type of tree you're trying to grow.

◄ To layer a spreading juniper, dig a trench under a low-growing shoot.

► Make a small wound in the underside of the shoot, apply rooting hormone, and secure the shoot to the soil with a wire.

◄ When roots form, dig up the rooted shoot and gently cut it away from the parent plant.

Collecting the seeds is the first step in planting. That seems obvious, but the timing of seed collection is the key. You must collect the seeds when they are ready but not too late or they will dry out and be worthless. When you notice the first of the seeds drop from the tree naturally, that's the time to harvest your seeds. Pick seeds right from the tree, not ones that have already fallen on the ground. The seeds on the ground may already contain fungi and larvae that swiftly infest the seeds that have

already dropped. Choose seeds that have begun to dry or have changed color—these are the ones that would be ready to drop naturally in a few days and are perfect for this process.

Clean all the debris from the seeds and throw away any that are damaged or broken. Let the seeds dry for a few days, then store them in a plastic zipper bag mixed with moist sand or vermiculite in the refrigerator for several months. This emulates the time the seed would spend on the ground in the winter—

EASY SHRUBS TO GROW BY LAYERING
Azalea
Butterfly bush
Dogwood, red-osier
Honeysuckle
Privet
Rose
Rose of Sharon
Spirea, vanhoutte
Viburnum
Weigela
Willow, pussy
Witch hazel, common

a sort of cold storage—which is called stratification. Once the seeds have been stored for a few months, they are ready to plant.

Plant seeds at the recommended depth into seed trays filled with potting soil. Water well and keep the soil moist but not wet. Place the container in a moist, humid environment, as this is critical to the germination process. Germination could take a few days or a few months, depending on the type of tree and the conditions in which the containers are kept. Keep the containers from direct sunlight, which can be drying, but leave them in a warm spot.

After about three to four months seedlings should be about 3 inches tall. At this point you can replant them into individual containers for the next stage of growth. Once the seedlings reach about 15 inches high and the trunks are about ¼ inch in diameter, they may be transplanted outside.

Following are three types of trees that are easy to grow from seed. Each seed type is different and while the basic methods apply to each tree, there are some differences that contribute to success.

Maple trees are very easy to grow from seed. The seeds should be harvested in spring, from April to May. Instead of placing the seeds in a plastic bag for a few months, plant maple seeds immediately in planting trays for best germination. The trays can then be placed in

FIVE EASY TREES TO GROW FROM SEED
Fir, white
Linden, American
Maple, Japanese
Oak
Pear, callery

direct sun, keeping the soil moist but not wet. Once germination occurs and the seedlings start to appear, add a liquid fertilizer at one-fourth strength every other watering and spray with a fungicide to stop mildew from forming. When the seedlings reach 3 inches high, replant them into individual containers, and when plants reach about 15 inches high, they're ready for planting outside.

To grow an **oak tree,** harvest the acorns for seeds in October when they are fully ripe, with no green color to them at all. Acorns can be gathered from the ground, but inspect them carefully for any weevil holes or for any that feel hollow. Let the acorns dry for a few days, then carefully remove the caps. Set the acorns in potting soil in planting trays, covered by about one-eighth inch of soil. Keep them in a sunny spot in moist soil and add a fertilizer (the same strength and timing as maple trees), then transplant into individual containers when the seedlings reach about 3 inches high. At about 15 inches high, plant them in the ground.

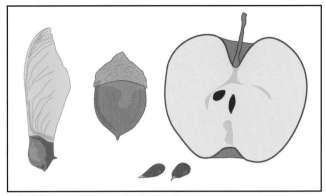

▲ Seeds from a maple, oak, and apple give this grow-your-own project its start.

Apple seeds require the stratification process to properly grow. Choose good apples from the tree (not from the ground) and carefully remove the seeds. Gently rinse the seeds a few times in fresh water to remove all the pulp. Place the seeds into a plastic zipper bag and add a drained mixture of three cups coarse perlite and three cups water. Seal the bag and place it in the produce bin in the refrigerator for at least 60 days. Watch for mildew and, if you find it on the seeds, mix a new batch of perlite and water; drain before placing it in a new bag, and rinse the seeds in a bleach mixture of 10 parts water to 1 part bleach before adding them to the new bag. Plant the seeds in planting trays as with other trees, but cover with a thin layer of sawdust or wood shavings to prevent mold. Keep the trays in the sun in the moist soil and transplant the seedlings

▲ Care for tree seedlings in pots until ready to plant in a permanent site.

into individual trays when they reach 3 inches high. Transplant seedlings into the ground when they reach 15 inches high.

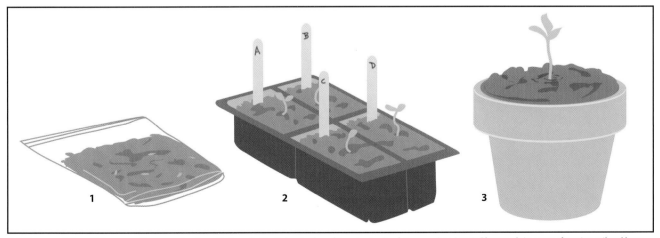

▲ 1. Some seeds benefit from spending a couple of months in a plastic zip bag in the refrigerator to simulate overwintering. 2. Plant seeds in a tray of potting soil and keep moist in indirect light for up to 4 months. 3. Plant seedlings in individual pots, then transplant to a permanent site when 15 inches tall.

Troubleshooting

When confronted with a plant problem, most gardeners assume that an insect or a disease is involved, then wonder what control to use. However most plant problems are due to environmental conditions and stresses rather than disease-causing agents (pathogens) or insects. More often than not many of these problems are caused by actions taken—or not taken—by gardeners.

Preventing problems

Healthy gardens consist of plants—along with bacteria, fungi, insects, and nematodes. Most of these organisms are benign and merely coexist with plants. And some of these organisms, such as fungi that form mycorrhizae, or nitrogen-fixing bacteria, are beneficial and necessary for healthy plant growth. Other fungi and bacteria are essential for breaking down dead plant material in the compost pile into humus. Beneficial insects and nematodes prey upon and parasitize pests in addition to playing important roles in pollination.

Healthy measures

The best defense against problems with pests and disease is to take good and regular care of your trees and shrubs. To keep them healthy during the growing season, do these five things:
1. Fertilize at least once a year to maintain appropriate levels of nutrients based on soil tests.
2. Water well, as necessary, especially during dry periods.
3. Mulch to conserve moisture and prevent weed growth.
4. Harvest fruit, if any, in a timely fashion. Unharvested fruit falls to the ground and attracts insects and creates an environment for disease.
5. Clean up every autumn. Rake and remove tree and shrub debris to eliminate opportunities for pests or disease to overwinter in your planting area.

Weeds

Weeds compete with more desirable plants in the lawn and garden. The pernicious ones vie for light, water, food, and space. Once weeds are identified they usually can be removed easily with little thought. However identifying the weed and determining why it has invaded is the first step in managing it.

Traditional weed control consists primarily of hand-

▲ Ladybugs do their part to keep the aphid population down.

▶ A healthy, well-cared for tree is its own best defense against pests and disease.

pulling and mulching. When properly timed this two-pronged approach is usually effective. Weeds are easiest to control when the seeds are germinating, thereby preventing the weeds from becoming established. They are most easily removed when the soil is moist but not excessively wet. Once the weeds are established, hard work, weed controls, or both may be needed. So focus on preventing the weeds from going to seed.

After identifying the weeds review your garden and lawn care practices. Consider what you need to change to maintain a healthy landscape.

◄ The praying mantis is one of the landscape's best natural pest control tools.

Insects

Scouting for insects is much more challenging than looking for weeds. In a matter of days, insects can arrive, damage your trees and shrubs, then seemingly disappear. Monitor your plants routinely to keep on top of the insect population and prevent infestations. You should spot check your trees and shrubs on a regular basis so you can take action before the damage reaches destructive levels. You can remove some pests physically by handpicking them off, using a garden hose to wash them from the plants, or spraying them with insecticidal soap or Volck Oil. These approaches are the least toxic ways to control insect problems. For them to be effective, you must be vigilant to prevent the insect from becoming established.

When scouting your yard or garden, include all plant groups (lawn, trees, shrubs, fruits, vegetables, annuals, and perennials), and inspect several plants within each group at random. Check the tops and undersides of several leaves or leaflets on each plant. Determine how much damage is acceptable to you. If the damage you observe is minimal, you may choose to handpick pests, avoiding the need for chemical control. If the infestation is severe, you may need to spray to prevent the problem from increasing, or to reduce insect populations to a level that becomes pickable.

Despite how carefully you maintain your trees and shrubs, you will inevitably confront an infestation of something. Problems in your neighbor's yard can become your problem in the blink of an eye. But before reaching for a control to spray, carefully examine the problem. Sometimes it will take care of itself. Insects are susceptible to disease too. Large populations of aphids are a food source for adult and immature ladybugs. Ladybug beetles are voracious; one can eat several hundred aphids. Praying mantises prey upon smaller insects, as do spiders. Remember that your garden and yard are part of the larger environment. When spraying to control an insect pest problem, consider that you may unintentionally kill beneficial insects as well.

Diseases

Leaf spots, discoloration, and wilting indicate plant distress. Early detection, accurate diagnosis, and understanding how chemical controls work are essential to manage plant diseases. By scouting regularly you can quickly discover disease problems, correctly diagnose them, and prevent further spread of a pathogen before the disease reaches epidemic proportions.

It can be difficult to accurately diagnose disease in the home landscape, so harvest a characteristic sample of the affected plant, wrap it in newspaper or a paper towel (plastic causes samples to rot), and take it to a reputable nursery or your cooperative extension service for identification.

▲ Handpick larger insects off of infested plants, then drop them in soapy water to kill them.

Diagnosing plant damage

▲ Even mature, healthy hemlocks (as in the above landscape) can be destroyed by the pernicious woolly adelgid.

You can take several steps to determine what pest or disease is causing damage to your trees and shrubs.

Know your plants

Start by knowing exactly what plants you're dealing with, including a plant's botanical (Latin) name, which is often more helpful in this situation than using its common name. Many types of cedars are planted throughout the United States for example: true cedar (*Cedrus*), eastern red cedar (*Juniperus*), western red cedar (*Thuja*), or incense cedar (*Calocedrus*). Even though all of these trees are called cedar, they are all very different, and they suffer from distinct pests and diseases.

You should also be familiar with the ordinary life cycles of your plants. For example, many conifers lose their needles in the fall, and certain hollies and rhododendrons drop their leaves in spring. Knowing what is normal and when it occurs allows you to recognize abnormalities. Keep in mind that many ornamentals have variegated leaves, brightly colored new growth, or double flowers. Understanding your plants' features and habits helps you decide whether there is a problem.

Finally be aware of the problems to which some of your plants may be susceptible. Knowing that hemlocks are generally vulnerable to woolly adelgids, for instance, will make you more aware of potential problems with *your* hemlock.

Look for symptoms and signs

Symptoms, which describe how a plant responds to damage, can be vague. Wilting, leaf spotting, and discoloration often appear and are difficult to distinguish from one another. But they may indicate different problems. Therefore diagnoses should be based upon more than symptoms alone. A conclusive diagnosis requires the presence of one or more signs.

Signs are direct evidence of the organism causing the damage that creates characteristic symptoms. A sign could be a mushroom, a tiny pustule caused by a fungus, the ooze of bacteria, living insects, webbing, frass (excrement), or insect exoskeletons. The presence of signs confirms that a particular pest is causing the symptoms you observed. But pests can be present even without signs.

Make as exhaustive and descriptive a list of signs and symptoms as you can. This will help determine if it is a combination of problems that needs to be addressed. Also look for patterns among groups of plants; examine plants of the same or similar type as well as plants of different types. Signs of problems on a group of plants of the same type likely indicates pest or disease problems, while problems across a range of types of plants usually indicates a cultural problem.

▲ A fungal growth on the trunk may be an indication of systemic damage happening to the tree.

▲ Leaves on trees are like hair and fingernails on humans; they're a place where signs of illness or other problems appear.

▲ Yellowed and chewed leaves may indicate a pest infestation.

▲ Coral spot fungus enters the plant through a wound. By the time the visible symptoms appear on the outside of the tree, the wood is usually already dead.

Also note details of the problems you observe as they develop over time. Rather than appearing suddenly, most problems have been developing over a period of time, and noting when and to what extent various signs and symptoms have developed can help accurately diagnose a problem.

Assess the damage

Generally the types of damage to your trees and shrubs will put the cause in one category or another. Pest insect damage is usually indicated by leaves chewed along the edges or holes chewed in the middle; branches that have lost their leaves in the middle of the growing season; wilted, discolored, or curled leaves; or holes in the bark.

Diseases to your tree or shrub are caused by a fungus, a virus, or bacteria. Disease damage is indicated by pale, wilted lower leaves, which are clues that roots are suffering or decaying; blight, dieback, or growths on the stems and twigs; and spots, blisters, or filmy coating or deformities on leaves and flowers.

Damage from pest animals is usually indicated by young trees or shrubs that have been nibbled down entirely; new growth nibbled off; lower stems of larger trees or shrubs defoliated; or chafed bark.

Damage from cultural problems—such as drought, flooding, or cold; equipment damage; chemical damage; salt spray; or surface roots—can take a variety of forms.

A general droop or scorch to the leaves or malaise in the whole tree or shrub signals stress from drought or flooding. Cold damage, which is usually caused by a plant being planted outside of its proper zone or by severe winter weather, can cause a tree or shrub to fail to leaf out or flower or to die. Foliage appears burned on cold-damaged evergreens, while sunscald causes a swelling, then a cracking of the trunk of a tree.

Wounds from lawn equipment generally take the form of nicks and abrasions to the trunk of a tree. Chemical damage, including excessive use of controls or improper use of fertilizers, is often indicated by bleached, discolored, or distorted foliage. Chlorosis, indicated by green veins with yellow in between, is due to high soil pH. Salt-spray damage can discolor foliage. Surface roots, which are roots exposed above the surface of the soil, show wounds from being skinned by lawn equipment or similar stress from the pressure of surrounding hardscape, such as sidewalks or driveways.

Finally it's common for trees or shrubs to suffer shock when transplanted to a new location after becoming established. Growth can become stunted and leaf drop, discoloration, or even death can occur.

▲ Flooding can cause short- and long-term damage to even the most healthy mature tree, if it is not suited to wet conditions.

Identifying causes and solutions of tree or shrub problems

▲ A woodpecker doing what woodpeckers do—causing countless tiny wounds to the bark that over time can weaken or destroy a tree.

▲ You don't need to be a detective to figure out that a webworm is busy decimating stems and leaves on this tree.

▶ Signs of mites include these unusual growths on foliage.

Plants require appropriate light, temperature, humidity, nutrients, and water, and they undergo stress when they receive too much or too little of these basic necessities, making them vulnerable to attack by insects and disease. So take care to choose the right plants for the right locations and provide proper care. Similarly you can prevent or correct most cultural problems, including environmental, mechanical, and chemical issues with plants or trees, through proper practices.

But problems brought on by living factors, including pest insects, diseases, or pest animals, are a different matter. Whether you helped cause these problems by neglecting to provide solid ongoing care for your trees or shrubs, or they appear through no fault of yours, you must become proactive, starting with identifying the cause of the problem. Here's where the real detective work comes in.

● **Insect damage:** Insects can cause great damage to trees and shrubs. When evaluating insect damage, be sure to identify the location and type of damage. It can be due to feeding, egg-laying, or both.

● **Disease damage:** Because the pathogens that cause most diseases are microscopic for most of their lives, disease problems are probably the most difficult to diagnose. Distinguishing between fungal, bacterial, viral, and nematode damage often requires a microscope or professional consultation.

● **Animal damage:** Small rodents and other animals can cause significant damage to plants while feeding. Small mammals commonly chew the bark and cambium tissue on small trees and shrubs. You can often find this damage above the snow line in winter. Larger mammals such as deer browse on lower branches, damaging the ends at the highest point they can reach. Birds, including woodpeckers and sapsuckers, cause considerable damage to trees, houses, and decks as they attempt to extract grubs and other larvae from the plants.

Insect pests

Insect damage is caused by chewing, piercing, sucking, or rasping.

● **Chewing damage:** Insects with chewing mouthparts feed on all parts of the plant.

● **Entire leaf:** If the entire leaf except for the midvein is eaten, examine the leaves for the presence of caterpillars, sawflies, or webworms.

● **Holes in flowers:** Indicates insect presence. Rose flowers are regularly damaged by rose chafers, Japanese beetles, and false Japanese beetles.

● **Pattern feeding:** Distinct notches on the leaf margin are often due to black vine weevils. Circular holes cut into the edge of the leaf are probably

▲ In sufficient numbers, beetles can defoliate an entire plant.

▲ Tent caterpillars devour foliage and branches on a devastating scale.

● **Root feeding:** Can be done by grubs and caterpillars, which are the larval stages of beetles, weevils, and moths. This damage results in a plant's loss of vigor and decline. Common root feeders include Japanese beetles and sod webworms.

● **Piercing-sucking:** Unlike chewing insects, those with piercing-sucking mouthparts pierce plant tissue and suck liquid, such as sap and water, into their stomachs. While piercing and sucking, they inject saliva into the plant to aid in feeding. The saliva can be toxic to the plants and can transmit viruses and other diseases to healthy plants. Piercing-sucking damage can cause various symptoms, such as small flecks, deformed plant or flower growth, wilting, or leaf damage.

● **Spittlebugs:** Pierces the stems of plants and feeds on the juice. Their presence is indicated by frothy spittle.

● **Leaf spotting and stippling**: An insect's toxic saliva can also cause lesions on leaves. Aphids, scale insects, mealybugs, and spider mites may cause spotting or stippling.

● **Galls:** Irregular plant growths that result when insects inject plant hormones and other growth-regulating chemicals into the plant. Galls occur on leaves, bark, flowers, buds, acorns, or roots. Oaks are quite susceptible to leaf and twig attack.

● **Leaf distortion:** Many insects inject toxins that result in curling or puckering of leaves or other deformities that mimic the symptoms of disease. Examples include honeysuckle witches'- broom aphids, eriophyid mites, and cyclamen mites.

● **Rasping damage:** The mouthparts of rasping insects rub out plant tissue to feed upon it.

● **Thrips:** Thrips feed and create a rasping injury called silvering from their rasping-and-sucking action. Depending on the host species, injuries occur on fruit, flowers, flower buds, leaves, and leaf buds. Thrips often carry tomato spotted wilt virus, a serious disease.

▲ Borers feed under bark, causing general wilt and dieback.

signs of leaf cutter bees.

● **Random damage:** If found throughout the leaf, it is often the result of feeding by beetles, grasshoppers, or weevils.

● **Skeletonized leaves:** Results when the inner green portion of the leaf is consumed by insects, leaving the vein structure visible

● **Leaf miners:** These insects tunnel between the upper and lower leaf membranes. Common hosts of leaf miners include columbine, hollyhock, aspen, birch, and elm.

● **Webbing:** Fall webworm is an example of an insect that encloses plant tips in webbing and feeds on blossoms, leaves, and buds.

● **Petiole borers:** Burrows into the petiole, the stem that attaches a leaf to the branch. The maple petiole borer is common where maples are planted.

● **Borers:** Includes several types of insects. Eggs laid at the base of the affected plant hatch, and larvae (grubs or caterpillars) chew their way into the plant. Wilting and dieback are common symptoms.

● **Bark borers:** Feeds on living tissue under the bark and forms beetle galleries. A general decline of the plant or a specific branch indicates damage. Close examination reveals holes in the bark and insect frass or sawdust. Conifers such as pine or spruce may produce large amounts of resin in response to the borer. Examples of bark borers include pine bark beetles, elm bark beetles, bronze birch borer, and emerald ash borers.

▲ The spittlebug leaves a frothy spittle that makes for quick diagnosis of infestation.

Common pests on trees and shrubs

While there are countless insect pests that can invade your yard and do damage to vulnerable trees and shrubs—many of them specific to your geographical region—there are several "usual suspects" in the average home landscape. Following are descriptions of nine very common pests, the telltale damage they cause, and the recommended action to take against each of them.

Aphids

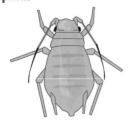

Aphids are tiny green, yellow, black, brown, or gray soft-bodied insects that cluster on bark, leaves, or buds of trees and shrubs. Aphids suck the juice from a plant, which causes curled, distorted, or discolored leaves. They also often leave behind a sticky substance known as honeydew, which coats the leaves and attracts ants, which is another sign aphids are at work. A sooty mold can also develop on the honeydew, causing the leaves to look dirty.

▲ Evidence of aphids includes discolored or distorted leaves.

While their damage is generally not fatal, in sufficient number aphids can cause plants to suffer a general malaise, leaf drop,

or dieback of branches. When you discover an aphid infestation, remove with a strong spray of water or water mixed with insecticidal soap. Repeat as necessary. Aphids proliferate during the cooler parts of the growing season, then reduce in number when the weather gets warm.

Bagworms

Bagworms are spring-hatched larvae that munch on the leaves of most types of trees and shrubs. Each larva builds a bag around itself that is attached to a branch. It emerges from the bag to feed on leaves; when it has eaten all the leaves from a branch, it drags its bag to a new spot on a fresh branch.

▲ The bagworm attaches to branches in a telltale sack.

Signs of the presence of bagworms are the bags, of course, and chewed leaves or defoliated branches. Unchecked, a bagworm infestation can stunt the development of deciduous trees or even kill evergreens. At the first sign of bagworms in late spring through mid summer, spray with Bt (*Bacillus thuringiensis*) to kill young worms. Handpick and destroy bags found on branches to eliminate the eggs of next season's bagworms.

Borers

Borers are larvae of certain moths and beetles that tunnel below and feed off of the bark of a tree, which can cause dieback or girdling of the trunk. Borers look for trees that are vulnerable due to stress from transplanting, drought, equipment or chemical wounds, or that are weakened from other insect infestation. Signs of the presence of borers

▲ Borers leave a sawdust like residue at the point of penetration on the wood.

are sawdust around the holes they bore in stems.

The best defense against borers is to avoid vulnerability by keeping up your tree's good health. Carefully timed applications of insecticide can be effective during the two weeks between when the eggs hatch and the borers enter the tree, beginning in late spring and through the summer, depending on the type of borer and your geographical location. If you suspect borers, consult a local tree professional for advice on the best strategy and timing.

Gypsy moth caterpillar

The hairy, dark caterpillars we know as gypsy moth larvae are voracious night feeders that damage a tree by chewing its leaves. Bothered in sufficient numbers by this pest, a tree can be almost entirely defoliated, which can make it more vulnerable to other pest insects or disease. Signs of this pest are first the golden rust-colored egg masses that appear on the trunks and branches of the tree, then,

▲ Gypsy moth caterpillars are voracious leaf feeders.

after hatching, chewed leaves or general defoliation.

This problem can be addressed by spraying an insecticide such as Bt after the eggs hatch in mid- to late spring. Spray weekly until infestation is diminished. You can also trap these caterpillars in burlap aprons arranged at the bottom of an infested tree, where they come down every day to find a shady spot to rest before the next evening's meal. Drop trapped caterpillars in a bucket of soapy water.

Japanese beetles

Japanese beetles are tough, metallic bronze winged pests

who are daytime feeders on the leaves of many types of plants. They chew leaf tissue between the veins, causing the leaves to look lacy or holey. They feed for about a month in early to mid-

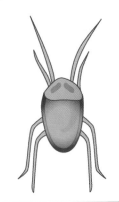

▲ Japanese beetles leave lacy holes on nibbled leaves.

summer and are capable of serious defoliation.

Luckily, these beetles are slow and easy to handpick off of leaves or to spray off with a strong jet of water. If the problem persists, an insecticide may be applied. Consult your local extension office for the most effective product in your area.

Leaf miners

Leaf miners are a kind of moth larvae, so named for the mines or tunnels they burrow into leaves for overwintering. These tunnels give the appearance of squiggly white lines on the

▲ Symptoms of leaf miners are a gradual discoloration and curling of leaves.

surface of the leaves, which become blistered, curled, or discolored from the infestation.

Because this pest does its damage from inside the leaf, ordinary topical insecticides are not effective. A tree care professional may recommend a synthetic systemic insecticide, but it's generally best just to trim and destroy leaves and branches that indicate infestation.

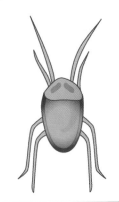

Spider mites

Spider mites are tiny pests that do big damage to trees and shrubs sucking sap from leaves and buds. The result is yellowed, discolored, or distorted leaf growth, and occasionally a general malaise or stunted growth for the plant. A silk webbing may be found on leaves or stems when spider

▲ Spider mites leave a silk webbing on leaves and stems after feeding.

mites are present, which you can confirm by shaking the leaves over a white piece of paper, on which tiny moving specks will appear.

Mites are hard to control, though an application of Volck Oil at the immediate onset of the problem can be quite effective.

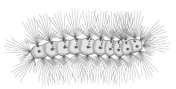

Webworms

Webworms are brown caterpillars with rust-colored stripes that appear in late summer and create webs around groups of leaves or entire branches, eventually destroying them. The webs are a sure sign of webworm, of

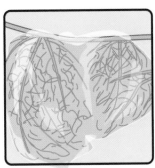

▲ Webworms create webs that surround entire leaves or branches.

course, as are bunches of dead leaves on individual branches.

In the case of minor infestations, webs may be removed by hand and disposed of in a bucket of soapy water. The application of Bt when the worms begin feeding is generally effective in larger infestations. Reapply until the problem is gone.

Woolly adelgid

The pale, aphid like woolly adelgid has single-handedly devastated the hemlock population in the East. This insect feeds on the base of the hemlock needles, causing discoloration and needle drop. Besides branch dieback and stunted growth, the presence of woolly adelgids is indicated by a cottony substance on the branches, especially near areas of new growth.

▲ Woolly adelgid leaves a cottony white substance on new growth of a hemlock.

Untreated, even mature trees infested with woolly adelgid can die in under 10 years. Control adelgids with a thorough application of insecticide spray or soap. Consult a local tree care professional for a recommendation of the appropriate product; consider professional application of the treatment on large trees.

Managing your pests

As with weeds in the landscape, it's unrealistic to attempt a total elimination of the problem; instead, consider how much you can stand, and how much you're willing to do to manage the problem. One or two beetles on a plant doesn't call for an all-out assault with an industrial-strength application of insecticide. But noticeable and rapid defoliation does call for immediate and decisive action.

There are four basic tools for pest management. First, do what you can, when possible, to address the problem by hand, picking off insects that have appeared on a small scale. You can also use natural insecticides, such as Bt *(Bacillus thuringiensis)* or neem, which are effective against certain pests. Insecticidal soaps are beneficial in certain cases as well. Sometimes synthetic insecticides are best in extreme cases, or when a systemic approach rather than just a topical approach is necessary. In every case, consult a local trusted nursery or tree care professional for recommendations on the best products for your problem in your area.

Diseases

Use a magnifying glass to locate and identify the signs and symptoms of plant disease. Pathogens that cause disease include fungi, bacteria, viruses, nematodes, and even other plants.

Leaves, flowers, and fruits

- **Angular, water-soaked leaf spot** Bacterial leaf spot is usually angular because the lesion is stopped by the leaf veins. Spots often appear water-soaked.
- **Anthracnose** This fungal leaf spot progresses through the leaf vein and into the woody stem of the plant. It can produce blightlike symptoms.
- **Leaf distortion** Infected leaves vary from their normal shape and size. This symptom is associated with plant diseases such as viruses and fungi or is due to infestations of insects such as mites.
- **Leaf spot** Circular lesions, with or without concentric rings, may appear and grow through leaf veins. Pimplelike fruiting bodies may appear on the diseased tissue. Most leaf spot disease is due to fungi.
- **Mosaic mottling** Viruses cause varying shades of green or yellow that produce an irregular, variegated appearance on leaves.
- **Powdery mildew** This white dusty substance on

▲ Powdery mildew is unsightly, but not generally life threatening to an infected tree.

▲ This massive oak tree died of sudden oak death fungus.

leaves is a sign of surface fungi.
- **Rust** This fungal disease is characterized by orange pustules that appear on the leaves. It may produce chlorotic symptoms around the pustule.
- **Ring spot** Round, target-shape spots are symptoms of viral disease.
- **Scattered, dry, angular leaf spot** Foliar nematodes cause angular leaf spot defined by the leaf veins.

Roots

- **Knot gall** Roots attacked by nematodes often have galls or knots. Nematodes are microscopic roundworms that cause diseaselike symptoms.

Symptoms of nematode damage include wilting and stunting. Some bacteria can cause galls or unusual root proliferation.
- **Rot** Roots appear darkened and soft, and plants may be easily pulled from the soil. Few root hairs are present. The earliest symptoms usually include wilting or stunting.

▲ Witches'-broom is a curious growth caused by a variety of parasites or fungi.

Fungus may be present. Root rot often develops due to overly wet or overly dry conditions.

Stem, trunk, and branches

● **Blight** Shoot blights result in the death of new growth, usually with shoots blackening, curling, and dying. Young shoots are more susceptible than older shoots.

● **Canker** These sunken or swollen dead areas in the stem may be target-shape in woody ornamentals. They are usually associated with wounds, which served as entrances for infection. Small pustules (fungal fruiting bodies) may appear; or bacterial ooze may occur during wet weather. Wilting may happen outward

▲ Typically, leaf galls do not seriously affect the overall growth of a maple tree.

▲ This growth is a cedar burl. It looks menacing but is completely harmless.

from the site of the canker.

● **Gall** This round or elongated swelling in the main trunk or branches can be small or large and, like canker, prevent nutrient flow. Galls can be fungal or bacterial.

● **Rot** Stem- and branch-rotting organisms are usually secondary attackers, invading previously damaged tissue.

● **Rust** Rust fungi affect leaves and branches. The fungal signs are usually visible for only a few weeks in spring.

● **Wilt** Wilt disease affects the water-conducting vascular tissue of the plant.

Discoloration of the vascular tissue is usually present. The problem may lie below ground. Common wilt diseases include Dutch elm disease, oak wilt, verticillium wilt, and fusarium wilt.

● **Witches'-broom** This proliferation of new growth from a single site may be due to parasitic plants, such as mistletoe or rust fungi. Phytoplasmas are wall-less bacteria that cause ash and elm yellows. These diseases also produce witches'-broom, but the signs are not visible.

Diseases *(continued)*

With insect pests, you can often see the cause of the problem (the pest!) along with the symptoms and signs of its presence. With disease, however, you only have the clues. So keep a watchful eye for the first sign of symptoms of any of these common diseases in the home landscape.

anthracnose affects leaves—there is no twig dieback.

Plant anthracnose-resistant varieties when possible. Otherwise, gather or prune and then destroy infected leaves and branches. Disinfect your pruning tools afterward. Also replace all mulch.

Anthracnose

Anthracnose is a disease that affects leaves and twigs, especially in ashes, dogwoods, maples, white oaks, and sycamores. It is a fungus that thrives in cool, wet weather and grows through the bud or leaf toward the wood, which it eventually kills. Evidence of anthracnose on a sycamore is canker on the wood and eventually a deformity in the shape of the tree due to the dead buds and stems. On maples, oaks, and ashes,

Fire blight

Fire blight is a bacterial disease that causes blooms and leaves to wilt, curl, and turn brown, as if scorched by fire. It is spread by insects during wet, humid weather. It can be particularly devastating to fruit trees, and has been known to kill even mature trees.

On small trees, thoroughly prune and destroy infected branches after the growing season, to a point at least 4 inches beyond visible damage. Disinfect pruning tools after each cut. For larger trees, hire a tree care professional to prune and spray with a bactericide.

Leaf spot

Leaf spot is a fungi that causes red spots that rot holes in foliage. Infected leaves develop spots, then turn yellow or brown and drop off the tree. Leaf spot spreads during cool, wet spring weather, when new foliage is developing. Ornamental cherry trees are especially vulnerable to leaf spot.

Shake infected leaves from the tree onto a disposable sheet or tarp and destroy. Prune tree to encourage better air circulation and mulch well to prevent the fungi from splashing up from the ground. Spray weekly with sulfur or copper fungicide after blossoms fall on a tree that has been known to suffer from leaf spot. Consider removing seriously infected trees, including the roots, because they pose a threat to others in your landscape.

Powdery mildew

Powdery mildew is an ashy white substance that appears on leaves and is caused by a variety of fungi that thrive in both humid and dry weather. The mildew is caused by fungal spores that are carried by the wind on to the leaves of healthy plants. The leaves are sapped of nutrients and the mildew appears. Infected leaves may eventually become distorted, discolored, and drop.

Plant mildew-resistant varieties when possible. Spray healthy foliage of infected trees with sulfur fungicide to halt the spread of infection. Gather and destroy all tree debris in autumn. Prune inside the canopy to promote light and better air circulation for the plant.

Plant verticillium wilt-resistant varieties whenever possible. Fertilize to stimulate vigorous growth. If new foliage has not appeared on wood infected by verticillium wilt within four weeks, prune out all affected wood, disinfecting tools after each pruning cut.

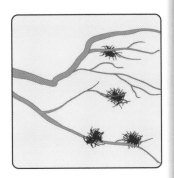

Witches'-broom

Witches'-broom is a strange viral disease that causes clusters of shoots to grow out of lateral buds on branches in the vague shape of a broom. They often pop up all over the tree, destroying the main branches and occasionally the whole tree. Trees are susceptible to infection at vulnerable points such as where pruning or injury has taken place.

Prune and destroy brooms and injured branches. Spray the affected tree with locally recommended fungicides in fall or early spring.

Rust

There are several kinds of rust, which is a very common fungal disease that causes powdery orange or red pustules to appear on leaves. Rust can cause significant leaf drop, as well as a die-off at the end of twigs and overall stunted growth of the plant.

While not as serious as some other diseases, it's a good idea to remove and destroy infected leaves and branches. Rake and destroy fallen leaves in autumn. Consult your local extension office for advice on the most effective fungicide for rust in your area.

Verticillium wilt

This soil-dwelling fungus causes a distinctive wilt that can disfigure many trees and shrubs. It enters the tree through the roots and spreads up into the branches through the trunk. It causes water and nutrients to be blocked from reaching the branches, which causes leaves to wilt and become discolored.

SYMPTOMS OF DISEASE

A variety of common diseases cause similar symptoms that can be observed in the home landscape.

● **Canker** is caused by dozens of species of fungi and is evidenced by blisters on bark, branches, or the trunk of an infected tree.

● **Galls** are growths that develop on leaves, shoots, or the trunks of trees infected by one of a number of fungal or bacterial conditions, as well as by several types of insects. Because it can be hard to determine the cause of these symptoms—and because treatment would be different depending on the cause—it's best to consult a tree care professional if you observe an outbreak of these symptoms.

● **Rot** is a general degeneration of stems and branches caused by organisms that are usually attacking tissue previously damaged by pests or disease.

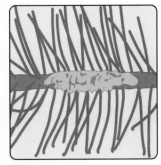

Canker

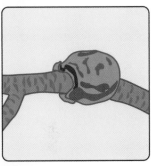

Gall

Rot

UNDER THE WEATHER

When trees and shrubs aren't drastically ailing but just don't look right, it's a little like when we feel vaguely unwell and suffer moderate or non specific symptoms. There are a handful of common characteristics of a plant that's "under the weather" and some familiar, mostly environmental causes:

Sparse flowering: The plant may not be mature enough yet to flower. It also may not be receiving an adequate cool or dormant spell in winter. Too much shade for a sun-loving plant can cause a lack of flowering, as can bad pruning and too much fertilizer.

Bud drop: Transplant shock or frost and cold injury can cause buds to drop, as can drought. Insects such as spider mites, which feed on buds, might also be the culprit.

Mild wilt: Most mild wilt is caused by extreme heat or drying wind, so water well and protect from harsh weather as necessary.

Salt burn: Foliage can be singed by salt spray from winter road treatment, as well as ambient salt in the air near the seashore. Too much fertilizer can cause the same fried edge to the foliage.

Pale foliage: This can be a result of an iron deficiency. Test soil for alkalinity and correct by spraying chelated iron fertilizer.

▲ A deer will devour foliage as high up a tree as it can reach.

While there are many additional pest insects to contend with in your landscape, the damage from only a few pest animals can be devastating. Deer, rabbits, mice, and voles are virtual wrecking crews when plants are vulnerable and conditions are right. Add to that occasional cultural problems, such as drought, flooding, or extreme cold, or equipment or chemical damage, and you may feel like you're on permanent patrol to protect your valuable trees and shrubs.

Plant with these potential problems in mind. If you have a large deer population in your area, for example, choose as many "deer-proof" plants as you can. Or if you know that a part of your property is prone to flooding during rainy periods, look for plants that tolerate the excess moisture. Take measures early on to protect against the damage of some of these factors.

Deer

Deer will eat almost anything if they're hungry enough. Or at least anything they can reach. Having been nudged out of their natural habitat in the wild and into developed areas, deer seem to devour landscape plants as fast as gardeners can plant them. Little makes the heart sink faster than the naked branches and nibbled form of a tree or shrub snacked upon by a deer.

How to address this problem? Fencing is the most expensive and dramatic way to deal with a deer problem. If built at least 6 feet high, fences are effective against deer, but be aware that the deer you successfully keep out of your yard will simply move on to your neighbor's yard, causing a rather unneighborly domino effect of deer destruction.

It's better overall to plant with care. Choose plants deer disdain and apply repellent strategies to keep them from nibbling your trees and shrubs down to the nubs. Mix repellents that disturb a deer's senses of smell, taste, sound, sight, and touch.

Odor repellents work, at least for a while. Home remedies said to be effective include human hair and certain brands of soap strung from mesh bags on or near the plants. Store-bought products can be effective as well, though you should mix them up regularly because if one repellent is used too long, the deer will become accustomed to the smell and eventually ignore it. The smell of the family pets, who do their "business" in the yard, can be an effective deterrent as well.

Motion-activated floodlights and water-spray devices will also keep the deer moving, at least temporarily. Employ a range of varied, year-round strategies against the deer. It may seem like a full-time job, but if you live in deer country, you have little choice.

DEER-RESISTANT TREES AND SHRUBS

Andromeda, Japanese	Enkianthus, redvein	Maple
Barberry, Japanese	Fir, douglas	Mountain laurel
Bayberry, Northern	Forsythia, border	Oaks
Bearberry	Ginkgo	Birch, paper
Beech, European	Grapeholly, Oregon	Pines
Black Gum	Hawthorns	Quince
Boxwood, common	Holly (American, inkberry)	Smokebush
Broom	Honeysuckle	Spirea
Chase Tree	Juniper, Chinese	Spruces
Chokeberry, red	Kerria, Japanese	St. johnswort, shrubby
Cinquefoil, bush	Leucothoe, drooping	Sweet gum
Cotoneaster	Lilac	Viburnum
Daphne, burkwood	Magnolia	Weigela
Dogwood, flowering		Willows
		Wintergreen
		Witch hazel

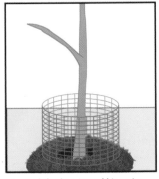

▲ Wrap young trees or surround with wire caging to defend against rabbits, mice, and voles that like to nibble the tender bark in winter.

◀ The thorny stems of barberry are a year-round natural deterrent to deer feeding.

▲ Sunscald is caused by a pattern of rapid freeze and thaw that blisters the trunk.

Rabbits

Cottontails are cute, sure, but less so when they're noshing on the plants in your yard. They're mostly after vegetables, annuals, and perennials, but they're fond of foliage and berries on shrubs as well as tree bark, especially on young trees. You can spot rabbit damage by the diagonal, sharply cut look to the wounds on branches and stems.

Use tree guards to protect young trees from rabbit damage. Wrap ornamental or fruit trees with commercial tree wrap or burlap, or with plastic cylinders. These wraps should extend at least 18 inches above the height of the season's average cumulative snowfall.

Mice and voles

Roots of young trees are extremely susceptible to feeding damage by mice and voles, which use mole tunnels in the soil (or dig their own) to gain access to the roots. These animals will also gnaw on the bark of certain trees at ground level, which can cause girdling and eventual death.

Use plastic tree shelters, tree bark guards, and tree wraps to protect the bark from these pests.

Cultural problems

Drought, flooding, and severe winter weather conditions are the most common causes of cultural problems for trees and shrubs. It can take a tree up to five years to recover from only one season of sustained drought, all the while being vulnerable to insect pests and diseases that will take advantage of its diminished health.

To protect against the effects of drought, amend the soil with good organic material and mulch well to keep the organic content working for the tree year-round. Water deeply at regular intervals as needed. If you are unable to water during drought, avoid fertilizing, pruning, or applying controls, as these further challenge the plant. Test soil occasionally to check for increasing pH and mineral imbalances that may lead to chlorosis or poor growth.

If you live in a region constantly or frequently in drought, plant only trees and shrubs you know to be drought tolerant, to give them a leg up from the start. Similarly avoid planting trees that are sensitive to too much moisture in areas prone to occasional flooding.

In the case of winter weather conditions, watch for sunscald, which happens when the trunk is warmed and expanded by sunlight during the day and then traumatized by fiercely cold temperatures at night. Prevent sunscald by wrapping vulnerable trees exposed to southwestern sun with light-color commercial tree wrap or burlap. This will minimize the dramatic fluctuations in temperature that cause sunscald.

▲ Cute? Maybe. Hungry? You bet. A rabbit will leave its mark on these tasty birch trunks.

Encyclopedia of trees and shrubs

Selecting trees and shrubs for your home landscape becomes one of the most enjoyable and challenging tasks you will face in the process of making the world around you a better place. With so many types of trees and shrubs to choose from, which ones will offer the most aesthetic appeal and potential value for your property? This is one of many questions you will ask as you consider the candidates that will most likely flourish in your home landscape and reward you with their benefits—from aesthetic appeal to shade, wildlife habitat, seasonal interest, and more. Begin now, using this encyclopedia as a guide to simplify the process, and then start dreaming.

This encyclopedia features trees and shrubs widely available for planting in home landscapes. You'll want to choose the best plants for the climate and site where you live as well as your particular landscaping needs. On the pages ahead, you'll find the information you need to help you determine whether a tree or shrub is suited to your landscape in terms of the site, climate, soil, and light conditions. You'll also find plenty of tips to help you ensure the success of your trees and shrubs and get the most enjoyment from your investment.

Begin by creating a list of the features that you desire in the landscape: fall color, shade for the patio, backbone for a wildlife garden, and so on. Narrow the list of possibilities to several appropriate choices by understanding the requirements and inclinations of the plants you are considering and then matching them to the situation.

You will learn the plants' common names and scientific names, which will help you in correctly identifying them when making your selections at the nursery. You will also be pointed to certain cultivars (or cultivated varieties), which represent only a few trees and shrubs you may use to shape and refine your landscape.

Each entry states the plant's primary features, growth rate, mature size, and correct growing zone. The plant description will help you assess its qualities, including its size, characteristics, appropriate uses, and potential limitations. You'll also find planting information and maintenance tips to make the trees and shrubs healthy and long lived—and to make the process enjoyable too.

▲ Plant for changing color and texture across all four seasons.

▲ Orchestrating winning combinations of trees and shrubs in your landscape is uniquely rewarding.

Abelia, glossy *(Abelia ×grandiflora)*

Features: Fragrant, trumpet like flowers and glossy leaves
Growth rate: Moderate to fast
Zones: 6 to 9

Glossy abelia *(Abelia ×grandiflora)*

Description: The deep green, glossy leaves of the abelia are the perfect backdrop to the delicate, pinkish-white flowers that bloom throughout the summer. Bronze fall foliage adds interest to the landscape. This rounded bush grows from 3 to 6 feet tall, with approximately the same spread. It is pest-free and drought tolerant.
Uses: Border, hedge, foundation planting, ornamental.
Site and care requirements: Plant in sun to partial shade. It prefers acidic, moist, well-drained soil but may tolerate drier soil with adequate watering. Winter dieback may be severely pruned because flowers develop on new growth.
Recommended varieties and related species: **'Compacta'** and **'Little Richard'** are dwarf varieties, growing only up to 3 feet high. **'Sherwoodii'** is a smaller variety (up to 4 feet) with purplish fall foliage. The **'Francis Mason'** variety is a heavy bloomer with yellow-green leaves that grows up to 5 feet tall.

Abies **spp.** (see Fir, white)

Acacia, sweet *(Acacia farnesiana)*

Features: The sweetly scented flowers of the sweet acacia look like little yellow puffballs; they emerge in the early spring
Growth rate: Moderately fast
Zones: 9 to 11

Sweet acacia *(Acacia farnesiana)*

Description: This shrub can grow to 10 feet in height. The fragrant flowers are sometimes used in the production of perfume, which demonstrates how intensely aromatic the blooms are. It is especially attractive to butterflies and would be a welcome addition to a wildlife-friendly landscape.
Uses: Accent, specimen.
Site and care requirements: Plant in full sun in well-drained soil. It can tolerate some shade. The sweet acacia is drought tolerant but will drop its leaves in the absence of adequate water.
Recommended varieties and related species: Bailey acacia (*A. baileyana*) is an Australian variety with golden yellow flowers. It can grow to 10 feet high. The catclaw (*A. greggii*) variety is a thorny bush that is useful for barrier plantings, but makes a bad choice for areas with a lot of foot traffic.

Acer **spp.** (see Maple)
Acer negundo (see Box elder)
Aesculus glabra (see Buckeye, Ohio)
Aesculus hippocastanum (see Horsechestnut, common)
Aesculus parviflora (see Buckeye, bottlebrush)
Albizia julibrissin (see Silk tree)

Almond, flowering *(Prunus glandulosa)*

Features: Glorious pink or white spring blooms
Growth rate: Moderate
Zones: 4 to 8

Dwarf flowering almond *(Prunus glandulosa)*

Description: Pink or white flowers cover the flowering almond before the leaves open in the spring. Showy single or double flowers are 1 to 2 inches in diameter. The shrub will grow 4 to 5 feet high and 3 to 4 feet wide.
Uses: Accent or row border.
Site and care requirements: Plants need full sun for best flowering, but tolerate partial shade. Adaptable to many soils, but thrives in rich, moist, acidic soil. Prune immediately after flowering to keep its shape and to encourage more blooms the next season.
Recommended varieties and related species: The **'Alba Plena'** has white double flowers, and the **'Rosea Plena'** has pink flowers. Tree-form flowering almond (*Prunus triloba*) grows 12 to 15 feet high and wide with a mounded shape.

Alder, European black *(Alnus glutinosa)*

Features: Upright, fast-growing, and suitable for wet areas of the landscape
Growth rate: Fast (2 to 4 feet a year in early years), then moderate
Zones: 4 to 8

European black alder *(Alnus glutinosa)*

Description: This large deciduous tree keeps its color until late fall, providing a nice green backdrop for other brilliant fall foliage. The male flowers that emerge in early spring resemble long, thin pinecones. These flowers stay on the tree well into fall and early winter, giving visual interest to what would otherwise be a bare landscape. The fast-growing alder reaches a height of 40 to 60 feet with a width of about 20 to 40 feet. The European black alder thrives in almost any soil and does especially well in the usually hard-to-plant, low wet areas of a landscape. It will survive planted next to bodies of water so it can help reduce erosion at the edge of a pond or swamp. Working well as an understory tree, it also takes to life in a lawn. The tree absorbs nitrogen from the air, producing its own fertilizer and improving the soil in which it's planted.
Uses: Use in a low-lying wet area or to edge a pond, stream, or swamp.
Site and care requirements: Plant in full sun or partial shade. It prefers well-drained soil, but will tolerate many different types of soil. The tree should be kept moist, which may require watering to maintain one in drier areas of the landscape.
Recommended varieties and related species: 'Imperialis' is a smaller tree with more delicate leaves, while 'Pyramidalis' is a larger tree that has a well-defined columnar shape.

Allspice, Carolina *(Calycanthus floridus)*

Features: Elegant, fragrant maroon flowers and deep green leaves on a solidly rounded shrub
Growth rate: Slow to moderate
Zones: 4 to 9

Carolina allspice *(Calycanthus floridus)*

Description: The most distinguishing characteristic of the Carolina allspice is its flowers. These deep reddish brown maroon flowers emit a sweet and spicy aroma, reminiscent of berries, melons, bananas, and cloves. The distinctive blossoms emerge in April and May, unfurling their colorful petals against dark green leaves. The Carolina allspice grows 6 to 10 feet high and 6 to 12 feet wide. It is drought tolerant and pest resistant. Buy the plant when it is flowering, because some plants (especially those grown from seed) may have less fragrance than others.
Uses: Plant under a window, next to a door, or anywhere you will most enjoy the fragrance as it wafts indoors. Good for a shrub border.
Site and care requirements: Plant in sun to partial shade in well-drained soil. Pruning may be necessary to keep the shrub from getting scraggly, particularly in a border. Prune after flowering.
Recommended varieties and related species: 'Athens' is a yellow-flowered, very fragrant cultivar whose green foliage turns yellow in the fall. 'Edith Wilder' and 'Michael Lindsey' both have darker leaves and are especially fragrant.

Alnus glutinosa (see Alder, European black)
Alpine currant (see Currant, alpine)
Amelanchier **spp.** (see Serviceberry)
Amur chokecherry (see Chokecherry, amur)
Amur cork tree (see Cork tree, amur)
Amur maackia (see Maackia, amur)

Andromeda, Japanese *(Pieris japonica)*

Features: This evergreen shrub boasts clusters of fragrant, urn shape flowers and rich green leaves
Growth rate: Slow
Zones: 5 to 8

Japanese andromeda *(Pieris japonica)*

Description: The Japanese andromeda or pieris blooms in early spring for 2 to 3 weeks. The flower clusters are 3 to 6 inches long and bloom in white, pink, and red, depending on the variety. In spring, foliage often emerges as red or bronze, giving color to the landscape before the flowers bloom. The haystack-shape shrub grows 8 to 12 feet high, with a spread of 6 to 8 feet. Japanese andromeda is prone to infestation from lacebugs, which suck the juice from the leaves, turning them yellow.
Uses: Use as an accent, foundation planting, or in a border, especially with other acid-loving evergreen shrubs.
Site and care requirements: This is the perfect plant for shady, moist spots in the landscape. Plant in areas protected from wind in more northern zones and from winter sun in warmer climates. Pruning is unnecessary, but deadhead old flowers as the new buds develop in midsummer.
Recommended varieties and related species: A more compact variety, 'Mountain Fire' has white flowers and fiery red leaves that turn green as they mature. 'Valley Valentine'

has showy deep pink flowers while **'White Cascade'** has long-lasting white flowers. Other cultivars, such as **'Variegata',** have variegated leaves that offer another twist of color in the garden.

Apple *(Malus* hybrids)

Features: Among the most popular fruit trees, apples provide years of fruit and beautiful blooms
Growth rate: Slow to fast, depending on variety
Zones: 3 to 9

An old apple orchard in bloom

Malus hybrid 'Anna'

Description: Attractive, abundant blooms give way to fruit that can be enjoyed right off the tree. Depending on the variety, apple trees can produce fruit from summer into early winter, while providing the landscape with several months of interest. Typical apple trees grow up to 20 feet high, while dwarf varieties reach 6 to 8 feet high. A mature dwarf tree produces from 60 to 100 apples a year, while a full-size tree produces more than 300 apples. Earliest apples begin ripening in August. Little is more gratifying than eating the fruit from your home orchard. With the hundreds of varieties available, it's possible to find an apple tree that will suit your landscape as well as any appetite.

A profusion of apple blossoms

Uses: For accent, grouping, fruit production.
Site and care requirements: Choosing the right variety of apple tree for the landscape is the first step toward growing a successful tree. First visit a nearby nursery to find out which are the hardiest and most disease-resistant apple cultivars for your region. Some varieties are self-pollinating, but most require at least one other apple cultivar blooming nearby for pollination. Plant more than one tree to ensure a successful crop. Apple trees should be planted while dormant—in the spring in central and northern areas and in the fall in southern climates. Follow planting directions for the tree regarding spacing. Generally dwarf apples should be planted 8 to 10 apart; others up to 20 feet apart. Apple trees prefer full sun and slightly acidic soil. Trees typically begin to bear fruit within 3 to 5 years after planting.

Recommended varieties and related species: Many of the most well-known apple cultivars have been made better through hybridization. Look for improved strains of old favorites and check their pollinization requirements. **'Esopus Spitzenberg'** is prized for its rich flavor and crisp flesh. **'Zestar'** is an excellent all-purpose white-fleshed red apple that is hardy to Zone 3. **'Jonathan'** is self-fruitful but susceptible to fire blight. **'Braeburn'** is a self-fruitful tree that bears late. **'Gala'** is a sweet midseason apple popular in many regions. **'Jonagold'** is a compact tree with juicy, sweet, all-purpose red fruits that ripen in early October. **'Stayman Winesap'** is a favorite red baking and cider apple in Zones 5 to 8 that keeps well. **'Irish Peach'** is an early variety for sauces and pies.

Fruit from *Malus* hybrid 'Irish Peach'

Arborvitae, American *(Thuja occidentalis)*

Features: Hardy evergreen, dense foliage makes beautiful hedges or privacy screens
Growth rate: Slow to fast, depending on variety
Zones: 2 to 7

American arborvitae *(Thuja occidentalis)*

Description: The evergreen American arborvitae is a soft-leafed shrub that can grow from a few feet high up to 60 feet high. When planted in a row, the pyramidal shape lends itself to making a very effective privacy screen. American arborvitae can also be planted with others to add height to a grouping, which makes it popular for providing visual interest in foundation plantings. Some varieties grow up to 4 feet a year, so it is often used to fill a space quickly. American arborvitaes have tiny green cones that appear in spring. The female cones turn a silvery color over time, which contrasts nicely with the green of the shrub.
Uses: Hedge, border, foundation planting, screen; or dwarf-variety accent planting.
Site and care requirements: American arborvitae can be grown in most any soil, but well-drained, moist soil is best. It can be planted in full to partial sun and grows best when protected from winter wind and snow. A weather-damaged shrub exhibits yellowing leaves. Pruning is unnecessary, but can be performed to shape the shrubs into a hedge or to control the silhouette and height.
Recommended varieties and related species: Varieties of American arborvitae include **'Emerald',** a slow-growing variety that is heat and cold tolerant, and **'Nigra'** and **'Techny',** which have dark green foliage throughout the winter. **'Rheingold'** is a dwarf variety that grows 3 to 4 feet high.

Arborvitae, oriental *(Platycladus orientalis)*

Features: Light evergreen foliage and exceptionally suitable for warmer climates
Growth rate: Slow to moderate
Zones: 6 to 10

Oriental arborvitae *(Platycladus orientalis)*

Description: The yellowish green foliage of the oriental arborvitae keeps its color throughout the winter. It is more heat tolerant than the American arborvitae, and therefore is perfectly suited for growing in warmer climates. It starts out somewhat compact but opens as the plant matures. It grows up to 25 feet high, and the round-edge, pyramidal shape boasts a large base up to 10 to 15 feet wide that fills empty spaces with ease. It is one of the best choices for evergreen hedges. Dwarf varieties grow up to 3 feet high.
Uses: Border, hedge, foundation planting, accent.
Site and care requirements: Oriental arborvitae grows in just about any soil. No pruning is needed, other than to shape a hedge or to control a specimen's overall shape and height. Protect trees from severe dry winds and cold that can damage foliage and cause it to turn brown and die.
Recommended varieties and related species: Blue and yellow dwarf cultivars are popular in the South and West. **'Baker'** and **'Blue Cone'** are examples of full-size varieties with green to blue-green foliage. **'Aurea Nana'** is a dwarf variety with yellowish foliage.

Arbutus menziesii (see Madrone, Pacific)
Aronia arbutifolia (see Chokeberry, red)

Ash, green (Fraxinus pennsylvanica)

Features: Best suited to provide shade; adaptable to many different conditions and soils
Growth rate: Fast
Zones: 3 to 9

Green ash (Fraxinus pennsylvanica)

Description: The green ash reaches 50 to 60 feet tall with a spread of about 25 feet, making it an excellent shade tree. The green ash is a popular choice for landscape planting because of its fast growing habit (up to 3 feet a year) and tolerance of heat and cold. Its dark green foliage turns golden yellow in fall. The shape is irregularly pyramidal, becoming rounded in maturity.
Uses: Shade, accent.
Site and care requirements: The green ash is adaptable to many different soils and grows best in full sun. The root system of the green ash may become intrusive so planting near sidewalks or driveways is not recommended. Choose a seedless variety, because the fruit can become a nuisance when it falls in abundance. Green ash is susceptible to borers and ash yellows. The emerald ash borer is a major problem in some areas of the country, and is rapidly spreading.
Recommended varieties and related species: 'Marshalls Seedless' is a male cultivar that bears no fruit. It is a hardy tree with dark green foliage. 'Patimore' is also fruitless, has a more regular shape, and is most tolerant to cold. 'Summit' has no fruit and produces the yellow fall foliage typical of the green ash.

Ash, white (Fraxinus americana)

Features: Adapts to many sites and offers shade with beautiful reddish purple fall foliage
Growth rate: Moderate
Zones: 3 to 9

White ash (Fraxinus americana)

Description: The white ash tree has a more regular form—from pyramidal in youth to more rounded in maturity. It grows 50 to 80 feet high and just as wide, providing a mass of welcome shade in the heat of summer. It is heat-tolerant, adapts to many different soil conditions, and grows about 18 inches a year. It can live well over 100 years and some last up to 200 years. The white ash, famous for its wood used to make baseball bats, makes a fine addition to a large landscape. Along with the red-purple fall foliage, the bark with a meshlike texture, and the deep purple blossoms in spring, the white ash offers an interesting display throughout the year.
Uses: Shade, accent.
Site and care requirements: Because of its size at maturity, the white ash should be planted in larger properties with plenty of room to grow. Select a male cultivar, which is fruitless to eliminate the litter and nuisance of the falling fruit. Plant in full sun. While the white ash tolerates many different soil conditions, well-drained soil is best. It is susceptible to scale, ash yellows, and borers, including the emerald ash borer, a major pest in parts of the country.
Recommended varieties and related species: 'Autumn Purple' has deep green foliage that turns reddish purple in the fall. The foliage of this variety is more brilliant in the northern areas than in southern climates. 'Autumn Applause', a slightly smaller white ash whose height reaches about 45 feet, is suitable for smaller landscapes. 'Rose Hill' features reddish purple fall foliage.

Asimina triloba (see Pawpaw)

Aucuba, Japanese (Aucuba japonica)

Features: Shade lover with leathery green leaves; purple-red flowers and red berries on female plants
Growth rate: Slow
Zones: 7 to 10

Japanese aucuba (*Aucuba japonica*)

Description: The leathery-looking, somewhat shiny leaves enliven the landscape with their dark green color. The tidy evergreen shrub reaches up to 10 feet when mature. Japanese aucuba does well when shaded by larger trees. It also makes a good foundation plant, shading a house or a similar structure. Some cultivars feature leaves with yellow or white markings and work to brighten a shaded location. The shrub is also salt tolerant, making it suitable for seaside planting. Female plants produce reddish purple flowers followed by bright red berries, which remain on the plant throughout the winter.
Uses: Foundation or as accent under large, shady trees. Also an appropriate container plant.
Site and care requirements: Best for warm-climate gardens. Plant in shade to partial sun. Well-drained, moist, and organically-rich soil is best. A plant of each sex is required for berry production. Keep soil evenly moist the first 2 years to encourage growth. Prune plants in spring to remove winter-damaged branches and enhance their rounded shape. Cut plants back to control their size.
Recommended varieties and related species: 'Variegata' is very shade tolerant and produces yellow-flecked leaves. 'Sulphura' sports variegated leaves with yellow-gold edges. 'Crotonifoli' is a variety with white-flecked leaves.

Azalea (see Rhododendron)
Baccharis pilularis (see Coyote brush)

Bald cypress (Taxodium distichum)

Features: Nicely pyramidal with fernlike texture and fall color, ideal for planting in wet conditions
Growth rate: Moderate
Zones: 4 to 10

Bald cypress (*Taxodium distichum*)

Description: This deciduous conifer loses its needles in the fall and grows a new crop in the spring. Before the needles drop, they turn brownish red, adding a blush of color to the landscape. The tree matures into a pyramidal shape and reaches 50 to 70 feet high and 20 to 30 feet wide. The bald cypress forms catkins in late winter and develops peeling reddish brown bark as it matures. The tree thrives in wet conditions, such as next to a pond or lake, but the tree can be planted away from water if the soil is kept moist. Once established, the tree is nearly carefree.
Uses: Next to a pond or lake, in a grouping, or as an accent in a home landscape.
Site and care requirements: Bald cypress does best in moist conditions. It prefers heavy soil or soil rich in organic matter. Plant in full sun or partial shade. Give the tree plenty of room to grow to mature size, and situate it away from areas where mowing or traffic can damage any knees that develop. Susceptible to neither pests nor disease, the bald cypress may need annual feeding with an acid plant food.
Recommended varieties and related species: 'Shawnee Brave' is a narrower version of the bald cypress. '**Monarch of Illinois**' is a larger, wider variety with yellowish foliage.

Barberry, Japanese *(Berberis thunbergii)*

Features: Dense, evergreen shrub with striking berries, thorns, and green to purple leaves that makes an excellent hedge
Growth rate: From slow to moderate, depending on type
Zones: 4 to 8

Japanese barberry *(Berberis thunbergii)*

Description: The Japanese barberry is a popular shrub in the South because it tolerates drought and various soil conditions. The leaves turn from green in the summer to reddish purple in the fall and winter, and the bright red berries that emerge in the fall can remain through the winter months. It is a thorny bush, so care must be used when choosing a planting site. Japanese barberry grows 3 to 6 feet high and 4 to 7 feet wide. The wintergreen barberry *(B. julianae)*, a larger variety that grows up to 10 feet tall, has leaves that turn golden yellow or dark red in the fall. Mentor barberry *(B. ×mentorensis)* grows to about the same size as the Japanese barberry, but the leaves turn an orangey red in the fall and drop off when winter arrives.

Uses: Hedge, barrier planting, foundation planting.

Site and care requirements: Plant in full sun to partial shade

Mentor barberry *(Berberis ×mentorensis)*

and almost any soil. Take advantage of barberry's natural fullness and use it in a privacy screen. The thorns will help make it a security hedge. The shrub adapts well to shearing and makes it a candidate for a formal hedge. Barberry also tolerates urban conditions and withstands wind.

Recommended varieties and related species: **'Crimson Pygmy'**, a dwarf variety of Japanese barberry, produces reddish purple leaves in fall. It grows up to 2 feet high and works well in small spaces. This variety displays the most vibrancy when grown in full sun. **'Aurea'** shows yellow foliage and reaches 3 to 4 feet high. **'Nana'**, a wintergreen barberry, reaches 4 feet high and has large thorns. Its dark green foliage turns red in winter. **'Spring Glory'**, a 6-foot-high mounding variety of wintergreen barberry needs no pruning and turns bronze to dark red in fall. **B. koreana**, or Korean barberry, has less spiney stems.

Wintergreen barberry *(Berberis julianae)*

Bayberry, northern *(Myrica pensylvanica)*

Features: Sweet-smelling berries and handsome green leaves on a nicely rounded form; adaptable to poor soil
Growth rate: Medium
Zones: 2 to 7

Northern bayberry *(Myrica pensylvanica)*

Description: Bayberry is common to coastal areas because it is adaptable to sandy soils. The added bonus of the aromatic berries and the dark green leaves adds color and character to an ordinary landscape. The berries emerge in the fall and may stay on the shrub until well into spring. It reaches 6 to 12 feet high and wide.

Uses: Hedge, grouping.

Site and care requirements: Northern bayberry should be planted in full sun to partial shade. It thrives in sandy soil and withstands salty spray and wind, typical of coastal areas. Prune bayberry to maintain its rounded shape. When trimmed regularly, taller varieties make handsome hedges.

Recommended varieties and related species: **M. cerifera,** or **wax myrtle**, is a related species that grows in Zones 3 to 7.

Beautyberry, Chinese (Callicarpa dichotoma)

Features: Hanging clusters of spring flowers and autumn color of vibrant, lilac-colored berries
Growth rate: Fast
Zones: 5 to 8

Chinese beautyberry (Callicarpa dichotoma)

Description: In spring small clusters of pink flowers hang from the slender branches that arch toward the ground. In mid to late autumn, the lilac berries clustered amongst the light green leaves attract birds and other wildlife. Native to China and Japan, Chinese beautyberry reaches a full height of 4 to 6 feet.
Uses: Use beautyberry in mass plantings, borders, and wildlife gardens, or as an accent plant to showcase the contrasting color of the berries.
Site and care requirements: Plant in moist, well-drained soil and full sun to light shade. Prune it to the ground in late winter or early spring after the berries are gone to promote dense growth.
Recommended varieties and related species: **Bodiner beautyberry** (*C. bodinieri*) is a taller variety, with larger berry clusters. **C. d. albifructus** is a white variety of the beautyberry. The related species, **American beautyberry** (*C. americana*), has the same vibrant fruit as Chinese beautyberry but is not as cold hardy.

Beautybush (Kolkwitzia amabilis)

Beautybush (Kolkwitzia amabilis)

Features: Charming pink, bell-shape flowers that bloom in late spring
Growth rate: Fast
Zones: 5 to 8

Description: Pretty clusters of pink, bell-shape flowers flourish on this gently arching shrub in late spring. The light brown bark on mature trunks splits vertically and exfoliates, adding distinctive texture to the garden during the fall and winter. Native to China, beautybush reaches a height of 6 to 10 feet, with a spread of about the same size.
Uses: Place it at the back of the garden, where it will form a background for flowering plants in summer and stand out in winter. It can be used in a border, but the distinctive shape of the arching branches may get lost in a crowded grouping.
Site and care requirements: Plant in full sun for best flowering, and allow plenty of room to grow. Prune out older stems immediately after flowering to promote new growth. It may also be cut to the ground to maintain its rounded shape and to keep it from reaching the form and size of a small tree as it matures.
Recommended varieties and related species: **'Pink Cloud'** and **'Rosea'** for clear, deeper pink flowers.

Beech, European (Fagus sylvatica)

Features: Copper-colored fall foliage and silvery bark
Growth rate: Slow
Zones: 5 to 7

European beech (Fagus sylvatica)

Description: This magnificently large, deciduous tree grows to 50 to 60 feet tall and 35 to 45 feet wide. It has bright green leaves with a silvery cast that turn a coppery color in the fall. Small nuts provide winter food for wildlife and the gray-silver bark adds color to the winter landscape.
Uses: Accent tree in large yards or landscapes.
Site and care requirements: The long-lived beech thrives in full sun, but tolerates light shade. It needs moist, well-drained, and acid soil as well as plenty of room to grow. The roots are somewhat shallow and may lift pavement as they grow if planted near sidewalks or driveways. Mulch widely to keep roots moist and protected. Pruning is unnecessary, but the lower branches of older trees may be pruned during winter dormancy to allow more of the bark to be visible.
Recommended varieties and related species: **'Asplenifolia'** has dark green, elegantly shaped leaves. **'Atropunicea'** is a general name for any of the purple-leaf

varieties such as **'Spaethiana'. 'Pendula'** has weeping branches. The **American beech** *(F. grandifolia)*, native to eastern North America, is larger than the **European beech.** Best grown in Zones 4 to 8, the American beech also needs plenty of space to grow. The dark green leaves turn a golden bronze in the fall, eventually turning brown, but hanging onto the tree sometimes until January.

Berberis spp. (see Barberry, Japanese)
Betula spp. (see Birch)

Birch *(Betula* spp.)

Features: Paperlike, peeling bark, which ranges in color from chalky white to red, yellow, and cinnamon brown
Growth rate: Moderate to fast, depending on variety
Zones: 2 to 9, depending on variety

Birch *(Betula* spp.)

Description: The delicate leaves of the birch nicely offset the peeling, curling bark. The trees reach 40 to 70 feet high with a spread of 20 to 60 feet. Birches are either pyramidal or rounded in shape and produce seeds that draw a variety of wildlife. They grow relatively quickly, making them desirable landscape specimens. Choose a variety proven adaptable to your locale or the tree will be short-lived.
Uses: Ornamental, shade, accent.

Weeping birch *(B. pendula)*

Site and care requirements: Birch trees need plenty of room to grow to accommodate their large and widespread root system. Planting in the fall is best, but birches may be planted in the spring if watered consistently. They are famously thirsty trees, so water and mulch to keep soil moist. Prune in the late summer or winter to remove dead or diseased branches. Birches are susceptible to leaf miners and bronze birch borers. Leaf miners damage the leaves, while bronze birch borer worms bore into the wood and can eventually kill the tree.
Recommended varieties and related species: European weeping birch *(B. pendula)* has a draping form and delicate cut leaves. This slow-growing tree is hardy in Zones 3 to 6 and is highly susceptible to leaf miners and bronze birch

borers. Varieties of European weeping birch include **'Roth'** and **'Youngii'**.

Paper birch *(B. papyrifera)*, also known as canoe birch, is best planted in Zones 2 to 7. The white bark peels off the tree as it matures, revealing cinnamon brown bark underneath. The dark green leaves turn a brilliant yellow in the fall, before dropping to reveal the creamy white bark that can beautifully offset evergreens if planted nearby. Paper birch prefers cooler climates and moist soil and is susceptible to heat stress and borers in hotter, sunny weather. This tree has a medium to fast growth rate, reaching full maturity and a height of up to 70 feet in 60 or 70 years.

Paper birch *(B. papyrifera)*

River birch *(B. nigra)*, also known as black birch, has cinnamon-colored peeling bark. The leaves do not change color in the fall, but drop to reveal the spectacular bark in the winter. This is the most borer-resistant birch variety. It grows well in moist soil and full sun to partial shade. Avoid very alkaline soils—pH 6.5 or higher. River birches grow best in Zones 4 to 9. The most common varieties of river birch for landscapes are **'Dura Heat'** and **'Heritage'.**

River birch *(B. nigra)*

Japanese white birch *(B. platyphylla japonica)* is a white-bark birch that does not peel as much as other birches. It grows well in Zones 4 to 7 and endures heat better than other white-barked birches. It is very resistant to borers but can become more susceptible to them in the hotter climates of the growing zone. Purchase cuttings from the variety **'Whitespire'**, as the seeds may not produce trees with the same characteristics of heat tolerance and resistance to bronze birch borers.

Japanese white birch
(B. platyphylla japonica)

Black gum *(Nyssa sylvatica)*

Features: Striking fall foliage that can range from yellow to orange, red, and purple—all on the same tree
Growth rate: Moderate
Zones: 4 to 9

Black gum *(Nyssa sylvatica)*

Description: The spectacular fall foliage show makes the black gum tree extremely attractive for home landscapes. This medium-size tree grows from 30 to 50 feet high with a spread of 20 to 30 feet. The pyramidal to full, rounded canopy provides plenty of shade from the hot summer sun. The bark, a dark gray to almost black color, is the basis for the name black gum. The bark looks like alligator skin in texture—thick and cracked—which adds its own interest to the winter landscape. The fruit of the black gum tree resembles small bluish black berries that are little more than a slightly messy nuisance for people but are very appetizing to birds and other wildlife. This tree is also known as the black tupelo.
Uses: Specimen tree or in a grouping for even more spectacular effect.
Site and care requirements: The black gum tree can be planted in full sun to partial shade. It prefers moist acid soil but can survive in dry soil as well. Prune lower branches to allow room to enjoy the excellent shade the tree provides.

Blueberry, highbush *(Vaccinium corymbosum)*

Features: Delicious fruit and colorful flowers and leaves that combine for year-round interest
Growth rate: Slow
Zones: 3 to 7

Highbush blueberry *(Vaccinium corymbosum)*

Description: This deciduous shrub provides four seasons' worth of reasons to grow in your home landscape. The small green leaves are the background for spring flowers that bloom in white and yellow. The flowers give way to the blueberries themselves, which ripen to a purplish blue in early summer. Fall brings a color burst from the changing foliage in colors ranging from golden yellow to orange to red. And the form and color of the stems provide winter interest. It's an excellent addition to a border or planted as an accent bush. Highbush blueberry grows 6 to 12 feet high, with a spread of 8 to 10 feet.
Uses: Border, accent, foundation planting.
Site and care requirements: Blueberries prefer full sun and acidic, sandy soil. Mulch around the base to retain moisture. Birds find blueberries as delicious as people do; cover bushes with commercially available netting to protect your crop.
Recommended varieties and related species: Highbush varietie are **'Blueray'**, **'Earliblue'**, and **'Jersey'**. Lowbush blueberry *(V. angustifolium)* grows 2 feet tall and wide in Zones 2 to 5.

Box elder *(Acer negundo)*

Features: Hardy, adaptable, and fast-growing shade tree for harsh climates
Growth rate: Fast
Zones: 2 to 9

Variegated box elder *(Acer negundo 'Variegatum')*

Description: The box elder grows 30 to 50 feet high, with a spread of 20 to 40 feet. This rapidly growing tree can be grown in a range of soil types, from moist to dry. Native to Canada and the eastern United States, it withstands harsh climate conditions such as wind, snow, and cold temperatures. It is susceptible to box elder bugs, which eat the seeds on the female trees. The wood is prone to breakage, so it may require more cleanup in the home landscape than in open areas. The large, rounded shape may grow irregularly as the tree matures. The leaves are particularly showy when they turn yellow in the fall, but certain varieties of box elder boast variegated leaves in various colors during the spring and summer.
Uses: Open areas and landscapes in harsher climates.
Site and care requirements: Plant in full sun or medium shade. Adaptable to most soil conditions.
Recommended varieties and related species: **'Flamingo'** has variegated pink and green leaves that are especially nice on this common tree. **'Variegatum'** has white and green variegated leaves and prefers a shadier site.

Boxwood, common *(Buxus sempervirens)*

Features: Versatile and known for lush green leaves and dense forms
Growth rate: Slow
Zones: 6 to 10

Common boxwood *(Buxus sempervirens)*

Description: Common boxwood is one of the most attractive and versatile shrubs for borders and hedges. It can be trimmed into just about any hedge shape or even used for topiary. It grows 15 to 20 feet high and about the same width. This densely packed evergreen provides a uniform green wall in mass plantings and hedges. Used as a foundation planting, common boxwood hides undesirable structural views. While boxwood solves all sorts of landscape woes, it needs to have dead twigs thinned to keep its growth uniform. It lacks tolerance to extreme hot and cold.
Uses: Hedge, screen, foundation planting.
Site and care requirements: Common boxwood grows best in well-drained, moist soil. Plant in full sun or partial shade and protect from extreme heat and drying winds. Mulch around the base of the boxwood and plant nothing else at the base because the roots are shallow and will not compete well with other plantings. Avoid cultivating around the roots. Remove dead twigs and leaves from inner branches.
Recommended varieties and related species: **'Northern Find'**, **'Northern Beauty'**, and **'Vardar Valley'** are hardier varieties that are recommended through Zone 5. **'Wintergreen'** *(Buxus microphylla)* and hybrids like **'Greenmound'** are top choices for northern locations.

Boxwood is a favorite plant for artful shaping in a formal garden.

Broom, Scotch *(Cytisus scoparius)*

Features: A fine-textured shrub with blooms that range in color from white to yellow and red
Growth rate: Moderate
Zones: 5 to 8

Scotch broom *(Cytisus scoparius)*

Description: Drought- and salt-tolerant Scotch broom also withstands dry, poor soil. Flowers develop in late spring, and soon the bush is covered in small blooms that resemble pea plant flowers. In some areas Scotch broom is considered a weed, because it proliferates through long seedpods that burst, throwing the seeds for several feet. The seeds can survive in the soil for years, until the conditions are right for germination. In the home landscape, Scotch broom adds color with springtime flowers as well as leafless twigs that remain green throughout the winter.
Uses: Border, mass planting.
Site and care requirements: Plant in sandy, poor soil. Scotch broom requires little care other than pruning to keep it from looking weedy and unkempt.
Recommended varieties and related species: **'Burkwoodii'** is a variety with red blooms. **'Moonlight'** flowers a creamy tan and grows from about 4 to 6 feet.

Broom, warminster *(Cytisus ×praecox)*

Features: Small yellow spring blooms and evergreen branches for winter interest
Growth rate: Fast
Zones: 6 to 8

Warminster broom *(Cytisus ×praecox)*

Description: Warminster broom tolerates challenging conditions, including windy and coastal climates. Its proclivity for survival in dry soil means it needs little upkeep and makes this shrub useful for far-reaching areas of the landscape. Plant it anywhere for its showy spring color and an evergreen accent in winter. The grasslike stems—with or without blooms—prove useful in cut flower arrangements. Warminster broom grows 3 to 5 feet high and up to 6 feet wide. The mounded shape provides an attractive form anywhere in the landscape.
Uses: Accent, border.
Site and care requirements: Plant in dry, poor soil. No pruning is necessary.
Recommended varieties and related species: **'Gold Spear'** is a smaller variety that grows up to 4 feet high with about the same spread. The sweet-smelling, yellow flowers bloom in spring, and in the fall the leaves drop to reveal the evergreen stems.

Buckeye, bottlebrush *(Aesculus parviflora)*

Features: Foot-long stems of spiky white flowers and handsome foliage
Growth rate: Slow to moderate
Zones: 5 to 8

Bottlebrush buckeye *(Aesculus parviflora)*

Description: The bottlebrush buckeye provides spectacular foliage and grows in the shade, giving a punch of color to otherwise dark areas. It produces spectacular, 1-foot-long flower spikes. The creamy-white flowers with red anthers emerge in June—relatively late compared to other flowering shrubs—and attracts hummingbirds to the yard. As if the striking flowers weren't enough, this deciduous shrub offers medium green leaves that turn a golden yellow in the fall, adding interest to the landscape through most of the year. It grows 6 to 10 feet high with a spread of 8 to 15 feet.
Uses: Accent or specimen in either sunny or shady landscape to showcase the unusual flowers.
Site and care requirements: Plant in sun to shade and well-drained soil. Amend the soil with plenty of organic matter. Allow lots of room for the shrub to spread as it grows.
Recommended varieties and related species: **'Rogers'** shows off flower stems of 18 to 30 inches long.

Buckeye, Ohio *(Aesculus glabra)*

Features: Showy flowers on a lovely rounded tree
Growth rate: Moderate
Zones: 4 to 7

Ohio buckeye *(Aesculus glabra)*

Description: The buckeye is best used as a singular accent to the landscape because of its wide crown. It grows from 20 to 40 feet high with a similar spread, but the short trunk and low branches make it appear much wider than other trees of similar height and width. It is often called a stinking buckeye because the leaves and twigs give off a foul smell when crushed or broken. The buckeye got its name from the appearance of the fruit—it resembles a buck's eye when fully mature. The bright yellow flowers bloom in late spring, giving way to the fruit that helps keep the population of squirrels alive throughout the winter, although the fruit is poisonous to humans. One of the first trees to lose its leaves in fall, its foliage turns yellow to bright orange before dropping.
Uses: Accent, specimen.
Site and care requirements: Plant in full sun or partial shade in moist soil, allowing plenty of growing room. Mulch to help preserve soil moisture because this tree tolerates drought poorly. Ohio buckeye is prone to leaf blight and scorch.
Recommended varieties and related species: **Red buckeye** *(A. pavia)*, a smaller tree than the Ohio buckeye, often resembles a large bush due to its low branches and short trunk. It reaches 15 to 20 feet high with about the same spread. The red flowers bloom in mid spring, attracting bees and hummingbirds. It does best in full sun but tolerates partial shade and should be planted in well-drained, loamy soil. **Yellow buckeye** *(A. octandra)*, a larger

Red buckeye *(A. pavia)*

buckeye, grows 60 to 70 feet high with a spread of up to 30 to 40 feet. The yellow flowers emerge in late spring, while the orange autumn leaves light up the landscape. It grows best in full sun and needs plenty of room to grow.

Buddleia davidii (see Butterfly bush)

Buffaloberry, silver *(Shepherdia argentea)*

Features: Silvery leaves that complement bright red, edible berries
Growth rate: Fast
Zones: 2 to 6

Silver buffaloberry *(Shepherdia argentea)*

Description: The buffaloberry is a loosely branched shrub with silvery green leaves. White flowers emerge in spring, giving way to the red berries that are popular for making jams and jellies. Harvesting the berries may be difficult though, due to the 1- to 2-inch thorns on the branches. Its open, rounded shape reaches 6 to 14 feet high with a width of 8 to 14 feet. This shrub tolerates poor, dry soil and withstands drought, wind, and salt spray, making it useful for coastal plantings.
Uses: Accent, fruit production.
Site and care requirements: Plant in full sun. Although buffaloberry is well-adapted to moderately alkaline and saline soil, it will not fare well in a wet, poorly drained spot.
Recommended varieties and related species: A similar species, **russet buffaloberry** *(S. canadensis)*, also has dark green leaves with a silvery cast and red fruit. This smaller shrub grows only to about 6 to 8 feet tall and wide.

Bunchberry *(Cornus canadensis)*

Features: Tightly bunched, edible berries and showy white flowers on a low-growing shrub
Growth rate: Slow
Zones: 3 to 6

Description: A relative of the dogwood, this shrub features blooms that appear in July and August and are actually made up of four white bracts around a small white flower, giving the appearance of one large flower. The berries that emerge in late summer are good for making jams and jellies, but watch for competition from the other creatures that enjoy them as well. The yellow to red fall foliage of the bunchberry makes this a seasonally appealing addition to the landscape. The creeping nature of the bunchberry growth makes it a perfect planting as bushy groundcover, as a single plant can grow up to 3 feet wide but only up to 8 inches high.

Bunchberry *(Cornus canadensis)*

Uses: Groundcover and mass planting for harvesting berries, for the color, and to attract wildlife.
Site and care requirements: Plant in partial sun to full shade. The most growth occurs in shade and cool, moist, acid soil. Prepare the site for planting by loosening the soil and mixing in plenty of organic matter.

Burkwood daphne (see Daphne, burkwood)

Burning bush *(Euonymus alatus)*

Features: Fiery red fall foliage and an attractive vase shape
Growth rate: Slow
Zones: 4 to 8

Burning bush *(Euonymus alatus)*

Description: Fall color is the main reason to plant a burning bush. The oval, 1- to 3-inch-long leaves provide a pleasant green throughout spring and summer, but when the foliage lights up scarlet in the fall, this shrub becomes a gem of the landscape. The vaselike shape develops to 10 to 15 feet high and to about the same width at maturity. Insignificant yellow-green flowers give way to red berries in the summer, adding another dimension of color and interest to the bush as the leaves turn in the fall.
Uses: Mass planting, border.
Site and care requirements: Plant in full sun to shade. Burning bush adapts to nearly all soils except wet soil. Allow burning bush to grow into its naturally mature form. Pruning may result in uneven growth. Because of the plant's distinctive natural shape, allow plenty of room between bushes when placing them in borders.
Recommended varieties and related species: **'Compacta'** is a dwarf variety that grows 5 to 10 feet high, with a denser form. **'Rudy Haag'**, an even smaller variety, grows to 4 to 5 feet high. The fall foliage is slightly less intense, with a more pinkish red color.

Butia capitata (see Palm, pindo)

Butterfly bush *(Buddleia davidii)*

Features: Lush drooping blooms that attract butterflies, bees, and occasional hummingbirds
Growth rate: Fast
Zones: 5 to 9

Butterfly bush *(Buddleia davidii)*

Description: The graceful, arching stems hold panicles of pink, white, yellow, or purple flowers that emerge in summer. This bush is heat and drought tolerant and is easily transplanted from containers. The rounded shape of the butterfly bush reaches 5 to 10 feet high, with a spread of 6 to 8 feet. The gray-green leaves are a pleasing sight even before the flowers appear.

Uses: Border, specimen.

Site and care requirements: Plant in full sun in moist, well-drained soil. Promote flowering by pruning in late winter, trimming the plant to as short as 12 inches. Flowers emerge from new growth. Plants often die back in the Midwest.

Recommended varieties and related species: **'Black Knight'** is a variety with dark purple flowers. **'Pink Delight'** produces fragrant pink flowers on longer panicles. **'White Bouquet'** and **'White Profusion'** are varieties with attractive white flowers.

A monarch butterfly and a bumblebee share a moment on a butterfly bush bloom.

Buttonbush *(Cephalanthus occidentalis)*

Features: Fragrant puffy white flowers on a wildlife friendly shrub
Growth rate: Moderate
Zones: 5 to 10

Buttonbush *(Cephalanthus occidentalis)*

Description: Buttonbush may not be the showiest shrub, but it grows in wet soil, giving it an edge over other plants in those areas of the landscape that catch and hold water. The large, loosely

Buttonbush bloom

rounded form gives an informal appearance, especially when it reaches a mature size of 6 to 10 feet high and wide. The musky-scented, creamy white flowers that emerge in late spring resemble small white puffballs. The medium green leaves turn yellow in the fall. Butterflies are attracted to the blooms. The fruit draws birds and other wildlife to the plant throughout the winter.

Uses: Mass planting, specimen.

Site and care requirements: Buttonbush needs moist or wet soil in order to flourish and cannot tolerate dry conditions. Promote best flowering by pruning severely—to 6 to 12 inches—annually.

Buxus sempervirens (see Boxwood, common)

Cabbage palm (see Palm, cabbage)
California fan palm (see Palm, California fan)
California incense cedar (see Incense cedar, California)

California lilac (*Ceanothus* spp.)

Features: Vibrant, fragrant blue flowers that are a highlight of the Western landscape
Growth rate: Fast
Zones: 8 to 10

California lilac (*Ceanothus* spp.)

Description: California lilac flowers are deep blue and crowd this plant to provide the perfect focal point in the Western garden. The flowers are reminiscent of the clusters of a common lilac (to which it is not related) and emerge in late spring or summer. Though lacking cold tolerance, this shrub can survive a light frost, but it does best in a warm, protected area of the landscape. While it grows to up to 5 feet tall, the California lilac's spreading form reaches 8 to 9 feet wide, making it a good groundcover as well.
Uses: Groundcover, mass planting, specimen.
Site and care requirements: Plant in a full sun in well-drained soil. Protect from harsh wind or heavy frost. Prune during a dry part of the summer to prevent disease.
Recommended varieties and related species: **'Puget Blue'** offers deep blue flowers and deep green leaves, as does the **'Julia Phelps'** variety.

Callicarpa dichotoma (see Beautyberry, Chinese)
Calluna vulgaris (see Heather, Scotch)
Calocedrus decurrens (see Incense cedar, California)
Calycanthus floridus (see Allspice, Carolina)

Camellia, Japanese (*Camellia japonica*)

Features: Large, colorful, elegant flowers are the belles of the ball in warm-climate landscapes
Growth rate: Slow to moderate
Zones: 7 to 10

Description: The large flowers of the camellia bush are set against glossy, dark green leaves and bloom in colors from white to pink to rosy red. This broadleaf evergreen grows 8 to 15 feet high and 5 to 10 feet wide, with a dense, pyramidal shape. Native to Japan and China, the camellia makes an outstanding specimen planting or a beautiful addition to a mixed border. The Japanese camellia does well in partial shade, so use it in a darker area of the landscape for a punch of color from the classic blooms in the winter or spring.

Japanese camellia (*Camellia japonica*)

Uses: Specimen, mixed border.
Site and care requirements: Camellias need soil that is moist, well-drained, slightly acidic and rich in organic matter. Plant in partial shade as the leaves may turn yellow if situated in direct sun. Pruning is unnecessary except to remove dead branches.
Recommended varieties and related species: For double pink blossoms, plant **'Debutante'**. Variegated red and white blooms are the signature coloring of **'Governor Moulton'**, a variety with disease resistance.

Camphor tree (*Cinnamomum camphora*)

Features: A classically rounded evergreen shade tree
Growth rate: Slow
Zones: 8 to 10

Description: The rounded shape and the size of the camphor tree make it a great shade tree. It grows 50 feet or more with about the same spread. The abundant shiny green leaves make for a dense canopy that provides a good windbreak. It produces tiny white flowers that give way to berries in the summer. The plentiful berries start out red,

Camphor tree (*Cinnamomum camphora*)

then turn black when fully ripened, providing food for the birds. The camphor leaves have a distinct fragrance when crushed, and have a slightly numbing effect when the oil is applied to the skin.
Uses: Specimen, windbreak.
Site and care requirements: Plant in full sun to partial shade. Camphor does best in moist, well-drained soil. Allow enough room for this tree because the roots can grow well away from the trunk and can easily disturb other plantings or pavement.

Canadian hemlock (see Hemlock, Canadian)

Canary Island date palm (see Palm, Canary Island date)
Carissa macrocarpa (see Natal plum)
Carolina allspice (see Allspice, Carolina)
Carolina silverbell (see Silverbell, Carolina)
Carpinus betulus (see Hornbeam, European)
Carya illinoinensis (see Pecan)
Carya ovata (see Hickory, shagbark)
Castanea **spp.** (see Chestnut, American)

Catalpa, southern *(Catalpa bignonioides)*

Features: Striking, elegant white flowers and distinctively long, narrow pods
Growth rate: Fast
Zones: 5 to 9

Southern catalpa *(Catalpa bignonioides)*

Description: The Southern catalpa is a fast-growing tree with large light green leaves. It grows up to 30 to 40 feet high, with a similar spread. The tubular, fluted white flowers are spotted with yellow and purple, growing together in clusters on 4- to 8-inch stalks. Long, beanlike pods appear after flowering. These 6- to 15-inch pods litter the yard, so locate the tree where this won't become a bother.

Southern catalpa blooms

Uses: Specimen, background planting.
Site and care requirements: Southern catalpa does well in a variety of soils and sites. Plant well away from buildings to avoid the mess from bean pods. No pruning or specific care are needed. Catalpa worms or catalpa sphinx moths can endanger catalpa trees. The moths lay eggs on the undersides of the leaves, and when hatched the larvae feast on the leaves. Take appropriate care to remove caterpillars if they appear. Once the caterpillars drop from the tree, they are often scooped up by Southern anglers to use as bait.

Northern catalpa (*C. speciosa*)

Recommended varieties and related species: '**Aurora**' is a variety with yellow leaves that usually keep their color in cooler climates. A smaller, bushier variety, '**Nana**' is grafted onto a standard catalpa.

Northern catalpa *(C. speciosa),* an especially hardy native to the Midwest, grows best in Zones 4 to 8. This adaptable tree, at home on farmland as well as in the city, grows 40 to 60 feet high with a 20 to 40 foot spread. No maintenance is needed after planting. The Northern catalpa does well in almost any soil and grows best in full sun. This tree has a moderate to fast growth rate. When planting, leave plenty of room for its mature size. The spectacular flowers bloom about two weeks earlier than Southern catalpa and are a favorite of bees and hummingbirds. The long bean pods appear after flowering and will also create litter in the landscape.

Chitalpa *(C. ×tashkentensis)* is a cross between desert willow *(Chilopsis linearis)* and the southern catalpa. The long dark green leaves are reminiscent of the desert willow, but the blooms are like those of the catalpa. The pale pink flowers that resemble orchids bloom from late spring until early fall. While the flowers do drop, there are no bean pods on the sterile chitalpa trees and therefore no yard litter. Hardy in Zones 6 to 9, chitalpa does well in sunny, dry sites. It grows quickly, reaching a mature height of 25 to 30 feet. The variety '**Pink Dawn**' has pale pink blooms, while the '**Morning Cloud**' variety blooms pale pink to white.

The extraordinary bloom of a northern catalpa

***Ceanothus* spp.** (see California lilac)

Cedar, atlas *(Cedrus libani atlantica)*

Features: A beautiful shape and unusual purple cones
Growth rate: Slow
Zones: 6 to 9

Atlas cedar *(Cedrus libani atlantica)*

Description: Atlas cedars have silvery blue to blue-green needles that lend a striking color to the landscape. The pyramidal shape tops out at 40 to 60 feet high and upwards of 30 to 40 feet wide. These trees can live

Deodar cedar *(Cedrus deodara)*

Cedar of Lebanon *(Cedrus libani)*

hundreds of years, and as they mature, a distinctive flat top develops. The purple cones appear in the fall—the smaller male cones grow at the bottom of the tree, while the larger female cones grow at the top. The wood of the atlas cedar is popular for building furniture and for use in construction, because it is durable and insect repellant. This is the least cold hardy of the cedars.

Uses: Specimen.

Site and care requirements: Atlas cedar prefers full sun but can grow in partial shade. Keep in mind the tree's potential size when choosing the planting site and provide plenty of space for it to fill out. Plant atlas cedar in moist, well-drained soil.

Recommended varieties and related species: **'Glauca Pendula'** is a weeping variety whose branches droop dramatically toward the ground. The **'Glauca'** variety has bright blue needles.

Deodar cedar *(C. deodara)* grows up to 70 feet high with a spread of 30 to 40 feet. It is a fast-growing tree whose dense branches become more open as it matures. The purple male cones form on the bottom of the tree while the females grow on top. Plant in full sun and moist, well-drained soil. Deodar cedar tolerates drought. Cold-hardy varieties, including **'Shalimar'** and **'Kashmir',** are available that will survive in warmer areas of Zone 5.

Cedar of Lebanon *(C. libani)* is the national tree of Lebanon and figures prominently in biblical lore. This cedar is known for its large trunk, graceful mature shape, and dark green foliage. It has large, open, irregular branches that spread to 20 to 30 feet. This is the most cold hardy of the cedars, and it is also drought tolerant. Although it can live in dry, infertile soil it prefers well-drained, fertile soil. The tree suffers in humid conditions. It takes three years for the cones to mature and turn brown.

Cedar, Japanese *(Cryptomeria japonica)*

Features: Bluish green needles, a thick trunk with peeling bark, and a graceful shape
Growth rate: Fast
Zones: 6 to 9

Japanese cedar *(Cryptomeria japonica)*

Description: Japanese cedars grow up to 60 feet high. This swift-growing tree has a pyramidal shape with horizontal branches that droop toward the ground nearer the bottom of the tree. The small 1-inch cones, which are both male and female, are distributed throughout the tree. Larger specimens living in the wild can have trunk diameters of 10 to 12 feet, with the peeling bark becoming more evident as the tree grows taller.
Uses: Ornamental, specimen.
Site and care requirements: Plant in full sun to partial shade. Allow plenty of room for the mature tree and its enormous trunk. Plant in well-drained, moist soil, and prevent the soil from drying. Japanese cedar can be severely cut back—as close as 2 to 3 feet from the ground—and it will grow back from the stump.
Recommended varieties and related species: 'Elegans' reaches about 30 feet high and 8 feet wide. **'Globosa Nana'** is a larger variety that grows in a more rounded shape. Dwarf varieties, such as **'Compacta'** and **'Compressa',** grow so small they are often used for bonsai.

Cedrus **spp.** (see Cedar, atlas)
Celtis occidentalis (see Hackberry, common)
Cephalanthus occidentalis (see Buttonbush)
Cercidiphyllum japonicum (see Katsura tree)
Cercis canadensis (see Redbud, eastern)
Chaenomeles **spp.** (see Quince, common flowering)
Chamaecyparis **spp.** (see False cypress, lawson)
Chamaerops humilis (see Palm, Mediterranean fan)

Chaste tree *(Vitex agnus-castus)*

Features: Fragrant purple summer blooms and pleasantly scented foliage
Growth rate: Slow to moderate, depending on climate
Zones: 7 to 9

Chaste tree *(Vitex agnus-castus)*

Description: This tree produces vibrant lavender to deep purple flowers on long spikes in early to midsummer. At the peak of the blooming season, the entire plant is covered with the flowers that give off a pleasant, almost spicy scent. The leaves have a faint aroma of sage, which adds another dimension of interest. The chaste tree grows 10 to 20 feet high with about the same spread. It starts to look unkempt as it grows to maturity, so shaping may be necessary when it is grown in a border. The tree grows more slowly in northern locations, and grows best when protected from the wind.
Uses: Border, specimen.
Site and care requirements: The chaste tree grows best in well-drained soil. Apply light applications of fertilizer in the spring, and mulch to retain moisture. Flowers grow on new shoots, so pruning should be done in the winter if the shrub needs to be tidied up.
Recommended varieties and related species: While varieties with white or pink flowers exist, they are not widely available. **'Vitex negundo',** a species of chaste tree, is commonly planted in the Zones 5 and 6 of the Midwest.

Cherry, flowering *(Prunus* spp.)

Features: One of the most beautiful and fragrant ornamental flowering trees you can plant in the home landscape
Growth rate: Moderate to fast, depending on type
Zones: 2 to 8, depending on type

Flowering cherry *(Prunus* spp.)

Description: Though a famous springtime attraction in Washington, D.C., the flowering cherry tree with its plentiful, aromatic blooms is a delightful addition to any landscape. Pink or white flowers appear in April or May before the foliage emerges. The foliage provides its own show, turning from green to golden yellow to muted red in the fall. Most flowering cherries are grown for their blooms and vaselike shape, but some types produce edible fruit.

Uses: Ornamental, specimen, border.
Site and care requirements: Flowering cherry trees prefer moist, well-drained soil and full sun. Depending on the type of tree as well as the site where it is planted, pruning may or may not be necessary to maintain its shape.
Recommended varieties and related species: Higan cherry *(P. subhirtella)* is hardy when grown in Zones 4 to 8 and is one of the longest-lived flowering cherry trees. With a moderate growth rate, this tree reaches 20 to 40 feet high and has a spread of 15 to 30 feet. Plant in full sun in well-drained soil. Varieties include **'Pendula'** or weeping higan cherry, whose branches gently bow to the ground, and **'Autumnalis',** whose upright form and pink flowers make it a classic flowering cherry tree.

Yoshino cherry *(P. ×yedoensis)* is the type of tree planted around the sights in Washington D.C. This tree's white or pink flowers emerge in the spring, making it a showy specimen planted in the yard or included in a cherry border. In fall the foliage turns yellow, adding to the tree's appeal. The fast-growing Yoshino cherry reaches 40 to 50 feet high and wide at maturity. It grows best in Zones 5 to 8. Varieties include **'Snow Fountain'** which grows to only about 12 feet high, **'Shidare Yoshino,'** a weeping variety, and **'Akebono',** which has a more spreading habit.

Yoshino cherry *(P. ×yedoensis)*

Nanking cherry *(P. tomentosa)*, a cold-hardy variety adaptable to Zones 2 to 6, is an especially showy tree that produces edible fruit. The white to pink flowers emerge in early spring, giving way to red fruit that ripens in midsummer. To produce fruit, there must be cross-pollination, so plant at least two trees in fairly close proximity to each other. For best flowering and fruit production, plant in full sun in well-drained soil.

Sargent cherry *(P. sargentii)* is among the first flowering cherry trees to bloom in the spring. The upright, rounded shape makes this a beautiful flowering specimen as well as an excellent shade tree. It grows 20 to 30 feet high with the same spread at maturity. The pink to deep-pink blooms give way to small dark red to purple fruit. The cherries ripen in the summer, providing neighborhood birds with a feast.

Higan cherry *(P. subhirtella)*

Sargent cherry *(P. sargentii)*

The tree's fall foliage—turning golden bronze to red—is another feature that make this one of the most popular flowering cherry trees. The cinnamon-brown bark has a smooth texture and glossy appeareance and is hardy in Zones 4 through 7. Look for **'Accolade'**, a variety with pink blooms that grows to about 25 feet high.

Cherry laurel *(Prunus laurocerasus)*

Features: Shiny, dark green, evergreen leaves and fragrant, milk-white flowers
Growth rate: Moderate
Zones: 7 to 8

Cherry laurel *(Prunus laurocerasus)*

Description: Also known as English laurel, the cherry laurel grows 18 to 20 feet tall with a similar spread. The flower clusters bloom in midspring, followed by small berries that ripen to a purple-black in the fall. The rounded shrubby form can be maintained by pruning, or the plant may be allowed to grow until it becomes the size of a small tree. The large, dark green leaves are a lighter green on the bottom, adding interesting color contrast to the landscape as the tree sways in the wind.
Uses: Mass planting, hedge, specimen.
Site and care requirements: Cherry laurel should be planted in moist, well-drained soil. Plant the tree in full sun in colder climates and partial shade in warm climates. It tolerates pruning, but trim individual branches because shearing damages the foliage.
Recommended varieties and related species: **'Otto Luyken'** is a small variety that grows up to 3 feet high and 5 feet wide. It is hardy to Zone 6 and is shade tolerant. **'Schipkaensis'** also grows in Zone 6 and reaches a height of 5 feet. **'Marbled White'** is a variegated variety with white-spotted leaves.

Chestnut, American *(Castanea dentata)*

Features: A classic shape, tasty nuts, and attractive fall color
Growth rate: Fast
Zones: 3 to 8

Chinese chestnut *(Castanea mollissima)*

Description: The American chestnut once flourished in the United States, but it was almost decimated by chestnut blight. This Asian bark fungus was first discovered in this country in 1904, and it is estimated that it killed more than 3 billion chestnut trees. The American chestnut is making a comeback, thanks to organizations that are breeding and hybridizing American chestnuts to resist blight. American chestnuts are rounded, stately trees that reach 30 to 40 feet high with a similar width. The flowers are white catkins that bloom in the early summer, giving way to the fruit that matures in the fall. When these spiny burrs fall off the tree, the nuts inside are ready for harvest. The trees will bear fruit within a few years of planting.
Uses: Specimen or in a grouping for the nuts.
Site and care requirements: While a single tree produces both male and female flowers, plant at least two trees to ensure pollination and a successful harvest of nuts. Plant in full sun and moist, well-drained soil.
Recommended varieties and related species:
Chinese chestnut *(C. mollissima)* grows in Zones 4 to 9. It is blight resistant and a popular choice for the nut production. Although male and female flowers grow on the same tree, several trees should be planted together for successful pollination to occur. Male flowers of the Chinese chestnut emit a foul smell. Plant the tree away from high-traffic areas of your yard. Chinese chestnuts grow 40 to 60 feet high and wide. The rounded shape is similar to that of the American chestnut, but the shorter trunk and serrated leaves are marked differences. Plant in full sun to partial shade and well-drained, moist soil.

   Japanese chestnut *(C. crenata)* is a small to medium-size tree that grows to about 30 feet tall and wide. It is hardy in Zones 4 through 9, but thrives in the hotter climates of these areas. It is blight resistant as well as drought tolerant. The flowers bloom in the summer, with the female flowers developing into the popular nuts. Plant in groupings to ensure pollination. Japanese chestnut should be planted in moist, well-drained soil and full sun to partial shade.

Chionanthus **spp.** (see Fringe tree, Chinese)
Choisya ternata (see Mexican orange)
Chinese beautyberry (see Beautyberry, Chinese)
Chinese pistachio (see Pistachio, Chinese)
Chinese tallow tree (see Tallow tree, Chinese)

Chokeberry, red *(Aronia arbutifolia)*

Features: Sweet blooms, punchy red berries, and appealing fall foliage
Growth rate: Slow
Zones: 4 to 9

Red chokeberry *(Aronia arbutifolia* 'Brilliantissima')

Description: The long, dark green leaves of this carefree shrub provide a background to small white flowers in the spring, and then give way to large, ripening berries. The gorgeous red berries stay on the shrub long after the foliage turns color in autumn. Chokeberry grows 8 to 10 feet tall with a similar spread. The rounded shape and open form may grow untidy and leggy as the shrub ages.
Uses: Border, mass planting.
Site and care requirements: Plant red chokeberry in full sun for best fruit production and in well-drained, acidic soil. Red chokeberry tolerates wet soil and proves drought tolerant, but it will not survive in dry, alkaline soil. The shrub is ideal at a woodland's edge or next to a sunny pond. Plant the shrub in a group to camouflage the legginess that occurs. Lacebugs are often a problem.
Recommended varieties and related species:
'Brilliantissima' has the most vibrant fall foliage, larger berries, and a fuller form.

Chokecherry, amur *(Prunus maackii)*

Features: Cinnamon brown bark provides distinctive winter interest
Growth rate: Moderate to fast
Zones: 2 to 6

Description: A rounded shape and spectacular bark make this a perfect specimen tree. Native to Siberia, the amur chokeberry is especially well-suited to colder climates. Small white flowers bloom in the spring, followed by small fruit that matures and blackens in the fall. Although it does not boast spectacular fall foliage, the amur chokecherry becomes its own winter color show once the leaves drop. The tree tolerates drought, but not extreme heat. It grows up to 35 feet tall with about the same spread.

Uses: Specimen, accent, or shade.
Site and care requirements: Plant in full sun to partial shade and well-drained soil.
Recommended varieties and related species: 'Amber Beauty' displays a more even form with somewhat ascending branches.

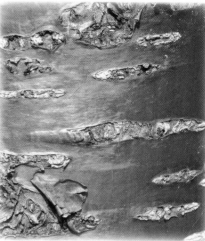

Bark of the amur chokecherry *(Prunus maackii)*

Cinnamomum camphora (see Camphor tree)

Cinquefoil, bush *(Potentilla fruticosa)*

Features: Long-lasting blooms on a shrubby form
Growth rate: Slow
Zones: 2 to 7

Bush cinquefoil *(Potentilla fruticosa)*

Description: The color and size of the blooms may differ from variety to variety, but the duration of the blooming season of the shrubby cinquefoil remains the same. From June until the first frost, a large number of flowers bloom continuously, making this a popular planting for color gardens. It is cold and drought tolerant but susceptible to mites. Bush cinquefoil grows from 3 to 4 feet high with a comparably equal spread.
Uses: Border, mass planting, foundation planting, garden edging.
Site and care requirements: Plant in full sun for best flowering, but this plant will survive in partial shade. It is adaptable to most well-drained soils. Plant red- or orange-flowering varieties in partial shade, as these flowers tend to bleach out in full sun.
Recommended varieties and related species:
'Abbotswood' has white flowers, while 'Goldfinger' and 'Coronation Triumph' bloom bright yellow. Red-flowering varieties include 'Gibson's Scarlet' and 'Red Ace'. 'Tangerine' blooms orange.

***Cistus* spp.** (see Rock rose)

Citrus (*Citrus* spp.)

Features: Pretty, aromatic blossoms, glossy foliage, and luscious fruit
Growth rate: Dependent on type of tree and variety
Zones: 10 to 11

Orange *(Citrus sinensis)*

Description:
Although citrus fruit is delicious, the trees stand out as wonderful additions to the landscape based on their other attributes. Glossy leaves, rounded overall form, and delicate, aromatic flowers also make citrus trees appealing plants for the home landscape. For harvesting, choices abound in types of fruit trees in the citrus family, including a wealth of varieties and sizes. The most popular trees are lemon, lime, orange, and grapefruit. All have rounded silhouettes, grow best in Zones 10 and 11, and produce edible fruit. Fragant blossoms emerge in February to March. Harvest times vary depending on the type of fruit being grown. Size is variable too, depending on whether you purchase a dwarf, semi-dwarf, or full-size tree. They range in height from about 5-foot dwarf varieties up to 20- to 30-foot full-size trees. Citrus trees are not at all cold hardy. An entire harvest can easily be lost to a frost or freeze. Help ensure your tree's well-being in case of a sudden frost or freeze by choosing a variety proven hardy to one zone colder than your locale. Be prepared to cover a citrus tree and provide supplemental heat when frost is in the forecast.
Uses: usually planted for fruit production or for the beauty of the tree.
Site and care requirements: Plant in full sun in well-drained soil. While they can survive in a variety of soils, it will do best in sandy soil. Leave enough room for the mature size of the tree and plant two or more citrus trees to ensure pollination. Citrus trees should be planted in late winter to early spring. New trees need special care—if you buy a tree already fruiting, remove the fruit at planting time. The tree expends a lot of energy growing the fruit, which is better spent developing the tree and the roots than in fruit production when the tree is young. Begin fertilizing a young tree after the first year of growth. Apply fertilizer in March, June, and September for the next 4 years, then fertilize occasionally as needed. Prune the citrus trees anytime of year except for winter. Prune for shape or to remove suckers from the bottom of the tree that may inhibit the tree from growing to its full potential.
Recommended varieties and related species:
Grapefruit *(Citrus paradisi)*, more than most members of the

Grapefruit *(Citrus paradisi)*

citrus family, is extremely temperature-sensitive and should be planted where it can be protected from cold and wind. Give it a sheltered microclimate such as a southern exposure between a house and a brick or stone wall. Varieties to consider are the **'Star Ruby'**, a seedless variety that produces red-fleshed fruit and **'Orlo Blanco'**, another seedless variety. **'Cocktail Hybrid Grapefruit'** is a variety crossed with a sweet orange, producing a sweeter grapefruit. A **'Marsh'** grapefruit tree yields white-fleshed fruit.

Lemon *(Citrus limon)*

Lemon *(Citrus limon)* trees will grow in fairly poor soil, surviving in the sandiest locations. Some popular varieties to plant are **'Meyer Lemon'** and **'Lisbon Lemon'** as both produce an acidic, very juicy fruit. **'Pomona Sweet Lemon'** produces a sweeter fruit. In colder areas of the growing zone, plant the **'Harvey'** variety, which is a slightly more cold hardy variety than many others.

Lime *(Citrus aurantifolia)*

Lime *(C. aurantifolia)* grows 7 to 13 feet high—smaller than the other citruses. It is also cold-sensitive, so plant a lime tree in a protected area of the landscape. **'Key Lime'** yields fruit with acidic juice that, combined with other key ingredients, is the basis of the famous key lime pie. **'Kaffir Lime'** produces acidic fruit with orange skin. The leaves of this tree are popular ingredients in Middle Eastern and Asian cooking. Try planting **'Sweet Lime'** for a sweeter fruit.

Orange *(C. sinensis)* production is nearly synonymous with the states of Florida and California. To get a taste of what is being grown there, try **'Satsuma'**, a consistently sweet-fruited variety with the bonus of some cold-hardiness. For a navel variety with minimal seeds, consider **'Fukumoto Navel Orange'** with deep orange-skinned fruit or **'Washington Navel Orange'** with time-tested popularity. Choose **'Valencia'** for the best juice production. **'Tarocco Blood Orange'** is known for its fruit's deep, reddish-orange flesh and sweet flavor.

Cladrastis kentukea (see Yellowwood, American)
Clerodendrum trichotomum (see Glorybower, harlequin)
Clethra alnifolia (see Summersweet)
Coprosma repens (see Mirror plant)

Cornus canadensis (see Bunchberry)
Cornus florida (see Dogwood, flowering)
Corylopsis pauciflora (see Winter hazel, buttercup)
Corylus avellana 'Contorta' (see Harry Lauder's walking stick)
Cotinus coggygria (see Smoketree)

Cork tree, amur *(Phellodendron amurense)*

Features: Gray-brown bark with a corky texture and a graceful, open habit
Growth rate: Slow to moderate
Zones: 3 to 7

Amur cork tree *(Phellodendron amurense)*

Description: The amur cork tree stars in the bark-interest category. The corky bark surrounds twisty, low-growing branches of a mature tree. The open form gives this tree a bold silhouette that stands out in the landscape. This medium-size tree grows to 30 to 50 feet high with a comparable width. Female trees have black fruit in the fall that lasts into winter. The yellowish bronze fall foliage is unremarkable but the tree's leafless winter form is its crowning glory.
Uses: Shade, specimen.
Site and care requirements: Plant in moist, well-drained soil and in full sun. Cork tree does best when kept moist, but tolerates some drought as it matures. Female trees need a male tree close by for pollination, but the resulting fruit litters and stains when it falls. Plant either a single tree or all male trees to avoid the potential mess.
Recommended varieties and related species: Lavalle cork tree *(P. lavallei)* grows a bit taller than the amur cork tree. Plant male varieties, such as **'Shademaster'** and **'Macho',** to avoid fruit production.

Amur cork tree bark

Cotoneaster *(Cotoneaster* spp.)

Features: Attractive flowers and berries on a versatile, popular shrub
Growth rate: Fast
Zones: 3 to 8, depending on the species

Bearberry cotoneaster *(Cotoneaster dammeri)*

Description: The wide selection of cotoneaster varieties makes it a popular landscape plant with diverse utility. Attributes shared by all of the species include white or pink flowers followed by red berries that contrast strikingly with the green foliage. Cotoneaster adapts to a variety of soils and sites as well as garden styles. Fast-growing bearberry cotoneaster, a broadleaf evergreen, appeals to gardeners seeking to quickly fill an empty area of the landscape.
Uses: Border, mass planting, groundcover.
Site and care requirements: Although cotoneaster survives in many types of soil, for best results, it should be planted in well-drained soil. Plant in a sunny to partially shady location for best results.
Recommended varieties and related species: Bearberry cotoneaster *(C. dammeri)* grows in Zones 5 to 8. It is a low-growing plant, reaching only 1 to 1½ feet high, but it grows 6 feet wide. Bearberry cotoneaster is a fast grower, which makes it perfect for quick groundcover. The white flowers blossom in May, giving way to sparse red berries in summer. The foliage turns an attractive reddish purple in the winter. Pruning may be necessary to keep it from becoming unruly. Watch for fire blight and lacebug

Many-flowered cotoneaster (C. multiflorus)

infestation. Popular varieties include **'Coral Beauty'**, which fruits freely, and **'Skogholm'**, a rapidly growing variety that grows up to 2 feet high and tolerates drought.

Creeping cotoneaster *(C. adpressus)* provides an ideal choice for a shrubby groundcover. The compact habit, dark green leaves, and red fruit make this species a colorful addition to the landscape. Although the flowers are less-than-showy, large red berries appear in the fall that constitute this plant's dramatic statement. Creeping cotoneaster's rigid branches and slightly mounded form help make it a handsome groundcover. The plant grows 1 to 1½ feet high with a 6-foot spread. It makes itself at home by rooting where the branches touch the ground, bolstering its reputation as a reliable groundcover. Plant it in sun to partial shade Zones 4 to 6.

Many-flowered cotoneaster *(C. multiflorus)* is known for its profusion of small, white flowers that appear in May. Because the flowers have an unpleasant fragrance, situate plants away from traffic areas. Hardy in Zones 3 to 7, this larger species of cotoneaster grows up to 8 feet high and 12 feet wide. Plant it in full sun to partial shade and moist, well-drained soil. A slightly mounded shape makes this an ideal shrub in a border or mass planting where its red berries add fall color to the landscape well into October. This species is less likely than others to be affected by disease and insects.

Rockspray cotoneaster (C. horizontalis)

Rockspray cotoneaster *(C. horizontalis)* is a low, dense shrub that grows in Zones 4 to 7. The branches grow horizontally in layers, producing a herringbone effect and adding textural interest to the landscape year-round. Growing 2 to 3 feet high and up to 8 feet wide, it can be espaliered on a fence or wall to create an especially interesting garden feature. Rockspray cotoneaster blooms in late spring to early summer, and then the pink flowers give way to bright red berries that can last well into the winter. This species works well in a rock garden or as a groundcover. Use it to help control soil erosion on a bank or slope. Plant it in sun to partial shade and moist, well-drained soil. This drought-tolerant plant may be more susceptible to fire blight than other cotoneaster species. Try planting the variety **'Variegatus'** for exceptional color in the garden. The creamy white-edged leaves produce a spectacular sight when planted as a groundcover.

Spreading cotoneaster *(C. divaricatus)* has the most attractive fall foliage and fruit of all the cotoneasters. The rose-colored flowers are followed by red fruit that last well into the fall. The leaves turn intense, reddish purple in the autumn, adding to the attractiveness of this shrub. It grows in Zones 4 to 7 and should be planted in full sun to partial shade. It favors moist, well-drained soil, but can tolerate somewhat-dry soil and windy sites as well. Use it for a hedge or screen. Spreading cotoneaster grows 5 to 6 feet high and 6 to 8 feet wide.

Willowleaf cotoneaster *(C. salicifolius)*, an evergreen shrub, grows 10 to 15 high and 8 to 10 feet wide. As one of the larger cotoneasters, this species has an attractive, arching habit with white flowers in early summer and fruit that stays through the winter. Dark green leaves provide a background for the berries and give the fall and winter landscape added color. Hardy in Zones 6 to 8, this shrub needs a warmer climate than other cotoneasters. Plant in sun to partial shade in moist, well-drained soil. Use it for a border or mass planting. **'Repens'**, a low-growing shrub, proves more suitable as a groundcover than the common willowleaf cotoneaster.

Willowleaf cotoneaster (C. salicifolius)

Cottonwood, eastern *(Populus deltoides)*

Features: A quick-growing source of shade
Growth rate: Fast
Zones: 2 to 9

Eastern cottonwood *(Populus deltoides)*

Waterside cottonwoods in fall color

Recommended varieties and related species: Seedless male cultivars, including **'Siouxland'** and **'Noreaster',** allow you to avoid the yard litter produced by female trees.

Coyote brush *(Baccharis pilularis)*

Features: An adaptable wildlife-friendly evergreen
Growth rate: Fast
Zones: 7 to 11

Description: The eastern cottonwood grows as much as 3 to 4 feet per year. At maturity, it reaches heights of up to 40 to 70 feet and a width of 50 to 70 feet. Also known as the eastern poplar, this tree makes a commanding—but not long-lived—sight in the landscape. The tree often dies within 70 years. At maturity, the cottonwood is susceptible to limb damage from wind and harsh weather, which accounts for its shorter life span. In spring small yellow flowers appear on a female tree; red flowers appear on a male tree. The flowers on the female tree dry and split open in autumn, releasing seeds with cottonlike wisps that float off and provide food for the area wildlife.

Uses: This fast-growing shade tree thrives in wet areas where other trees won't survive.

Site and care requirements: Plant in moist soil and full sun. The tree may tolerate drier sites. Prune to remove deadwood.

Cottonwood bark

Description: Native to California, coyotebrush tolerates almost any type of soil as well as drought, especially once established and mature. The shrub grows from 4 to 8 feet high with a comparable spread. Its upright form lends itself to plantings as a hedge and screen. Coyote brush also responds well to pruning and shearing. White flowers that appear in the fall are not especially showy but provide a welcome sight late in the growing season.

Uses: Hedge or screen; or for erosion control.

Site and care requirements: Adaptable to many soil types and climates, coyote brush will grow best in well-drained soil and full sun. Provide supplemental water during extremely hot and dry summers. Prune to shape a hedge or to keep plants tidy looking.

Coyote brush *(Baccharis pilularis)*

Crabapple, flowering (*Malus* spp.)

Flowering crabapple (*Malus spp.*)

Features: A showy flowering tree that's popular in the northern landscape
Growth rate: Slow
Zones: 4 to 8

Description: Crabapple trees are famous for their splendid flowers and small, attractive fruit. The flowers range in color from white to pink to red and bloom beginning in midspring. The decorative value continues with fruit that comes in colorful hues ranging from yellow to orange, orange, red, and deep red. Lovely, colorful buds precede the flower and fruit show.

Berries of the sargent crabapple

Malus 'Centurion' flowers

The trees are available in a range of sizes. Full-size varieties can grow up to 20 feet high with a spread of 6 to 15 feet. Most dwarf varieties grow from 8 to 15 feet high. Crabapples are self-pollinating, so if you plant only one in the landscape it will produce beautiful blooms and attractive fruit. Many crabapple trees are quite susceptible to scab, fire blight, and leaf spot. Choose cultivars that possess disease resistance.

M. sargentii 'Jewelberry'

Uses: Ornamental specimen, border.
Site and care requirements: Plant in full sun to light shade and fertile, well-drained soil.
Recommended varieties and related species: There are so many to choose from, but a few cultivars to check out include **'Adirondack'**, **'Bob White'**, and **'Mary Potter'** for white blooms. Pink-flowered cultivars include **'Louisa'** and **'Strawberry Parfait'**. For interesting red fruit, try **'Prairiefire'** or **'Red Jewel'**.

Japanese flowering crabapple (*M. floribunda*), one of the most profuse-flowering crabapples, also boasts a handsome form, making it a must-have for many homeowners. Midspring brings on the flowers. The fragrant pink blossoms turn white as they mature. By the end of summer the fruit appears in all its red and yellow glory. The Japanese crabapple reaches heights of up to 20 feet with a similar or greater spread. Plant in full sun and well-drained soil. Prune in late spring or early summer after flowering.

Sargent crabapple (*M. sargentii*), a dwarf species that grows 6 to 10 feet high, spreads 6 to 12 feet. Pink buds open to white blooms, which in turn give way to small, bright-red fruit that lasts well into the fall and winter. Plant in full sun and moist, well-drained soil. **'Tina'** grows to only 5 feet high and produces attractive white flowers.

Japanese crabapple blooms

Crape myrtle *(Lagerstroemia indica)*

Features: Showy, long-lasting summer blooms
Growth rate: Fast
Zones: 7 to 9

Crape myrtle *(Lagerstroemia indica)*

Description: This flowering tree puts on a show all year long. The long-blooming flowers come in a range of colors—pink, red, white, and lavender—and can bloom throughout the summer. The pleasing vaselike shape and fall foliage also make the crape myrtle an attractive choice for the landscape. The leaves turn yellow, orange, or red in the fall, and then drop to reveal peeling gray and brown bark. Crape

Crape myrtle 'Natchez'

myrtle is drought tolerant once established, but susceptible to mildew. The tree grows 15 to 20 feet high with a spread of 6 to 15 feet. An exceptionally ornamental specimen, crape myrtle provides an even more spectacular sight when planted in clusters or a hedge.

Uses: Specimen, ornamental, screen, grouping.

Site and care requirements: Plant in full sun to partial shade and moist, well-drained soil. When planting in groups, leave 3 to 4 feet between the trees. Remove suckers and complete pruning by late summer. Pinch spent flowers to encourage more blooms.

Recommended varieties and related species: Many mildew-resistant cultivars are available, including **'Cherokee'** with red flowers and **'Tuskegee'** with deep pink blooms. **'Natchez'** has beautiful, peeling bark and white blooms. **'Comanche'** has hot pink flowers and dark foliage.

The fine winter bark of the crape myrtle

***Crataegus* spp.** (see Hawthorn)
Cryptomeria japonica (see Cedar, Japanese)
×*Cupressocyparis leylandii* (see Cypress, leyland)

Currant, alpine *(Ribes alpinum)*

Features: A hardy, carefree shrub suitable for the northern regions of the United States
Growth rate: Moderate
Zones: 2 to 7

Golden variety of alpine currant *(Ribes alpinum* 'Aureum')

Description: Alpine currant is a great shrub for hedges and borders in the northern United States. Cold hardy and drought tolerant, it can be planted in sun or shade and requires little additional care

Alpine currant blooms

during the year. An alpine currant hedge can be pruned at any time to keep it tidy year-round. The shrub grows 3 to 6 feet high with a comparable spread. The yellowish green flowers aren't showy, but they give way to small berries that ripen in the summer and attract birds. Glossy green leaves and a dense growth habit make this an excellent shrub for planting in a hedge or border.

Uses: Hedge, border, mass planting.

Site and care requirements: Plant in sun or shade. Prune any time of the year to maintain shape. Plant in virtually any type of well-drained soil. Little upkeep is required.

Recommended varieties and related species: 'Green Mound' is a smaller variety that grows 2 to 3 feet high with the same spread. Try the varieties **'Nana'** and **'Compacta'** also. **Clove currant** *(R. odoratum)* bears flowers with a clovelike fragrance. **Red-flowering currant** *(R. sanguineum)* has colorful blooms on a compact form and grows in warmer climates from Zones 6 to 10.

Cycas revoluta (see Palm, sago)

Cypress, leyland *(×Cupressocyparis leylandii)*

Features: A columnar evergreen with time-tested utility
Growth rate: Fast
Zones: 6 to 10

Leyland cypress (×*Cupressocyparis leylandii*)

Description: This dense, fast-growing evergreen tree offers
a solution for areas of the landscape that need a screen.
It protects landscapes and gardens from salt spray and wind,
or hides unwanted views. It grows up to 3 feet a year,
reaching 60 to 70 feet high and spreading 6 to 12 feet.
The needles turn dark bluish green when the tree matures.
It is susceptible to bagworms and canker.
Uses: Screen, hedge.
Site and care requirements: Best when planted in full sun,
but it tolerates some shade. Plant in almost any soil, as long
as it is well-drained. Pruning is required in the first year of
growth, as well as throughout the next few years to keep it
tidy and to encourage dense growth.
Recommended varieties and related species:
'Castlewellan' has yellowish foliage, while **'Green Spire'**
displays green foliage and a narrower growth habit.
'Haggerston Grey' has gray-green foliage, while
'Naylor's Blue' has the bluest foliage of the leyland
cypress varieties.

Italian cypress (*Cupressus sempervirens*)

Italian cypress *(Cupressus sempervirens)* has a distinctive,
narrow, columnar form made famous by postcards from
the Tuscan hillsides of Italy. Its architectural form proves
most useful in formal settings and warm, dry climates.
This fast-growing tree, hardy from Zones 7 to 9, reaches 30
to 40 feet tall and 3 to 6 feet wide. Trees form an effective
screen when several are planted alongside one another.

Italian cypresses on a formal estate

Cytisus spp. (see Broom)

ENCYCLOPEDIA OF TREES AND SHRUBS | 125

Daphne, burkwood *(Daphne ×burkwoodii)*

Features: Lovely, fragrant flowers on a handsomely rounded
  shrubby form
Growth rate: Slow to moderate
Zones: 4 to 8

Burkwood daphne *(Daphne ×burkwoodii)*

Description:

The small, densely formed burkwood daphne is a delight when the flowers bloom in the spring. The pinkish white blooms play against blue-green leaves that endure well into the fall and early winter. The dizzying fragrance of the flowers makes this plant desirable for any garden. As a bonus, clusters of blooms snuggled among the daphne leaves offer visual delights too.
It excels as a specimen plant or when combined with other plants in a fragrant

Burkwood daphne 'Carol Mackie'

border. On the flip side, this shrub can be fussy about its environment. It needs exceedingly well-drained soil for an even chance of survival. It cannot tolerate oversaturation or flooding. It grows up to 3 feet high and about 4 feet wide with a densely branched habit.
Uses: Specimen, border, rock garden.
Site and care requirements: Burkwood daphne performs best in well-drained, pH-neutral soil, protected from scorching sun and drying winds. Plant the shrub in partial

Rose daphne *(D. cneorum)*

sun to shade. Avoid cultivating around the roots or moving the plant once it is established. Plant in an area where the fragrance can be enjoyed, but not where foot traffic or landscape machinery might damage it.
Recommended varieties and related species: Cultivars include **'Carol Mackie'**, which has yellow-edged green foliage. The yellowish leaves of **'Briggs Moonlight'** are edged in green.
  Rose daphne *(D. cneorum)* grows from ½ to 1 foot high and spreads to 2 feet. The vibrant pink flowers show off in May, clustering among the dark green leaves. Rose daphne requires exceptionally well-drained soil for survival. It grows best in Zones 4 to 7. Varieties include **'Alba'** which has white flowers, while **'Ruby Glow'** and **'Eximia'** have rosy-pink blooms that demonstrate the classic color of the rose daphne.
  Winter daphne *(D. odora)* grows best in Zones 7 to 9. The rosy pink flowers bloom in late winter to early spring against shiny, dark evergreen leaves. This shrub grows from 3 to 5 feet tall with a similar spread. Its dense, compact form makes this a stellar shrub for a perennial garden. Winter daphne requires well-drained soil. Plant it in sun to partial shade. Varieties include white-flowering **'Alba'** and **'Aureomarginata'** with yellow-edged leaves and dark pink flowers.

Winter daphne *(D. odora)*

Davidia involucrata (see Dove tree)

Dawn redwood *(Metasequoia glyptostroboides)*

Features: A gloriously huge, conical form with glowy fall foliage
Growth rate: Fast
Zones: 5 to 8

Dawn redwood *(Metasequoia glyptostroboides)*

Description:
Once thought to be extinct, the dawn redwood was discovered in China in the early 1940s and has since been planted across the United States. This extraordinary tree has persisted since the time of the dinosaurs and is known as a living fossil. A commanding tree, it grows 70 to 100 feet high with a spread of about 25 feet. The green needles of

Dawn redwood

this deciduous tree turn orange-brown in autumn before falling. Young bark is a reddish brown, and turns a deeper brown and peels when mature. This fast-growing tree adds up to 3 feet in height a year in even, balanced growth and needs plenty of space to reach its mature size.
Uses: Specimen in larger landscapes.
Site and care requirements: Plant in moist, well-drained, somewhat acidic soil. This tree suffers in alkaline soils. It needs full sun for best growth. Allow ample space for growth. Pruning is unnecessary.
Recommended varieties and related species: Two varieties, **'National'** and **'Sheridan Spire'**, have thinner growth habits but the same uniform, pyramidal shape.

Deutzia, slender *(Deutzia gracilis)*

Features: A profusion of small, white flowers in May on a low, mounded shrub
Growth rate: Slow to moderate
Zones: 4 to 8

Slender deutzia *(Deutzia gracilis)*

Description: The low growth habit of this plant makes it ideal for a shrub border and mass plantings. It grows 2 to 4 feet high and 3 to 4 feet wide. The burst of blooms in midspring dominates the delicately branched shrub and leaves an arching, green-leafed plant when flowering is complete. The shape becomes ragged over time and requires pruning every few years to restore its graceful shape. Slender deutzia tolerates drought and withstands wintry cold.
Uses: Shrub border, mass planting, specimen in a rock garden.
Site and care requirements: Plant in full sun for best flowering, but can withstand partial shade. Will survive in moist, well-drained soil. No real care needed other than renewal pruning every few years.
Recommended varieties and related species: **'Nikko'** *(var. nakaiana)* is a small shrub that grows up to 2 feet high. The blue-green foliage is a nice background to the small white double flowers that bloom in midspring. The leaves turn a reddish purple in the fall.

Lemoine deutzia *(D. ×lemoinei)* is a hybrid deutzia with loads of white flowers and a twiggy, informal shape. It grows up to 7 feet tall and is very hardy in colder temperatures, from Zones 4 to 10.

Fuzzy deutzia *(D. scabra)* is a larger, old-fashioned oval-shape shrub with panicles of white flowers tinged with pink. It grows from 6 to 10 feet tall and about half as wide, in Zones 5 to 7.

Deutzia blooms

Diospyros kaki (see Persimmon, Japanese)
Diospyros virginiana (see Persimmon, common)

Dogwood, flowering (Cornus florida)

Features: Beautiful blooms and striking bark on a wildlife-friendly favorite
Growth rate: Slow
Zones: 5 to 9

Flowering dogwood (*Cornus florida*)

Description: Flowering dogwood is recognized for its flowers, which are actually four-leafed bracts surrounding tiny flower clusters. These bracts can be seen from a distance but you need to get a closer look to see the flowers. Ranging from white to deep pink, the bracts emerge in late spring before the leaves. The tree displays another season of color in the landscape in mid- to late fall when its small red fruit ripens and foliage turns red to purplish red. Although the fruit attracts attention, it also draws birds and other wildlife to feast on it. The mature flowering dogwood features textured, almost scaly bark that adds appeal to the winter landscape. The tree can reach 30 to 40 feet high with a similar spread. Flowering dogwood is susceptible to the fungal disease anthracnose, which affects trees in the home landscape as well as those in the wild. Avoid transplanting dogwoods from the wild as they might be infected with this disease.

Uses: Specimen, grouping, border.

Site and care requirements: Flowering dogwood prefers partial shade and well-drained soil. In addition, the soil should be slightly acidic and allow excellent drainage. A 2-inch layer of mulch helps ensure soil moisture. Avoid damage to the trunk while mowing or trimming because this can make the tree more susceptible to disease.

Flowering dogwood in fall

Recommended varieties and related species: 'Cherokee Chief' has deep pink to red flowers, while 'White Cloud' has traditional white blooms. Try 'Pluribracteata' for double white flowers or 'First Lady', which has variegated leaves and yellow-and-white flowers.

Kousa dogwood (*C. kousa*) is a slightly smaller tree than the flowering dogwood. Growing 20 to 30 feet high with a similar spread, this tree is hardy in Zones 5 to 8. The growth habit is less uniform than that of flowering dogwood—the young vaseshape tree matures to a more open, broader-reaching form that is lower to the ground. The shape doesn't detract from the beauty of the flowers, which range in color from creamy white to pink. Red fruit, shaped like raspberries, stand out among purplish scarlet late-fall leaves. Kousa dogwood is more resistant to cold temperatures

Kousa dogwood (*C. kousa*)

and anthracnose than flowering dogwood. Consider planting 'Milky Way', which has white flowers, or 'Samaritan', which has variegated leaves and cold tolerance. 'Satomi' offers less cold tolerance than other varieties and produces pink flowers.

Fruiting kousa dogwood

Red-osier dogwood (*C. sericea*) is a shrubby dogwood that grows 7 to 9 feet high and up to 10 feet wide. This red-stemmed plant provides winter color after the leaves have fallen. The attractive mounded shape

Red-osier dogwood (*C. sericea*) foliage

makes this a nice choice for hedges or border plantings, and the tough root system makes it a good planting for sloping areas of the landscape. The real highlight is the red bark, which may darken to a grayish brown as the plant matures. Prune back a third of old growth each spring to spark new growth. It's hardy in Zones 2 to 7. Plant in full sun to partial shade in moist, well-drained soil. Consider planting unusual varieties such as yellow-stemmed 'Flaviramea' or 'Kelseyi,' a smaller and more compact variety that grows only to about 2 feet high and wide.

Downy serviceberry (see Serviceberry, downy)

Dove tree *(Davidia involucrata)*

Features: Unusual fluttering blooms and foliage
Growth rate: Slow to moderate
Zones: 6 to 8

Dove tree *(Davidia involucrata)*

Description: The May blooms that bring to mind handkerchiefs are actually two white bracts that surround a smaller purple flower. The beauty of the dove tree is in the movement of the bracts and leaves in the lightest breeze, swaying gently and creating the illusion of hundreds of doves flitting through the tree. It grows from 20 to 40 feet high in a pyramidal shape. The leaves retain their green color in fall, and then the scaly, orangey-brown bark provides winter interest after the leaves have fallen.
Uses: Specimen.
Site and care requirements: Plant in full sun to partial shade in moist soil; mulch to retain soil moisture. Prune only to maintain the tree's overall shape as it develops.
Recommended varieties and related species: Somewhat more cold hardy, **D. vilmoriniana** has bluish-gray leaves.

Eastern redbud (see Redbud, eastern)
Eastern red cedar (see Red cedar, eastern)
Elaeagnus pungens (see Silverberry)

Elder, American *(Sambucus canadensis)*

Features: Delicate summer blooms and edible late-summer berries
Growth rate: Fast
Zones: 3 to 9

American elder *(Sambucus canadensis)*

Description: American elder, or elderberry, is a familiar sight on the side of roadways. In early summer, broad clusters of tiny white flowers appear, followed by dark purple berries in mid- to late summer. The flavorful berries are a favorite of birds. The berries are also favored by people for making jelly and elderberry wine. The large shrub or small tree grows 5 to 12 feet high with a similar spread. American elder has multiple stems with a spreading or arching growth habit that may become unruly. The plant is best used for native plantings or low-traffic areas of the landscape where its unkempt growth habit will be allowed. If you plan to use the berries for jelly or wine, plant several bushes for the best fruit production.
Uses: Fruit production, native planting.
Site and care requirements: Plant in full sun to partial shade. It will tolerate a variety of soils, but prefers moist to wet conditions. Prune to maintain the shape and remove suckers that shoot up from the plant's base.

Elder, common *(Sambucus nigra)*

Features: A fragrant flower with dark purple-black berries
Growth rate: Fast
Zones: 5 to 7

Common elder *(Sambucus nigra)*

Description: Small, white, fragrant flowers bloom in early summer, followed by deep purple to almost black fruit that appears in late summer. The fruit is particularly attractive to birds, but may also be used to make jellies and wine. Also known as common elderberry, it is less heat tolerant than its cousin, American elder, and grows larger—10 to 20 feet high and 8 to 12 feet wide. Some cultivars have purple leaves, but the main species' leaves are light green to yellow-green.
Uses: Specimen, fruit production.
Site and care requirements: Plant in full sun to partial shade. It prefers moist, well-drained soil, but can tolerate wet soil. Common elder may need pruning to maintain its shape.
Recommended varieties and related species: **'Laciniata'** has variegated leaves, while the **'Gerda'** (Black Beauty) is a cultivar with deep purple, almost black leaves.

Elm, American *(Ulmus americana)*

Features: A stately, once-common urban tree in America that's making a welcome comeback
Growth rate: Fast
Zones: 2 to 9

American elm *(Ulmus americana)*

Description: The American elm that once flourished across the United States was nearly decimated in the 20th century when Dutch elm disease was introduced into the country. Although disease continues to be a problem, breeders have begun developing disease-resistant varieties and homeowners are rediscovering the trees long-valued for their urban hardiness and strong streetside presence. The American elm's thick foliage and arching habit make this an ideal shade tree. Planted in a row lining a long, wide driveway or neighborhood boulevard, the trees create a lovely canopy. The American elm grows 60 to 80 feet high and 30 to 50 feet wide. Small flowers bloom in early spring, giving way to winglike seeds in fall. The fall foliage is golden yellow, hanging onto the tree well into the season. Other potential problems include elm leaf beetle, elm leaf miners, stem cankers, and elm yellows, but the tree tolerates saline soil and soil compaction.
Uses: Shade, specimen, streetside and boulevard planting.
Site and care requirements: Plant in full sun or partial shade. It tolerates different soils, but prefers moist, well-drained, slightly acid soil. This tree is easily transplanted at any size. Plant multiple trees at least 30 feet apart and at least 15 feet from any building. Prune in the first few years to cultivate a strong tree. Pruning only in late fall, winter, or early spring—not summer—helps the tree resist disease. Prune any diseased branches and immediately remove and destroy any debris to eliminate bark beetles (carriers of Dutch elm disease) that can live and breed in cut wood.
Recommended varieties and related species: **'Valley Forge'** and **'New Harmony',** released from the National Arboretum, have disease tolerance, enabling them to recover from Dutch elm disease if infected.

Chinese or lacebark elm *(U. parvifolia)* is a medium- to fast-growing tree that reaches a height of 40 to 50 feet with a similar spread. Best grown in Zones 5 to 9, this alternative to American elm is generally resistant to Dutch elm disease. Named for its lacy-looking, multicolored, exfoliating bark, this elm proves especially decorative in the winter landscape. Its fall foliage colors range from golden yellow to deep reddish purple. Plant **'Dynasty',** a cold-hardy variety or **'Emer II'** (Allee), whose showy bark colors provide a welcome contrast to a drab winter landscape. Both makes excellent shade trees.

Variegated lacebark elm *(U. parvifolia 'Variegata')*

Empress tree (Paulownia tomentosa)

Features: A compelling, open form and striking, fragrant flowers
Growth rate: Fast
Zones: 5 to 9

Empress tree (Paulownia tomentosa)

Description: The open growth habit of the empress tree, coupled with the unusual bell-shape blooms, make it an extraordinary choice for landscape planting. Although widely regarded as a weed species, this tree has become increasingly popular. The empress tree's purple flowers bloom in April and May and have a rich fragrance of vanilla, giving it a colorful, somewhat-tropical appeal. It grows 30 to 40 feet high with about the same spread. The tree is adaptable, surviving in all types of conditions. It also grows 2 feet or more a year, making it a good choice for those seeking a fast-growing tree.

Uses: Specimen, border.
Site and care requirements: Plant in full sun to partial shade and any type of soil. Prune only to remove dead branches. Flowers bloom on 2-year-old wood. Allow room for its mature size if placing among other trees or shrubs. It may die back in sudden, early-fall freezes.

Empress tree blooms

English walnut (see Walnut, English)

Enkianthus, redvein (Enkianthus campanulatus)

Features: Small, bellshape spring blooms and dazzling fall foliage
Growth rate: Slow
Zones: 4 to 7

Redvein enkianthus (Enkianthus campanulatus)

Description: The narrow, vertical growth habit, along with the striking blooms and fall foliage, makes the redvein enkianthus well-suited to planting as a specimen near an entryway or outdoor living area, or as part of a shrub border or woodland garden. Creamy white bell-shape flowers—with veins of pink or red running through them—bloom in May and June. The glossy green leaves of redvein enkianthus turn brilliant yellow to orangey-red in the fall. The shrub grows 6 to 12 feet high and has a spread of up to 8 feet. As the plant matures, it develops a more horizontal branching structure.
Uses: Specimen, shrub border, woodland planting.
Site and care requirements: Plant in moist, well-drained soil that is acidic and enriched with loads of organic matter. This shrub is not salt tolerant and needs additional water during periods of drought.
Recommended varieties and related species: 'Albiflorus' or *E. perulatus* is a smaller, white-flowering shrub that grows to about 6 to 7 feet high and is hardy to Zone 6.

Erica spp. (see Heath)

Escallonia, red (Escallonia rubra)

Features: Striking red blooms and evergreen leaves make this an ideal plant for the southern landscape
Growth rate: Fast
Zones: 8 to 10

Escallonia (Escallonia rubra)

Description: The glossy, dark green leaves provide a dense background for the rosy red flowers that come along in the summer. The shrub grows 10 to 15 feet high with about the same spread, but it can be kept to a more compact shape with selective pruning. If left to grow larger, the mounded growth habit makes for an excellent screen or windbreak. Escallonia is not drought tolerant, so give it supplemental watering in times of drought. It tolerates salt spray and makes a dependable candidate for planting in coastal areas.
Uses: Shrub border, windbreak, screen, mass plantings.
Site and care requirements: Plant in sun to partial shade and moist, well-drained soil. It dislikes alkaline soil. Escallonia does not fare well in extreme heat and humidity, so plant it in partial shade in hot climates.
Recommended varieties and related species: 'Frades' has deep-pink flowers and a more compact form, growing up to 6 feet high. 'Balfourii' also has pink blossoms and a slightly drooping growth habit.

Eucalyptus *(Eucalyptus* spp.)

Features: A fast-growing, hardy tree that's a classic in the western United States
Growth rate: Fast
Zones: 9 to 10 in the West

Eucalyptus *(Eucalyptus* spp.)

Cider gum *(E. gunnii)* foliage

ranging from white to gray to pink. As indicated by the name, the oil in the leaves hints of lemon.

Red-flowering gum *(E. ficifolia)* has red blossoms that stand out among the foliage. It grows up to 25 feet high with a spread of up to 10 feet.

Cider gum *(E. gunnii)* is another species with showy flowers. The yellow blooms appear in the fall, adding to the interest of the already appealing green and white bark. This tree can reach 70 feet high at maturity.

Snow gum *(E. pauciflora niphophila)* has both peeling bark and a trunk that bends as it grows, which gives it structural interest. Growing up to 25 feet high, this species is wind tolerant, making it useful as a windscreen.

Silver dollar gum *(E. polyanthemos)* acquired its name from the round, silvery leaves resembling silver dollars that hang from the tree. The speckled, flaky bark also adds interest. This species grows up to 50 feet tall and does best in drier soil and climates.

Description: Also known as a gum tree, eucalyptus provides fast growth, plenty of shade, and fragrant leaves in western landscapes. Depending on the species, these trees can grow 20 to 70 feet high with a spread of 10 to 30 feet or more. They are hardy trees, but don't fare well in the damp areas of Zones 9 and 10 in the Southeast. The long, dull green leaves are studded with glands that release fragrant oil, much sought after for its antiseptic and disinfectant qualities. The bark of the tree actually dies off each year, producing some of the most interesting textures, which differ from species to species. Some bark becomes long and stringy, other bark more ribbonlike, while still others are flaky, deeply grooved, or smooth but colorfully speckled. Some species have showy flowers that also bring interest to the landscape.
Uses: Shade, specimen, screen.
Site and care requirements: Eucalyptus survives in various types of soil, but not in areas with high humidity or extreme climatic changes. Locate the tree where it has ample space to grow to maturity. It will produce leaf and branch litter, so keep that in mind as well. Prune only in the winter to avoid infestation of the eucalyptus longhorn beetle.
Recommended varieties and related species: Argyle apple *(E. cinerea)* is a large species with ruddy, reddish bark that turns grayer when the tree matures. It can grow up to 50 feet high with a vaselike shape. **Lemon-scented gum** *(E. citriodora)* is another large species, growing up to 70 feet tall. The bark has a chalky appearance in colors

Eucalyptus leaves and flowers

Euonymus alatus (see Burning bush)

Euonymus, wintercreeper *(Euonymus fortunei)*

Features: A creeping shrub with colorful foliage
Growth rate: Slow to fast, depending on cultivars
Zones: 5 to 9

Wintercreeper euonymus *(Euonymus fortunei* 'Emerald 'n' Gold')

Description: Wintercreeper euonymus can have different growth habits, depending on the cultivar. Some grow 3 to 4 feet high and wide, making them useful in a border. Other cultivars work well as groundcovers or climbers. This evergreen shrub is known for its colorful foliage: Vibrant, dark green leaves feature white to silvery-colored veins. It flowers in the summer and displays small, orangey-red fruit in the fall. This plant is susceptible to scale.
Uses: Border shrub or climber on trees and buildings.
Site and care requirements: Plant in full sun to shade and moist but not wet soil.

Recommended varieties and related species: Plant **'Coloratus'** for a groundcover with leaves that turn purple in the winter. **'Emerald Gaiety'** has white to silvery-colored variegated leaves and grows up to 5 feet high and wide, while

Wintercreeper euonymous 'Emerald Gaiety'

'Emerald 'n' Gold' grows to about the same size and has yellow variegated leaves. **'Kewensis'** is a delicate variety with small, green leaves, as are **'Longwood'** and **'Minimus'**. One of the best varieties for fruit display is **'Vegetus'**.

European beech (see Beech, European)
European black alder (see Alder, European black)
European hornbeam (see Hornbeam, European)
European larch (see Larch, European)
European mountain ash (see Mountain ash, European)
Exochorda racemosa (see Pearlbush, common)
Fagus sylvatica (see Beech, European)

False cypress, lawson *(Chamaecyparis lawsoniana)*

Features: A lovely pyramidal evergreen with unusual red flowers
Growth rate: Slow
Zones: 5 to 7

Lawson false cypress
(Chamaecyparis lawsoniana)

Description: The drooping branches covered in lacy foliage are much of the appeal of false cypress. In the early spring red blossoms cover the tips of the foliage, giving an added dimension of color to the already attractive deep green. This tree grows 40 to 60 feet high, with a spread of up to 15 feet.
Uses: Specimen, screen.
Site and care requirements: Plant in sun to partial shade, and moist, well-drained soil. If necessary, prune minimally to control growth.
Recommended varieties and related species: **'Allumii'** is a cultivar with deep blue-green foliage and a faster growth rate than the species. **'Elwoodii'**, a dwarf variety, grows to about 8 feet high, while **'Golden King'** grows up to 30 feet high. **'Silver Queen'** boasts variegated foliage.

Nootka false cypress *(C. nootkatensis)*

Nootka false cypress *(C. nootkatensis)* grows 30 to 40 feet high and up to 20 feet wide. It is best grown in areas of Zones 4 to 7 that have sufficient soil and air moisture. The tree has a looser, more draping habit than lawson false cypress but features a similar overall pyramidal or conical shape. **'Pendula'** has a weeping form with foliage that dangles from the branches.

Hinoki false cypress *(C. obtusa)* grows 50 to 75 feet high and to a width of 10 to 15 feet. The pyramidal shape and drooping, fernlike branches make this a spectacular specimen or accent tree for a spacious landscape in Zones 4 to 8. This adaptable species prefers moist, well-drained, and acid soil. Smaller cultivars, such as **'Nana Gracilis'** and **'Filicoides'**, grow up to 6 feet tall.

Hinoki false cypress *(C. obtusa)*

Fir, douglas (Pseudotsuga menziesii)

Features: A stately evergreen that's a seasonal favorite
Growth rate: Moderate
Zones: 4 to 6

Douglas fir (Pseudotsuga menziesii)

Description: This hardy evergreen is particularly attractive for its blue-green needles, large cones, and stately presence in the landscape. It can live to be hundreds of years old, as evidenced by the huge, old-growth trees found in wild areas of the Pacific Northwest. It grows 40 to 80 feet high and from 12 to 20 feet wide in a home landscape, but can grow up to 100 feet or higher in the wild. Douglas fir is often grown commercially for use as a Christmas tree because of its pyramidal shape and the fact that the needles tend to stay on the tree longer in dry conditions. The shape of the tree changes to a more conical form as it matures, opening to reveal the bottom of the trunk. The blue-green needles are a lovely background to the flowers, or cones, that appear at the top of the tree in spring. These 3- to 4-inch-long cones eventually turn brown in the late summer, often hanging on to the tree well into winter.
Uses: Specimen, ornamental, and screen if planted in a row.
Site and care requirements: Plant in full sun to partial shade in moist, well-drained soil. Douglas firs are susceptible to damage from high winds, so plant in protected areas of the landscape. Choose a variety with cold hardiness appropriate to the region where you live.
Recommended varieties and related species: 'Fastigiata' is a variety with a more columnar habit and *P. menziesii glauca* is a more cold-hardy variety.

Fir, white (Abies concolor)

Features: A classic conical evergreen with blue-green needles
Growth rate: Slow to moderate
Zones: 4 to 7

White fir (Abies concolor)

Description: The light-colored bark and blue-green to silvery green needles are what make the white fir distinct from other fir trees. It grows from 30 to 50 feet high with a mature spread of up to 20 feet in the home landscape, but grows up to 100 feet high in the wild. White firs are also grown for use as Christmas trees, but don't retain their needles as long as the douglas fir. Red flowers appear in spring, growing into 3- to 6-inch-long cones that turn from green to brown as the season progresses. White fir is the most drought tolerant of all the firs.
Uses: Specimen, screen.
Site and care requirements: Plant in full sun to partial shade in moist, well-drained, and acid soil. Plant firs in the spring and prune only when necessary to remove dead or diseased branches.
Recommended varieties and related species: 'Candicans' is a splendid variety of white fir, but try 'Violacea' for the silver-blue needles or the dwarf variety, 'Compacta', which has bluish needles.

Balsam fir (*A. balsamea*) has a distinctly pyramidal shape when young that makes it popular for Christmas trees. It can become a bit messy-looking as it matures but should retain its overall shape when planted in colder climates. The foliage becomes thin in warmer conditions. This slow-growing tree is hardy in Zones 3 to 6 and grows best in full sun to light shade in moist, well-drained, acid soil. Balsam fir is susceptible to wind damage, canker disease, spruce worm, and spruce wooly aphid. Provide adequate water during drought conditions.

Dwarf balsam fir (A. balsamea 'Nana')

Firethorn *(Pyracantha* spp.)

Features: White spring flowers and stunning, long-lasting orange-red berries
Growth rate: Fast
Zones: 6 to 10

Firethorn *(Pyracantha coccinea* 'Mohave')

Description: Named for its fiery red fruit and wicked thorns, firethorn is best used to provide colorful interest in the winter landscape. Growing 6 to 18 feet high and up to 10 feet wide, this versatile shrub can be used for an informal hedge or barrier planting, or trained into espalier. Profusions of white flowers appear in spring on last year's growth but their scent can be unpleasant. Clusters of berries ripen in late summer and often persist into winter, adding their fiery red glory to the setting. Scarlet firethorn is heat and drought tolerant.

Firethorn *(P. atalantoides* 'Alexandra')

Uses: Hedge, specimen, espalier.

Site and care requirements: Plant in partial sun or light shade for best fruit production. Plant away from heavily trafficked areas because of the thorns. Provide well-drained soil. Firethorn tolerates dry conditions and can be grown in a container. Wear gloves when you prune in the winter or early spring, shaping the plant overall and removing diseased or dead branches. Because the plant is vulnerable to fire blight and scab, select a disease-resistant variety for best results.

Recommended varieties and related species: Choose a disease-resistant variety, such as **'Apache'**, **'Fiery Cascade'**, **'Navaho'**, and **'Shawnee'**. **'Gnome'** is a slightly smaller shrub, growing to about 6 feet high. A more cold-hardy variety called **'Lalandei'** is available, but it can be susceptible to scab. Nearly thornless **'Tiny Tim'** is a very small variety that reaches about 3 feet high.

Forsythia, border *(Forsythia ×intermedia)*

Features: Bright yellow blooms that signal the arrival of spring
Growth rate: Fast
Zones: 5 to 8

Border forsythia *(Forsythia ×intermedia)*

Description: The deep yellow flowers of forsythia are a sure indication that spring has arrived. The open, somewhat untamed growth habit of this shrub is enhanced by the abundance of flowers that cover it in early spring before the foliage develops. Ideal in borders and mass plantings, forsythia's dramatic flowers provide one of the best shows in town at bloom time. The small green leaves turn yellowish to reddish purple in fall. This shrub does well in a variety of adverse conditions and has drought tolerance, making it a popular plant for a variety of home landscapes. Forsythia grows 8 to 10 feet high and 10 to 12 feet wide. It can be pruned to retain a desired shape but is most striking when left to its natural growth habit.

Uses: Border, mass planting.

Site and care requirements: Plant in full sun and almost any type of soil. Adequate watering and feeding promote the best flowering. Protect forsythia from early spring frosts. Prune after flowering to remove the oldest stems or cut back to the ground to renew an older plant.

Recommended varieties and related species: **'Lynwood'** and **'Spring Glory'** are proven varieties with lighter yellow flowers, while **'Beatrix Farrand'** has more vibrant yellow blooms. Hybrids with developed cold hardiness include **'Meadowlark'** and **'Northern Gold'**. They are suitable for planting in Zone 4.

Forsythia blooms

Fothergilla, dwarf *(Fothergilla gardenii)*

Features: Small stature, fragrant flowers in early spring, and vibrant foliage in fall
Growth rate: Slow
Zones: 5 to 9

Dwarf fothergilla *(Fothergilla gardenii)*

Description: An attractive shrub for small spaces, dwarf fothergilla shows off in the early-spring garden with its bright white tassellike flowers, before the leaves fill out. The honey-scented blossoms give you plenty of reasons to plant the shrub near a window or walkway, where they will be most appreciated. In the fall the foliage turns fluorescent yellow, orange, and red, typically on the same leaf. Dwarf fothergilla grows from 3 to 5 feet high with about the same spread. Use this drought-tolerant plant in a border or mass planting to attract bees and butterflies; or as an accent plant to showcase its seasonal appeal.

Uses: Mixed border, shrub grouping, foundation planting.

Site and care requirements: Plant in sun for best flowering but tolerates partial shade. Best planted in moist, well-drained, acid soil.

Recommended varieties and related species: **'Blue Mist'** has bluish-green foliage with less-than-showy fall color.

Large fothergilla *(F. major)* is essentially the same plant as dwarf fothergilla but larger all over. Growing 8 to 10 feet high

Large fothergilla *(F. major)*

with the same spread. The plant's flowers and leaves are larger than those of dwarf fothergilla but with the same characteristics of the smaller plant. **'Mount Airy'** grows a bit smaller, reaching 6 feet high. It has great fall foliage and large, fragrant blooms.

Franklin tree *(Franklinia alatamaha)*

Features: Large, fragrant white flowers, brilliant fall foliage, and interesting bark
Growth rate: Moderate
Zones: 5 to 8

Flowers of the franklin tree *(Franklinia alatamaha)*

Description: Native to Georgia and named for Benjamin Franklin, the franklin tree has vanished from the wild and cannot be grown for long in the Southeast due to a root pathogen that inhabits the region's soil. Yet it is prized for the large, white, camellialike flowers that appear in summer and continue into fall. The glossy dark green leaves turn a vivid orangey-red to purple in the fall. The foliage hangs on into winter and then drops, revealing gray

Franklin tree

fissured bark. The tree's upright, open form makes it an attractive accent or a background plant for smaller shrubs. It grows from 10 to 25 feet high and about 6 to 15 feet wide.

Uses: Accent, specimen.

Site and care requirements: Plant in sun to partial shade, but does best in full sun. The soil should be well-drained and acidic. Keep the soil consistently moist but not wet.

Fraxinus **spp.** (see Ash)

Fringe tree, Chinese *(Chionanthus retusus)*

Features: Profusions of puffy white blooms
Growth rate: Slow
Zones: 6 to 8

Chinese fringe tree *(Chionanthus retusus)*

Description: The Chinese fringe tree is similar in size to the white fringe tree but has a more shrubby growth habit and smaller leaves. It grows reliably well in Zones 6 to 8, flowering a bit later than the white fringe tree. The sweet-smelling, white flowers bloom on new wood and grow at the tips of the branches instead of throughout the limbs. Female trees produce dark blue fruit that attracts birds. A male and female tree are needed for pollination and fruit production but not for flowering. The bark of the tree develops grooves and ridges as it matures, providing winter interest.
Uses: Accent, specimen, shrub border.
Site and care requirements: Plant in sun to partial shade and well-drained soil. For best results ensure consistent moisture. Prune after flowering to enhance the shrub's rounded, bushy form.

Fringe tree, white *(Chionanthus virginicus)*

Features: Delicate, cottony, fragrant white blooms and colorful fruit
Growth rate: Slow
Zones: 4 to 9

Description: The most striking feature of the white fringe tree is the fragrant, white flowers that bloom in spring and resemble the tree's nickname, old man's beard. Following the blooms, the fruit on the female trees matures into blue-black berries that are very attractive to birds. Although male and female trees are for pollination to produce fruit, either will flower if planted singly. The white fringe tree grows

White fringe tree *(Chionanthus virginicus)*

12 to 20 feet high and wide, and takes the shape of a large shrub to a small tree with a broadly rounded form. The large waxy green leaves turn a pale yellow to yellow-brown in the fall.
Uses: It is particularly striking when planted near a dark building and illuminated by nightlights to show off the unusual blooms. Plant it as a specimen, accent, or in a shrub border or along a stream or pond.

White fringe tree bloom

Site and care requirements: Plant in full sun to partial shade and moist, well-drained soil. The flowers form on old wood, so if you choose to shape the tree, prune only after flowering. The white fringe tree tolerates wind, air pollution, and urban situations but needs some winter protection in Zone 4.

Fuchsia, common *(Fuchsia ×hybrida)*

Features: Showy blooms in a range of colors where the climate is generally warm
Growth rate: Fast
Zones: 10 to 11

Common fuchsia *(Fuchsia ×hybrida)*

Description: The bountiful, two-toned flowers range in color from pink to red, purple, white, and coral, and bloom from late spring to early fall. Attractive to hummingbirds, the often-lengthy flowers prove ideal for nectar retrieval. The shrub grows to 3 feet high and wide with a rounded habit. It works well in perennial borders or trained into an espalier. Common fuchsia requires specific care to ensure

Fuschia blooms

flowering and survival. Easily injured by cold, it is susceptible to fuchsia gall mites, spider mites, and whiteflies.
Uses: Specimen, shrub border, espalier.
Site and care requirements: Plant in partial shade in a cool area of the landscape, protected from summer heat and strong winds. Plant in moist, fertile soil. Mulch around the plant to retain soil moisture. Water plants thoroughly and mist them during hot, dry weather. Fertilize every 10 to 14 days, from spring through early fall. Prune established plants in early spring, leaving at least two buds on each branch. Pinch stems of young and mature plants regularly to promote dense growth.
Recommended varieties and related species: Consider **'Alice Hoffman'**, **'Island Sunset'**, **'Red Spider'**, or **'Voodoo'** for various colors. *F. magellanica,* or hardy fuchsia, grows to a graceful, rounded shrub in Zones 6 to 10 and produces small, red flowers with blue inner petals. It dies back over winter in the north.

Gardenia *(Gardenia jasminoides)*

Features: Waxy white, ultrafragrant flowers with dark, emerald green leaves
Growth rate: Moderate
Zones: 8 to 10

Gardenia *(Gardenia jasminoides)*

Description: The delightfully intense fragrance of gardenia flowers makes the beautiful shrub worth the maintenance it requires. In summer the waxy white blossoms nestle among glossy green leaves, producing a striking contrast. The blooms turn yellow-white as they age, but the fragrance persists until they die. The shrub grows to about 6 feet high and wide, forming a densely rounded shape. As a specimen in the landscape of warm-summer climates, gardenia flowers best in areas with

Shrubby gardenia

warm evenings. Otherwise, it grows well in a container and can be moved indoors to protect it from chilly conditions.
Uses: Specimen, container, hedge, low screen, espalier.
Site and care requirements: A gardenia needs well-drained acid soil, richly amended with organic matter. Plant the shrub in partial shade and protect it from full sun and winter winds. Feed with an acid plant food every 3 to 4 weeks. Spray for sucking insects and provide good air circulation to prevent infestation. Mist regularly in the early morning when the shrub is not in bloom to boost humidity.
Recommended varieties and related species: Plant **'Radicans'** for a lower-growing shrub or **'Radicans Variegata'** for a variegated leaf with creamy white to pale yellow leaf margins. Double-flowering **'August Beauty'** is a robust beauty that reaches 4 to 6 feet high.

Gaultheria procumbens (see Wintergreen)

Gingko *(Gingko biloba)*

Features: Fan-shape leaves and golden fall foliage
Growth rate: Slow to moderate
Zones: 4 to 9

Gingko *(Gingko biloba)*

Description: Gingko trees have been around for millions of years and provide shade and a colorful fall display to this day. The characteristic fan-shaped leaves make the gingko unmistakable in the landscape. Eventually growing to be 50 to 80 feet high and 30 to 40 feet wide, the young trees often have an open, almost gangly growth habit that ultimately fills out into a lovely shade tree as it matures. At about 20 years old, male and female trees produce separate and distinct flowers, which are small, almost unnoticeable green blooms. The female trees eventually bear nuts that emit a foul odor as the flesh decomposes, so plant a male tree unless you can stand the unpleasant odor. The real show comes in the fall when the leaves turn a golden yellow, making the tree look positively aglow with the color. Be sure to catch the color show while it lasts, because just one gusty night can blow all the leaves off the tree. Gingko trees are very good for street planting, as they are tolerant of heat and drought and the root system will not disrupt sidewalks or pavement.
Uses: Specimen, shade, street trees.
Site and care requirements: Best planted in full sun in moist, well-drained soil. Plant in the spring for best results, and prune only to remove dead limbs.
Recommended varieties and related species: 'Autumn Gold' is a male variety that produces wonderful fall color, while 'Fastigiata' can be either male or female. 'Saratoga' grows into a more oval shape.

Gleditsia triacanthos inermis (see Honeylocust, thornless)

Glorybower, harlequin *(Clerodendrum trichotomum)*

Features: Beautiful, fragrant blooms and showy, colorful fruit on a multistemmed plant
Growth rate: Fast
Zones: 6 to 8

Harlequin glorybower *(Clerodendrum trichotomum)*

Description: This upright, treelike shrub produces clusters of sweetly scented flowers from mid- to late summer. Berries follow from late summer into early fall. The plant has an open, rounded and spreading shape. It reaches 10 to 20 feet high and wide. The flowers bloom on new wood, so prune the plant to shape it in early spring before growth emerges. When bruised or crushed, the leaves and branches exude an unpleasant odor, redolent of peanut butter. Harlequin glorybower can become invasive because of its tendency to form suckers. Prune the suckers to control invasiveness and crowding. In northern climates, the plant may die back to the ground over winter, but it recovers quickly come spring.
Uses: Shrub border, or allow suckering and train the plant up and over a trellis or pergola.
Site and care requirements: Plant in full sun to partial shade in well-drained, enriched, and acid soil. Keep the soil moist but not wet.
Recommended varieties and related species: Plant *C. ugandense* for its stunning blue to purplish blue blooms or the somewhat hardier *C. trichotomum fargesii*.

Glorybower bloom

Goldenchain tree *(Laburnum ×watereri)*

Features: Stunning, pendulous, yellow spring flowers and lovely olive-colored bark in winter
Growth rate: Moderate
Zones: 6 to 8

Goldenchain tree *(Laburnum ×watereri)*

Goldenchain tree bloom

Description: This small, dense, upright tree is best known for the glorious yellow flower chains that hang from its branches in May and June and last as long as two weeks. Fruit pods mature in fall. This highly desirable specimen tree can be fussy about site and climate and may be tricky to grow. Careful siting is necessary because the goldenchain tree prefers a sunny location with shade during the hottest time of the day. Intolerant of wet soil, the tree grows best in cooler, moderate climates. It reaches 12 to 15 feet high and 9 to 12 feet wide.
Uses: Specimen, shrub border, foundation, grouping.
Site and care requirements: Plant in moist, well-drained, and alkaline soil. Goldenchain tree prefers full sun with light late-afternoon shade. All parts of the tree—especially the fruits—are poisonous, so plant it away from areas with foot traffic. It can be trained over a pergola or espaliered.
Recommended varieties and related species: **'Pendulum'** is a weeping form, while **'Vossii'** has a denser habit and longer flower chains. **'Aureum'** features golden leaves.

Goldenraintree *(Koelreuteria paniculata)*

Features: Showy midsummer yellow flower clusters, attractive bright green foliage, and interesting fruit pods
Growth rate: Moderate to fast
Zones: 5 to 9

Goldenraintree *(Koelreuteria paniculata)*

Description: This tree is a treat in the summer landscape because the goldenraintree blooms profusely when other flowering trees have long passed their moment in the spotlight. Covered with tiny yellow blossoms in foot-long clusters, the tree appears as if it has been showered with golden rain. The flowers are followed by green, lanternshape fruit pods that eventually turn yellow, then brown. The foliage, striking lime green throughout the summer, turns yellow and golden orange in autumn. In winter the twisted branches make an interesting silhouette. The tree grows from 30 to 40 feet high and almost as wide in an irregular rounded shape. The goldenraintree proves adaptable once established by handling challenging conditions, including poor or compacted soil, drought, and excessive heat. Plant it where it can be easily seen as an admirable specimen.
Uses: Specimen, shade.
Site and care requirements: Plant in spring in moist, well-drained soil and full sun. Prune lightly during winter dormancy in the first few years to encourage growth of new branches.
Recommended varieties and related species: **'September'** is nicely rounded and blooms later, in August or September. **'Rose Lantern'** features pink seedpods and **'Fastigiata'** offers a handsome upright form, though it's a less dependable bloomer.

Goldenraintree bloom

Grapefruit (see Citrus)

Grapeholly, Oregon (Mahonia aquifolium)

Features: Glossy green, hollylike leaves, lovely yellow spring blooms, and distinctive purple-blue berries on an evergreen shrub
Growth rate: Moderate to fast
Zones: 5 to 9

Oregon grapeholly (Mahonia aquifolium)

Description: Attractive glossy green foliage and striking yellow flower clusters make Oregon grapeholly a springtime highlight whether situated in a foundation planting or shrub border. Its hollylike leaves and blue fruits make it equally appealing in winter. This evergreen shrub reaches 3 to 6 feet high and about as wide, forming an upright or low-spreading silhouette. Somewhat cold hardy, depending on care and conditions, Oregon grapeholly grows in protected sites in Zone 4.
Uses: Shrub border, foundation.
Site and care requirements: Oregon grapeholly adapts to sun or shade and moist, well-drained, and acid soil, although it must be protected from the sun in winter. Fertilize in springtime to maintain proper acid level. Mulch to maintain moisture and cut back one or two older stems each winter to encourage denser growth and flowering.
Recommended varieties and related species: 'King's Ransom' has an upright form and blue-green leaves that turn to purple in winter. 'Compactum', 'Apollo', and 'Moseri' are dwarf forms that grow to around 3 feet.

Gum tree (see Eucalyptus)

Hackberry, common (Celtis occidentalis)

Features: A hardy, wildlife-friendly shade tree
Growth rate: Moderate to fast
Zones: 3 to 9
Description: This is a tough, dependable tree that withstands all kinds of abuse, from pollution to poor soil to harsh, windy conditions. Known for its ability to grow where other trees would surely fail, it reaches 40 to 60 feet tall and nearly as wide, and offers quality shade with

Common hackberry (Celtis occidentalis)

its upright, rounded form. It has corky bark and unremarkable leaves that turn yellow in autumn. The hackberry provides a snack bar for birds that eagerly devour its fruit. It often provides a home for various nesting birds that take up residence in the crooks and crotches of its limbs. It is ideal for use in large yards or in a spacious fencerow.

The last of the hackberries in winter

Uses: Shade, planting for wildlife, difficult conditions.
Site and care requirements: Plant in just about any type of soil and full sun. Prone to witches'-broom, powdery mildew, and hackberry nipple gall. None of these ailments will kill the hackberry, but they can make it appear bedraggled. Take care to water a young tree during its first couple of seasons and you will rarely need to give a second thought about this extremely drought-tolerant tree.

Hackberry blooms

Prune carefully in early years to eliminate weak limbs or multiple trunks.
Recommended varieties and related species: 'Prairie Pride' is an especially rugged variety with dark green, leathery leaves that is resistant to witches'-broom and gall. The **sugarberry** (C. laevigata) is similar to the common hackberry but it is quicker-growing and resistant to witches'-broom.

Halesia tetraptera (see Silverbell, Carolina)
Hamamelis ×intermedia (see Witch hazel, hybrid)
Harlequin glorybower (see Glorybower, harlequin)

Harry Lauder's walking stick (Corylus avellana 'Contorta')

Features: Distinctive twisted stems and leaves, nuts and catkins
Growth rate: Moderate to fast
Zones: 4 to 8
Description: A cultivar of the larger European filbert (C. avellana), Harry Lauder's walking stick is a tangle of twisted stems that makes a striking impression. Also known as a corkscrew hazel or contorted filbert, it is of special interest in winter. This 8- to 10-foot tall and wide irregular-shape shrub or small tree has dangling male catkins. It is an ideal specimen tree in informal or woodland landscapes. Wildlife flocks to the tree for shelter and eats the nuts.
Uses: Specimen, wildlife.

Harry Lauder's walking stick (Corylus avellana 'Contorta')

Site and care requirements: Plant in moist, well-drained soil and full sun to light shade. Supplement the soil with organic matter, and mulch to keep it evenly moist until winter. If planted in Zone 4, this tree needs to be planted only in a protected site.
Recommended varieties and related species: The **Turkish filbert** (C. colurna) is a larger species with a more formal, pyramidal-shape tree that grows 40 to 50 feet high and about half as wide in Zones 4 to 7. It has glossy dark green leaves and gorgeous peeling bark. Brown male catkins appear in late winter. Use it as a specimen tree or in a naturalistic grouping.

Hawthorn, cockspur *(Crataegus crus-galli)*

Features: Bright red to nearly black berries and excellent fall color
Growth rate: Slow to moderate
Zones: 4 to 7

Cockspur hawthorn *(Crataegus crus-galli)*

Description: A classic in the Midwestern home landscape, this tree withstands the intense heat of summer as well as harsh winter conditions. It offers loads of visual appeal, including glossy green leaves that turn bronze and purple in the fall, bright red to dark purple berries that hang on through the winter, and an attractive broad, low-branched form. It grows to 25 feet high and 30 feet wide and can be cultivated into a loose hedge or screen or planted as a specimen or in a grouping.
Uses: Specimen, grouping, screen, hedge.
Site and care requirements: Plant in well-drained, somewhat acid soil in full sun. Mulch to keep the soil evenly moist throughout the growing season. Prune dead, crossed, or rubbing branches. Site away from foot traffic, where the thorns can present a problem. Susceptible to cedar-hawthorn rust, leaf miners, and aphids.
Recommended varieties and related species: **Var.** *inermis* is similar to the species but thornless.

Hawthorn, Indian (see Indian hawthorn)

Hawthorn, Washington *(Crataegus phaenopyrum)*

Features: Popular and adaptable with colorful flowers, berries, and foliage
Growth rate: Moderate
Zones: 4 to 8

Washington hawthorn *(Crataegus phaenopyrum)*

Description: The Washington hawthorn offers hardiness to Zone 4 and utility for smaller home landscapes. It features creamy white, slightly musty-smelling blooms in late spring, followed by plentiful clusters of orange-red berries. It grows to 20 or 25 feet tall and 15 to 20 feet wide in an oval to rounded shape. Glossy dark green leaves turn orange and red to almost purple in the fall. More tolerant of heat than other hawthorns, the Washington hawthorn has been widely planted in the South.
Uses: Specimen, screen, hedge.
Site and care requirements: Plant in moist, well-drained soil in full sun to part shade. Site away from foot traffic, as bees love the blooms. The thorns, which can be up to 3 inches long, can be problematic.
Recommended varieties and related species: **'Toba'** *(C. ×mordenensis)* is a cockspur hawthorn-Washington hawthorn hybrid that produces white blooms that turn a rosy pink and is nearly thornless, though it produces fewer fruits and is particularly vulnerable to cedar-hawthorn rust.

Hawthorn, 'Winter King' *(Crataegus viridis)*

Features: Dark green foliage, clusters of white spring blooms, and long-lasting red-orange fruit
Growth rate: Moderate to fast
Zones: 4 to 7

'Winter King' hawthorn *(Crataegus viridis)*

Description: Also known as green hawthorn, this cultivar of *Crataegus viridus* makes a popular choice for the home landscape with its broad, rounded vaselike shape. It features clusters of applelike blooms in spring. The lustrous green leaves turn gold to red or bronze in fall. In the winter it reveals silver to gray-green bark. A terrific ornamental or specimen planting, it grows 20 to 25 feet high and wide. 'Winter King' has fewer and smaller thorns than other hawthorns as well as resistance to common diseases.
Uses: Specimen, ornamental, group with evergreen plantings, wildlife.
Site and care requirements: Plant in moist, well-drained soil and full sun to part shade. Remove lower branches to maintain the rounded vaselike form. Prune to cultivate a single trunk, or allow it to develop multiple trunks.

Heath (*Erica* spp.)

Features: Hardy, compact shrubs with colorful spring blooms
Growth rate: Slow to moderate
Zones: 4 to 10, depending on variety

Heath (*Erica* spp.)

Description: These colorful, shrubby evergreens rarely disappoint. Most noted for their unusual bloom times—winter through early spring, depending on the variety and climate—heaths are a welcome source of color especially in the winter garden. Their tiny bell- or urn-shape flowers range from white to pale pink, rosy pink, magenta, and purple. They usually form buds in spring or summer but don't bloom until many months later. The small glossy evergreen foliage appears on the dense, compact plants, which grow from 1 to 7 feet tall and about 3 feet wide. There are literally hundreds of species, ranging from sun- and heat-loving Mediterranean varieties to brisk alpine-friendly types. Almost all are hardy and very low maintenance once established. They're well worth making room for in shrub borders—especially the winter-blooming heaths, which can even begin blooming under the snow, peaking out to offer a nice hint of spring to come.
Uses: Border, grouping, rock garden.
Site and care requirements: Heaths have shallow roots, so plant them in sandy, well-drained, slightly acid soil. They handle partial shade, although the blooms are more robust when the shrubs are planted in full sun. Keep plants tidy by pruning as soon as blooms are past their prime and not later because buds set soon thereafter for the next season.
Recommended varieties and related species: Winter heath (*E. carnea*), the most winter-hardy type, is adaptable to a sloping planting site. The dwarf shrubs work well as a groundcover, growing to less than 1 foot high and spreading to 2 feet wide. Also known as snow heather, winter heath is most likely to provide glorious winter blooms that appear from late November through midspring in creamy white, pink, magenta, and purple. Bloom times depend on the climatic conditions of the season: A harsh winter brings later blooms, while a mild winter prompts blooms to appear weeks or months earlier than usual. Pink blooms of **'Foxhollow Fairy'** appear from January to March. **'Sherwood's Early Red'** blooms ruby red from November to February. **'Springwood White'** features a profusion of white blooms and is hardy from Zones 5 to 7.

Bell heather (*E. cinerea*), hardy from Zones 6 to 8, includes cultivars that bloom in late summer and early fall. **Irish heath** (*E. erigena*) blooms in late winter and spring. It is less hardy than other heaths but grows 3 to 10 feet tall.

Heather, Scotch (*Calluna vulgaris*)

Features: Lush, dense, colorful blooms on an evergreen shrub
Growth rate: Moderate
Zones: 5 to 7

Scotch heather (*Calluna vulgaris*)

Description: Densely covering an area and forming a blooming carpet, Scotch heather is a favorite in cool, moist climates. Growing to 2 feet high and 3 to 4 feet wide, Scotch heather makes a bold impression whether massed on a slope or clustered in rock gardens. Small bell-shape blooms grow along the flower stalks and range from purple to red to pink and white. The flowers appear in late summer and attract bees to gather their nectar. Scotch heather's evergreen foliage and its dense, compact form gives the plant year-round aesthetic appeal in the home landscape.
Uses: Border, grouping, slope, rock garden.
Site and care requirements: Plant in moist, well-drained, somewhat-acid, sandy soil and full sun. Mulch to retain even soil moisture. Prune in the fall after flowering to

Scotch heather bloom

maintain the plant's shape and encourage future blooms.
Recommended varieties and related species: There are hundreds of cultivars featuring countless bloom colors and foliage variations.

Heavenly bamboo (*Nandina domestica*)

Features: Bright red berries, lacy evergreen foliage on an upright form
Growth rate: Moderate
Zones: 6 to 10

Heavenly bamboo (*Nandina domestica*)

Description: A favorite in Southern gardens, heavenly bamboo is put to good use as a mass planting or screening hedge. It features clusters of white flowers in summer, followed by bunches of bright red fruit that stay with the plant throughout the winter and provide visual interest. This dependable, moderate-size shrub fills bare or exposed spots nicely over time.
Uses: Specimen, grouping, screen, hedge, container.
Site and care requirements: Plant in early spring in moist, well-drained, fertile soil and full sun to part shade. Water well during the first couple of years. Once established heavenly bamboo will be drought tolerant. Prune to retain its upright shape. Cut back two or three of the oldest stems to the ground each spring to spur new growth.
Recommended varieties and related species: **'Harbour Dwarf'** forms a dense, 2- to 3-foot mound and displays purplish winter color. **'Firepower'** features bright red leaves in winter, as does **'Gulf Stream'**. **'Alba'** has white berries. **'Compacta'** is a dwarf form.

***Hebe* spp.** (see Veronica, shrubby)
Hedge apple (see Osage orange)

Hemlock, Canadian *(Tsuga canadensis)*

Features:
A large graceful, pyramidal evergreen
Growth rate: Moderate
Zones: 3 to 7

Canadian hemlock *(Tsuga canadensis)*

Description:
The Canadian hemlock is a striking specimen with its graceful pyramidal form, delicate deep green needles, and classic brown cones. It grows from 40 to 70 or more feet high and 25 to 35 feet wide. The tree's cones as well as its lush habit attract various of songbirds seeking food and shelter. Grouped with other hemlocks, it forms an effective screen. Well sited, mulched, and protected from lawn care injury, it is less susceptible to disease and pests such as the woolly adelgid insects that have badly damaged hemlocks in the eastern United States.

Uses: Specimen, grouping, screen, hedge, wildlife.

Site and care requirements: Purchase trees from reliable local sources for the greatest success. Plant in part shade and moist, well-drained, acid soil. The Canadian hemlock survives in full sun but only when it is protected from drying winds and the soil is richly amended with organic matter. It tolerates winter cold but can be damaged by unseasonable frosts. Water young trees as needed and established trees during drought. Watch for woolly adelgid infestation and address with an oil spray or systemic pesticide.

Recommended varieties and related species: Among the many cultivars of Canadian hemlock: **'Pendula'** has a weeping form. It makes either a handsome specimen or a screen that grows 10 to 15 feet high and twice as wide.

Carolina hemlock *(T. caroliniana)* has a more narrowly pyramidal form and somewhat less dense foliage than the Canadian species; and is not as cold tolerant. It grows 40 to 60 feet high and 20 to 25 feet wide in Zones 4 to 7. The prettiest detail on a Carolina hemlock is its large, irregular-shape cones that open

Carolina hemlock *(T. caroliniana)*

outward from the cone's center.

Western hemlock *(T. heterophylla)*, also known as the Pacific hemlock, does especially well in the Northwest. It is the tallest of the hemlocks, reaching up to 75 feet, even in the domestic landscape. It has sweeping branches and a more open pyramidal form than other hemlocks. The Western hemlock requires a moist environment and does not tolerate hot summer temperatures, hence its affinity for the cooler Pacific Northwest, where it is hardy from Zones 2 to 8.

Western hemlock *(P. heterophylla)*

Heptacodium miconioides (see Seven-son flower)
Hibiscus syriacus (see Rose of Sharon)

Hickory, shagbark *(Carya ovata)*

Features: Distinctive thick peeling bark and golden bronze fall color
Growth rate: Slow to moderate
Zones: 4 to 8

Description:
A massive stature and peeling gray bark make the shagbark hickory easily recognizable. This stately tree, with its wide, spreading form, grows 60 to 80 feet high and 35 to 50 feet wide. It has yellow-green oblong leaflets that turn golden brown in autumn. The sweet and plentiful nuts—attractive to people and

Shagbark hickory *(Carya ovata)*

squirrels—litter the lawn in autumn and may present a mowing hazard until the neighborhood squirrels come along to handle the cleanup. Chips of the bark are used to flavor smoked food.

Uses: Shade, wildlife.

Site and care requirements: Plant in well-drained loamy soil and water generously during the first two years to keep evenly moist. Mature trees will take care of themselves. Fertilize for vigorous nut production and prune to establish and maintain a central leader as the tree matures.

Recommended varieties and related species: Pecan hickory *(C. illinoinensis)* is a superior choice for nuts, though hardy only to Zone 6. **Shellbark hickory** *(C. laciniosa)*, which is hardy to Zone 5, is not as large as the shagbark and requires wetter soil.

Hippophae rhamnoides (see Sea buckthorn)

Holly, American *(Ilex opaca)*

Features: Showy red fruit and glossy evergreen foliage
Growth rate: Slow to moderate
Zones: 5 to 9

American holly *(Ilex opaca)*

Description:
A classic in the domestic landscape, the American holly is prized for its stiff, glossy evergreen foliage and luminous red fruit that appears in autumn and stays on the plant until spring. As with all hollies, the berries are a favorite of birds but poisonous to humans. Densely pyramidal when young, it becomes more open and irregular as it matures. The lower branches are often pruned to reveal part of the lower trunk. The largest of all the hollies, this species grows 40 to 50 feet tall and 20 to 40 feet wide. It works nicely as a specimen or planted in groups.

Uses: Specimen, grouping, hedge, wildlife.
Site and care requirements: Plant in moist, fertile, slightly acid, and well-drained soil; and in full sun to part shade. The more sun it gets, the denser this holly will grow. It's vulnerable to harsh winter wind and extreme summer heat, so take care when choosing a site for your American holly. Consider planting away from heavily trafficked areas where the sharp-edge leaves and poisonous berries could present a hazard. Plant one male for every three female plants to ensure abundant fruit production. Water generously during the growing season, fertilize annually, and prune to maintain a neat shape.

Recommended varieties and related species: Because there are so many available cultivars of American holly, it's most important to choose one suited to your growing region. Some favorites include fast-growing **'Merry Christmas'** and compact and abundantly fruiting **'Croonenburg',** as well as the adaptable female cultivars **'Miss Helen'** and **'Jersey Princess'.**

English holly *(I. aquifolium)* tends to be somewhat smaller and less tolerant of heat and cold than its American cousin. It does best in temperate coastal regions of Zones 6 and 7.

English holly *(I. aquifolium)*

Chinese holly *(I. cornuta)* is much smaller and bushier than American holly. Dense and rounded, it grows from 5 to 15 feet tall and wide. Chinese holly berries are the largest of all the hollies and grow in clusters all over the plant. Unlike other hollies, female plants don't require the presence of male plants to set fruit, although the berries will be more plentiful if there is a male plant in the vicinity.

Holly, meserve *(Ilex ×meserveae)*

Features: Shiny red fruit and evergreen foliage
Growth rate: Slow
Zones: 4 to 8

Meserve holly *(Ilex ×meserveae)*

Description: These hybrid hollies offer all the pleasure of holly berries and evergreen foliage on dense, shrubby, rounded forms. More cold-hardy than other hollies, it's a great choice for northern gardens. They generally grow from 8 to 12 feet tall and wide and are extremely attractive to wildlife, especially robins, bluebirds, and mockingbirds.

Uses: Specimen, foundation, grouping, hedge, wildlife.
Site and care requirements: Plant in moist, acid, and well-drained soil. Give this holly a location in full sun to part shade where it is sheltered from winter wind and intense summer sun. Water consistently throughout the growing season, fertilize annually, and prune as necessary in spring before buds form for the following season.

Recommended varieties and related species: **'Blue Princess'** features dark red fruit and dark blue-green foliage. **'Blue Prince'** has a compact form and grows to 12 feet with dark green foliage. It is a top-notch pollinator, as is **'Blue Boy'.** **'China Boy'** and **'China Girl'** are extremely cold hardy.

Holly, inkberry *(Ilex glabra)*

Features: Black fruit and broadleaved evergreen foliage on a compact form
Growth rate: Slow to moderate
Zones: 4 to 10

Inkberry holly *(Ilex glabra)*

Description: Inkberry is a super choice for foundation planting and hedges across a broad range of climate zones, with its rich evergreen foliage and dense, compact form. The distinctive fruit ripens to black in the fall and remains on the plant throughout the winter. Excellent for massing, the broad, thick shrub grows to 8 feet tall and 10 to 12 feet wide.

Uses: Foundation, massing, hedges.
Site and care requirements: Plant in moist, well-drained soil in full sun to part shade. Pinch back to encourage dense growth. Shear the plant to shape a hedge; prune it to minimize legginess.

Recommended varieties and related species: Compact forms include **'Shamrock', 'Compacta',** and **'Nordic'.**

Honeylocust, thornless *(Gleditsia triacanthos inermis)*

Features: Fine-textured leaves, unusual fruit pods, and a pleasantly open, spreading form
Growth rate: Fast
Zones: 4 to 9

Thornless honeylocust *(Gleditsia triacanthos inermis)*

Description: A popular shade or specimen tree in eastern and midwestern landscapes, the thornless honeylocust has a graceful form and fine overall texture. Its delicate foliage creates filtered shade, allowing grass and other plants to grow beneath it. The leaves turn golden yellow in fall. The twisted 8- to 12-inch-long fruit pods appear in spring, turn brown and drop in fall and winter, and require cleanup. Adaptable to most any soil, the thornless honeylocust grows relatively quickly, reaching up to 60 feet tall and 45 feet wide. It is a desirable candidate for a landscape where improved shade is needed.
Uses: Specimen, shade.
Site and care requirements: Plant your thornless honeysuckle in moist soil and then water it consistently during its early years in your landscape. Mature trees tolerate adverse conditions, including poor soil, compacted soil, drought, and even flooding. Wrap young trees to protect their tender bark. The tree is susceptible to several cosmetic foliage problems (leaf spot and spider mites), as well as some serious diseases (trunk, bark, and twig cankers) and insects (foliage webworms and trunk borers). Fertilize in spring to shore up the tree's good health against these threats.
Recommended varieties and related species: 'Sunburst' has appealing lemon yellow foliage. Smaller and more compact 'Imperial' grows to 30 feet tall and wide. 'Shademaster', 'Skyline', and 'Majestic' are favorites.

Honeysuckle *(Lonicera* spp.)

Features: Deeply fragrant blooms on an adaptable, informal shrub
Growth rate: Fast
Zones: 3 to 9, depending on the variety

Honeysuckle *(Lonicera* spp.) and roses

Description: Honeysuckle is a tough, fragrant plant with widely ranging forms, from low and densely bushy to openly spreading to delicately billowy to vining. Take your pick. In the absence of flowers—the highlight of any type or variety—the foliage also varies from pretty to nondescript. Honeysuckles grow 4 to 15 feet high depending on the variety. Allow the plant's intended use and location to help you determine the most suitable variety.
Uses: Border, grouping, mass planting, screen, hedge.
Site and care requirements: Plant in well-drained soil and full sun to light shade. Water the plant consistently in the first few years, until it becomes established. From then on, it will be drought tolerant. Fertilize a young plant annually, and prune after flowering to maintain its desired shape. Honeysuckle tends to become invasive if not kept in check.
Recommended varieties and related species: Blueleaf honeysuckle *(L. korolkowii)* has delicate blue-green leaves and a delicate, arching form. Rose-color blooms appear in late spring. Although they are not fragrant, the flowers attract butterflies, hummingbirds, and bees. The blooms are followed by bright red berries in summer. This plant grows from 6 to 12 feet high in Zones 4 to 7 and tolerates some shade.

Tatarian honeysuckle
(L. tatarica) is popular for its hardiness and spring blooms that range from white to pink. It grows up to 10 feet tall and wide, and it can be invasive. Birds love the showy berries that appear in June. Tatarian honeysuckle is appropriate for an informal hedge or screen. While it is adaptable in most soils in Zones 3 to 8, it needs full sun to bloom well and may be susceptible to aphids.

Tatarian honeysuckle *(L. tatarica)*

Winter honeysuckle
(L. fragrantissima) features loads of tiny lemon-scented cream-color blooms that appear for almost a month from late winter into early spring. It has dark red berries and dark green foliage on an irregular, open form. Tough and adaptable, it grows up to 10 feet tall and 6 feet wide, in full sun to part shade in Zones 6 to 10. Try **Trumpet** *(Lonicera sempervirens)* or **'Goldflame'**.

Hornbeam, European *(Carpinus betulus)*

Features: Hardy, low-maintenance ornamental tree with a handsome oval form
Growth rate: Slow to moderate
Zones: 4 to 7

Description:
The European hornbeam's elegant oval form and distinctive slate gray bark make it a terrific specimen tree in the home landscape. It also works well in a grouping as a screen. The deep green foliage is dense and stays on the tree until late autumn, when it turns a pleasant golden yellow before falling. It grows 40 to 60 feet tall and 30 to 40 feet wide.

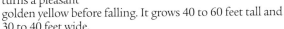

European hornbeam *(Carpinus betulus)*

Uses: Specimen, grouping, screen.
Site and care requirements: Plant in moist, well-drained, acid soil and full sun to light shade. Mulch around the tree to protect the bark from lawn equipment. Fertilize in spring. Prune in winter to shape a specimen or create a dense hedge.
Recommended varieties and related species:
'Globosa' is a more rounded and compact variety.
'Fastigiata' has a lovely upright form that makes it a good choice for smaller spaces.
American hornbeam *(C. caroliniana)*, or ironwood, is smaller and somewhat hardier than the European hornbeam, growing 15 to 20 feet tall in Zones 3 to 9. It has distinctive fall foliage that turns yellow to orange to scarlet.

Hornbeam bark

American hornbeam *(C. caroliniana)*

Horsechestnut, common *(Aesculus hippocastanum)*

Features: Showy flowers and a large, stately rounded form
Growth rate: Moderate
Zones: 4 to 7

Description:
This large, old-fashioned tree is common in the eastern half of the United States, the horsechestnut is impressive in stature. It has a dense canopy of dark green leaves that turn a fine yellow in fall. The white panicled springtime blooms are a favorite of hummingbirds and butterflies, though the spiny nuts that follow can be messy. It grows 50 to 70 feet tall and about as wide. With a tendency toward invasive roots, this tree needs room to grow far away from pavement or sidewalks.

Common horsechestnut *(Aesculus hippocastanum)*

Uses: Shade, wildlife.
Site and care requirements: Plant in moist, fertile, well-drained soil and full sun to part shade. Water as necessary to keep soil uniformly moist throughout the growing season, especially when the tree is young. Prune in early spring to remove dead branches. Dispose of fallen leaves in autumn to minimize fungal diseases, such as leaf blotch or powdery mildew, which might become problematic the following season.
Recommended varieties and related species:
'Baumannii' is an exceptional cultivar that does not produce the spiny fruit. **Red horsechestnut** *(A. ×carnea)* is a hybrid of the common horsechestnut and the red buckeye *(A. pavia)*. It features flashy red late-spring blooms. The red horsechestnut grows to 40 feet tall and 30 feet wide in Zones 4 to 8 and provides a handsome accent tree.

Red horsechestnut

Hydrangea, bigleaf *(Hydrangea macrophylla)*

Features: Spectacular late-summer flowers
Growth rate: Fast
Zones: 5 to 10, depending on the variety

Bigleaf hydrangea *(Hydrangea macrophylla 'Merritt's Beauty')*

Description: The appearance of the plush, showy, colorful blooms of the bigleaf hydrangea provides one of summer's most pleasant milestones. Ranging in color from white to pink to blue and purple, the flowers take over the otherwise unassuming rounded shrub and hold court over the garden for several weeks. Blooms take the form of either *lacecaps*, with a cluster of tiny flowers surrounded by larger flowers, or *hortensias,*

Bigleaf hydrangea
(H. macrophylla 'Nikko Blue')

which feature a cluster of same-size flowers. When not in bloom, the dark green foliage of bigleaf hydrangea offers minimal visual interest. Plant it among other shrubs that can pick up the aesthetic slack. The shrubs grow from 3 to 10 feet tall and wide, and works well in mixed shrub borders or grouped in foundation plantings. Hydrangea blooms make wonderful cut flowers, whether fresh or dried.

Uses: Specimen, foundation, border.

Hortensia-type blooms

Site and care requirements: Plant bigleaf hydrangeas in moist, fertile, well-drained soil and full sun. The plant variety and soil pH determine whether flowers tend toward pink or blue. For adaptable varieties and pink flowers, decrease soil acidity by applying lime to the soil; for blue flowers, add aluminum sulfate or peat moss to increase acidity. Water well and regularly because hydrangeas wilt during hot, dry periods. Mulching helps plants retain moisture. Fertilize once in early summer and prune right after flowering to remove flowerheads. Flowers bloom on the previous year's growth, so avoiding cutting back later.

Recommended varieties and related species: With hundreds of bigleaf hydrangea cultivars to consider, start by investigating those available and proven reliable in your region. Features that may influence your selection include color and type of bloom, color of foliage, hardiness, and the shrub's mature size. Some favorite hortensia-type bloomers include blue-flowering **'Endless Summer'**, **'Nikko Blue'**, and **'All Summer Beauty',** and the compact pink bloomers **'Forever Pink'** and **'Pia'**. **'Glowing Embers'** features cheerful red hortensia blooms. Lacecap favorites include **'Blue Billow'** and **'Mariesii',** which display dusty pink or pale blue flowers, depending on the soil pH.

Hydrangea, oakleaf *(Hydrangea quercifolia)*

Features: White flowers and oaklike leaves that offer distinctive fall color
Growth rate: Fast
Zones: 5 to 8

Oakleaf hydrangea *(Hydrangea quercifolia)*

Description: This fine shrub has handsome dark green oaklike foliage that turns burgundy and deep purple in autumn. Its white paniclelike blooms dry on the plant and remain until winter. The oakleaf hydrangea's roundish mounded form provides a strong presence whether placed singly in a shrub border or massed in a group, especially along a property edge. It grows to 6 feet high and 8 feet wide.

Oakleaf hydrangea in fall color

Uses: Specimen, border, massed grouping.

Site and care requirements: Plant in moist, fertile, well-drained acid soil in sun or part shade. In warmer zones it requires some shade. Mulch to help plant retain moisture.

Recommended varieties and related species: '**Snow Queen**' is a superior cultivar with oversized white flowers that point upward and deep red fall foliage. '**Snowflake**' has double flowers, while '**Pee Wee**' is a smaller shrub, growing under 4 feet tall, with fine flowers. '**Alice**' grows to 12 feet tall and wide and has oversized blooms that turn pink over time.

Hydrangea, panicle *(Hydrangea paniculata)*

Features: Panicled long-lasting midsummer blooms on a spreading form
Growth rate: Fast
Zones: 3 to 8

Panicle hydrangea *(Hydrangea paniculata* 'Grandiflora')

Description: This old-fashioned hydrangea distinguishes itself by its blooms, which appear in July and linger through the fall, going from white to a dusty pink to a rust color. The heavy flowers cause the branches to dip with their weight, which creates a pleasant, abundant effect. This large shrub, which grows to 20 feet tall and wide, can take the form of a small tree, depending on pruning habit. This hydrangea is hardier than others and works well in a mixed shrub border.

Uses: Specimen (if pruned to form a tree), border.

Site and care requirements: Plant in moist, rich, well-drained soil and sun to part shade. Prune to shape or tidy up dead stems in winter or early spring. This hydrangea blooms on new growth.

Recommended varieties and related species: '**Pink Diamond**' features pinkish blooms and easily reaches 20 feet tall. '**Grandiflora**' grows to a dense tree form and features a profusion of large blushing blooms.

Hydrangea, smooth *(Hydrangea arborescens)*

Features: Snowball-shape flowers and deep green foliage
Growth rate: Fast
Zones: 3 to 9

Smooth hydrangea *(Hydrangea arborescens* 'Annabelle')

Description: This low-growing hydrangea has a clumpy habit, but the lush round white blooms last from midsummer to early fall. The large dark green leaves are a handsome backdrop to the flowers, which go from lime green to white to brown over several weeks. Smooth hydrangeas work especially well in a grouping or a border, or as a specimen. It makes a handsome container plant.

Uses: Specimen, border, group, container.

Site and care requirements: Plant in moist, fertile, well-drained soil in part shade. Prune in winter or early spring to maintain the plant's compact shape. It blooms on new growth. Protect from exposure to extreme cold or wind.

Recommended varieties and related species: '**Annabelle**' is a superior cultivar that prefers full sun and features round snowball blooms up to a foot wide and a compact form that grows about 4 feet tall and wide. '**Grandiflora**' features smaller, less uniformly round, creamy white clusters that last through autumn.

***Ilex* spp.** (see Holly)
Ilex verticillata (see Winterberry, common)

Incense cedar, California *(Calocedrus decurrens)*

Features: A tall, columnar, formal shape and elegant evergreen leaves
Growth rate: Slow to moderate
Zones: 5 to 8

California incense cedar *(Calocedrus decurrens)*

Description:
The upright, slightly conical shape of this tree adds a certain refinement to the landscape. Along with the elegant evergreen foliage, the bark of the incense cedar becomes furrowed and peeling as the tree ages, adding additional appeal to the winter scenery. A bonus: The scent of cedar fills the air during the summer. California incense cedar grows from 30 to 50 feet tall and 8 to 10 feet wide. It proves adaptable to various soil conditions.
Uses: Accent, specimen, screen.
Site and care requirements: Plant in full sun to partial shade, and while it will adapt to many different types of soil, it grows best in moist, well-drained acid soil.
Recommended varieties and related species: The most common cultivar, **'Columnaris'**, has a narrower shape than the species. Try the dwarf variety, **'Compacta'**, which grows to about 6 feet tall. **'Aureovariegata'** has pretty yellow-variegated foliage.

Indian hawthorn *(Rhaphiolepis indica)*

Features: Spring blooms and evergreen foliage
Growth rate: Slow
Zones: 8 to 10

Description: Small, white or pink flowers dominate this versatile shrub in the spring, almost hiding the dark green, leathery leaves. Come fall the small, purplish black fruit emerges, almost hidden amongst the same leaves that were only the background to the flower. This shrub grows 4 to 6 feet high and wide, and the mounded habit lends itself to many landscape uses, from borders to groundcover.

Indian hawthorn *(Rhaphiolepis indica)*

Uses: Border, massing, hedge, groundcover.
Site and care requirements: It does best planted in full sun and moist, well-drained soil, but is adaptable to drier soil. It can be planted in partial shade, but its susceptibility to fire blight and leaf spot increases if the leaves don't dry fully when they get wet. Avoid wetting the leaves when watering.

Recommended varieties and related species: A larger form, ***R. umbrellata***, grows up to 6 feet tall with a similar spread. **'Minor'** and **'Enchantress'** are smaller version. For more interesting foliage color, plant **'Clara'**, whose new leaves emerge red.

Jacaranda *(Jacaranda mimosifolia)*

Features: A profusion of violet-blue flowers and fernlike leaves
Growth rate: Moderate
Zones: 9 to 11

Jacaranda *(Jacaranda mimosifolia)*

Description: The spectacular display of jacaranda flowers that bloom in the late spring continue into the summer. Its fernlike leaves give the tree a delicate appearance. The rounded, upright habit of a young tree develops into a more open, almost asymmetric form as it matures. The tree grows 25 to 50 feet high and 25 to 35 feet in width. Intolerant of salt, the jacaranda is not suitable to planting in coastal areas.
Uses: Ornamental, accent or shade.
Site and care requirements: Plant in full sun in sandy, well-drained soil. Planting it in partial shade results in fewer flowers.

Jacaranda bloom

Japanese aucuba (see Aucuba, Japanese)
Japanese camellia (see Camellia, Japanese)
Japanese cedar (see Cedar, Japanese)
Japanese kerria (see Kerria, Japanese)
Japanese pagoda tree (see Pagoda tree, Japanese)
Japanese pittosporum (see Pittosporum, Japanese)
Japanese snowbell (see Snowbell, Japanese)
Japanese stewartia (see Stewartia, Japanese)
Japanese umbrella pine (see Umbrella pine, Japanese)

Japanese zelkova (see Zelkova, Japanese)
Juglans nigra (see Walnut, black)
Juglans regia (see Walnut, English)
Juniperus spp. (see Juniper)
Juniperus virginiana (see Red cedar, eastern)

Juniper *(Juniperus* spp.)

Features: Infinitely versatile and adaptable evergreen shrub or tree
Growth rate: Slow to moderate
Zones: 2 to 10, depending on the species

Chinese juniper (*Juniperus chinensis* 'Hetzii')

Description: Junipers range in form from low-growing spreading groundcover to broad open mounds to upright trees, which means there is probably a juniper for every landscape situation, such as specimen, mass plantings, hedges, or foundation plantings. They have needle- or scalelike foliage, depending on the species, in all shades of green to blue. They are agreeable to just about any

Soft juniper foliage

soil and climate condition, generally requiring only a good start when they're planted and attention to common issues, such as bagworms, spider mites, and juniper blight.
Uses: Specimen, border, mass grouping, hedge, foundation, groundcover.
Site and care requirements: Plant in moist, well-drained soil in full sun. Water well when young; after established, junipers tend to prefer drier soil. Fertilize every spring with acid plant food, and trim spreading junipers in early summer to maintain size and proper growth habit. Tend to problems noted above through appropriate control of pests or cutting away of diseased areas.
Recommended varieties and related species: Chinese juniper (*J. chinensis*) is a favorite among the junipers. It features blue-green needlelike foliage on an open, spreading form. Plants range in size 5 to 50 feet tall and 5 to 20 feet wide, depending on the cultivar. They grow in dense spreading mounds, columnar or pyramidal upright forms, or as a low-growing cover, in Zones 4 to 10. **'Pfitzeriana'**

is a superior cultivar that's broad and sprawling, growing 4 to 6 feet tall and wide. **'Saybrook Gold'** has an upright, pyramidal habit, while **'San Jose'** is a dense, low form that grows 2 feet tall and up to 10 feet wide. **'Sea Green'** grows 6 to 8 feet tall and wide and features gracefully arching branches.

Common juniper (*J. communis* 'Depressa Aurea')

Common juniper (*J. communis*) has blue-green spiny foliage that turns a dull purple in winter. It generally grows 5 to 10 feet tall and 8 to 12 feet wide in Zones 2 to 7, depending on the cultivar. Favorites include: **'Depressa Aurea'**, with a fine low-growing spreading habit and golden green needles; **'Hibernica'**, which has a columnar form and grows to 15 feet tall; and **'Compressa'**, which has a dwarf conical form, growing only to 2 or 3 feet tall.

Shore juniper (*J. conferta* 'Blue Pacific')

Shore juniper (*J. conferta*), known as a dependable groundcover particularly in coastal areas, likes dry, sandy soil. Its prickly blue-green foliage and dense habit make it a good choice for barrier groundcover or planted on a slope. It grows up to 2 feet tall and 8 feet wide in Zones 6 to 10. **'Blue Pacific'** is favored for its fine green foliage and compact habit. **'Silver Mist'** has silvery needles and an appealing openly spreading habit.

Creeping juniper (*J. horizontalis*) features soft silvery blue-green needles on a low-spreading form. It grows 1 to 4 feet tall and as wide as 10 feet in Zones 3 to 9. Watch for juniper blight in this susceptible species. **'Bar Harbor'** and **'Blue Chip'** feature shades of silvery blue-green foliage that turns darker blue or purple in winter. **'Blue Rug'** resembles a flat, dense carpet.

Japanese garden juniper (*J. procumbens* 'Nana')

Japanese garden juniper (*J. procumbens*), another groundcover-type species, distinguished by its spreading tendency and stiff foliage, grows from 2 feet high to up to 12 feet wide in Zones 4 to 9. **'Nana'** features tiny foliage, grows only 1 foot tall, and drapes nicely over walls.

Savin juniper (*J. sabina tamariscifolia* 'New Blue')

Savin juniper (*J. sabina*) grows as a spreading groundcover or into a tall columnar form. It features bright green foliage that turns brown in winter. This hardy juniper is good for massing in groups or as groundcover over a large area in Zones 5 to 9. **'Broadmoor'** is a popular low-growing form that reaches only 1 or 2 feet tall and 6 feet wide. **'Arcadia'** is a true groundcover with bright green foliage.

Rocky Mountain juniper (*J. scopulorum* 'Skyrocket')

Rocky Mountain juniper (*J. scopulorum*) grows in an upright form 10 to 50 feet tall, depending on the culivar, in Zones 4 to 8. It has silvery or blue-green foliage and works well in a group as a screen or hedge, or alone as an accent. **'Skyrocket'** is a popular very narrow cypresslike form that grows as high as 12 feet. **'Tolleson's Weeping'** has a willowy habit, with silvery-blue stringy foliage. It reaches 20 feet tall and makes a fine accent plant.

Kalmia latifolia (see Mountain laurel)

Katsura tree *(Cercidiphyllum japonicum)*

Features: Colorful foliage from spring to fall, peeling bark, and a spreading silhouette to provide winter interest
Growth rate: Moderate
Zones: 4 to 8

Description:
Katsura is a four-season tree. Springtime brings the emergence of its leaves in all their reddish purple splendor. As summer approaches the leaves change again, turning the tree into a dense, blue-green wonder that provides plenty of shade. In the fall, the tree's foliage turns golden yellow to apricot, bringing with it a spicy fragrance that scents the autumn air.

Katsura tree *(Cercidiphyllum japonicum)*

When the leaves fall, the attractive trunk and branches, along with gray peeling bark, add interest to the winter landscape. Katsura grows 40 to 60 feet high and wide and has a shallow, spreading root system that needs plenty of unimpeded room to grow. While pyramidal-shape in youth, the mature tree takes on a more open, spreading form, which can be either rounded or pyramidal in shape and gives the scenery some winter interest when the leaves are gone. Young katsura trees are susceptible to sunscald or splitting bark in colder temperatures.

Katsura tree spring foliage

Uses: Specimen, shade in large yards or parks.
Site and care requirements: Plant in the spring in full sun or partial shade in moist, well-drained soil. Water young trees regularly during times of drought and mulch well, as the younger trees aren't as drought tolerant as the mature tree. Plant in an area protected from the wind and prune only to shape the tree when young.
Recommended varieties and related species: **'Pendula'** is a smaller, weeping variety. **'Ruby'** is a dwarf form that grows only to about 30 feet tall. The leaves of **'Aureum'** turn yellow during the summer instead of the regular blue-green.

Kerria, Japanese *(Kerria japonica)*

Features: Bright yellow blooms and green winter stems
Growth rate: Slow to moderate
Zones: 5 to 9

Japanese kerria *(Kerria japonica)*

Description: Late April and May bring vivid yellow blooms, with periodic blooms throughout the summer. The green leaves can turn a yellowish green in autumn, but when they fall the bright green stems are revealed, bringing a delightfully unique color to the plant and to the winter landscape. The upright, slightly mounded form makes the kerria useful in a shrub border or in shadier spots in the yard. Kerria grows 3 to 6 feet high and 6 to 9 feet wide.
Uses: Shrub border, massing, grouping.
Site and care requirements: Plant in full sun to partial shade, but flowers blooming in full sun will tend to bleach out. Kerria will tolerate almost any soil as long as it is well-drained. Prune the shrub right after flowering. It flowers on new growth. Cut the plant to the ground to rejuvenate it.
Recommended varieties and related species: **'Kin Kan'** stems turn yellow instead of green in winter. **'Picta'** has white variegated leaves and is a slightly smaller plant. **'Shannon'** and **'Golden Guinea'** produce single blooms, while **'Plenifora'** has double flowers.

Koelreuteria paniculata (see Goldenraintree)
Kolkwitzia amabilis (see Beautybush)

Laburnum ×watereri (see Goldenchain tree)
Lagerstroemia indica (see Crape myrtle)

Larch, European (*Larix decidua*)

Features: Lovely pyramidal shape with golden yellow fall color
Growth rate: Moderate to fast
Zones: 2 to 6

European larch (*Larix decidua*) fall color

Description:
The uniformly pyramidal shape of the young tree is an attractive addition to the landscape. Its shape becomes more irregular and open as the tree matures but pruning helps

New larch foliage

maintain the youthful form. The spectacular golden yellow to orange needles in the fall virtually set the tree alight with color before they drop for the winter. The tree grows from 70 to 75 feet high and 25 to 30 feet wide. Intolerant of air pollution and dry, alkaline soil, the European larch is also susceptible to larch casebearer in the Northeast.
Uses: Specimen, grouping.
Site and care requirements: Plant in full sun to partial shade in moist, well-drained soil. Prune in winter to retain shape.
Recommended varieties and related species: '**Fastigiata**' has a narrower, more columnar form. '**Pendula**' has a weeping form.

Japanese larch (*L. kaempferi*) grows 50 to 70 feet tall and about half as wide. It grows best in Zones 4 to 7, favoring warmer climates than the Eastern larch. The needles also turn a beautiful golden yellow in the fall, but this species of larch has a more open, pyramidal growth habit.

Japanese larch (*L. kaempferi*)

Larix decidua (see Larch, European)
Larix laricina (see Tamarack)

Lavender, English (*Lavandula angustifolia*)

Features: Evergreen shrub with aromatic spikes of purple flowers
Growth rate: Slow
Zones: 5 to 8

English lavender (*Lavandula angustifolia*)

Description: This shrub produces intensely fragrant purple flowers that bloom in summer. The blue-green to silvery green leaves are highly fragrant as well. It grows 1 to 2 feet high and 2 to 3 feet wide. The rounded growth habit makes it a pretty, aromatic addition in a shrub border or as a low hedge. It works well in mixed perennial plantings, herb beds, and rock gardens.
Uses: Shrub border, hedge, herb garden.
Site and care requirements: Plant in full sun in drier, well-drained soil. Do not overwater lavender. Prune flower stalks when blooms begin to turn brown.
Recommended varieties and related species: '**Rosea**' has pink flowers, while '**Hidcote**' has deep purple blooms. A more cold hardy variety, '**Nana**,' has traditional lavender purple flowers and cold hardiness.

Leptospermum scoparium (see Tea tree, New Zealand)

Leucothoe, drooping (*Leucothoe fontanesiana*)

Features: Evergreen shrub with graceful, drooping branches
Growth rate: Slow to moderate
Zones: 5 to 8

Drooping leucothoe (*Leucothoe fontanesiana*)

Description: Long, dark green leaves grace the limbs of this beautiful shrub. It grows 3 to 6 feet high and wide with a drooping, almost flowing yet mounded growth habit. White flowers bloom in spring but are usually hidden by the profuse foliage. The shrub can be temperamental if not planted in acid, moist, well-drained soil. Sensitive to wind, hot sun, and drought, the shrub must be sited in a protected area. Climate stress makes drooping leucothoe susceptible to leaf spot.
Uses: Border, foundation planting.
Site and care requirements: Plant this shrub in partial to full shade in moist, acid, well-drained soil. Prune drooping leucothoe to manage its height and shape.
Recommended varieties and related species: '**Nana**' is a dwarf variety that grows to about 2 feet high. '**Scarletta**' boasts foliage that emerges glossy, reddish purple in the spring and an even deeper maroon color in the fall. '**Girard's Rainbow**' has variegated foliage in combinations of white, copper, and pink.

Ligustrum **spp.** (see Privets)

Lilac, common *(Syringa vulgaris)*

Features: Ultrafragrant spring blooms and dark green foliage
Growth rate: Moderate
Zones: 3 to 7

Common lilac *(Syringa vulgaris)*

Description: The fragrant blooms on this upright, leggy shrub scent the spring air. Blooming in May, the flowers range from white to rose, pinkish purple, lilac, and deep purple. Once the blooms fade, the dark green foliage

Common lilac 'Alba'

remains until fall but may become sprinkled with powdery mildew during summer's hot, humid weather. Common lilacs grow 8 to 15 feet high and 6 to 12 feet wide.
Uses: Shrub border, specimen for the fragrance.
Site and care requirements: Plant in full sun in well-drained soil for best results. Deadhead the flowers for best flowering and prune to renew the shrub when necessary.
Recommended varieties and related species: There are hundreds of cultivars of common lilac, but try **'Avalanche'** or **'Edith Cavell'** for white flowers, **'President Grevy'** for blue flowers, or **'Krasavitsa'** for pink flowers. **'Katherine Havemeyer'** and **'Charles Joly'** produce pinkish purple to red-purple blooms. Choose a cultivar based on its size,

bloom color, and growth habit to best fit your landscape needs.
Korean early lilac *(S. oblata dilatata)* is a similar species to common lilac but it blooms earlier and is more cold hardy (to Zones 2 and 3). Cultivars of Korean early lilac include **'Maiden's Blush'** with pink blooms or **'Mount Baker'** with white flowers. Choose **'Pocahontas'** for hard-to-find deep purple blooms.

Lilac, meyer *(Syringa meyeri)*

Features: Dense, mounded growth habit with a profusion of fragrant, lilac-colored blooms
Growth rate: Slow
Zones: 4 to 7

Meyer lilac *(Syringa meyeri* 'Palibin')

Description: An abundance of pink to purple flowers and a smaller, rounded growth habit make this shrub a wonderful addition to the landscape. Meyer lilac blooms form on 4-inch-long panicles and nearly cover the entire plant in May. The dense foliage of the meyer lilac brings a welcome fullness to a shrub border or mass planting. It grows 4 to 8 feet high and 6 to 10 feet wide.
Uses: Shrub border, mass planting.
Site and care requirements: Plant a meyer lilac in full sun and well-drained soil. This shrub does not tolerate wet soil.
Recommended varieties and related species: **'Palibin'** grows up to 5 feet high and up to 7 feet wide with pink blooms. A related species, **littleleaf lilac** *(S. microphylla)*, grows up to 5 feet high and features pink flowers that bloom periodically throughout late summer and into fall. **'Superba'** is a cultivar of littleleaf lilac that features pretty pink blooms.
Korean lilac *(S. patula)* is another related species of meyer lilac. **'Miss Kim'**, a larger form of **'Palibin'**, showcases the same flowers and foliage but grows to about 8 feet high and wide.

Linden, American *(Tilia americana)*

Features: A stately, well-formed tree with deep green foliage
Growth rate: Moderate
Zones: 2 to 8

American linden *(Tilia americana)*

Silver linden *(T. tomentosa)*

rounded shape as is matures. The leaves are smaller than other lindens, developing from dark green in spring and summer to yellow in the fall. This tree grows best in Zones 3 to 7. Good candidates include **'Chancellor'**, **'Glenleven'**, and **'Greenspire'**.

Silver linden *(T. tomentosa)*, has dark green, glossy leaves with silvery undersides. After leaf fall the tree's silvery bark enhances the winter landscape. It grows 50 to 75 feet tall and 25 to 45 feet wide and the dense, pyramidal growth habit becomes more rounded with age. The silver linden makes an outstanding specimen tree in lawns and along streetsides. Its dense canopy does not encourage underplanting. The tree tolerates drought, heat, and pollution better than most lindens, and grows best in Zones 4 to 7. **'Green Mountain'** is a dense, fast-growing variety. **'Sterling Silver'** shows off both the silvery leaves and bark of the species.

Description: The strong, pyramidal form of the American linden lends itself to planting in a larger landscape. It grows from 60 to 80 feet high with a spread of 20 to 40 feet wide. It lives from 100 to 150 years and develops into a more rounded shape as it matures. Dark green leaves showcase fragrant, pale yellow flowers in the summer, followed by small brown fruit in the fall. The leaves turn yellowish brown in the fall before dropping to reveal the tree's striking winter silhouette.
Uses: Specimen, shade.
Site and care requirements: Plant the tree in full sun and deep, moist, well-drained soil. The American linden tolerates clay soil; it benefits from deep watering in dry summers.
Recommended varieties and related species: Littleleaf linden *(T. cordata,)* is a good tree for shade or street planting. Growing 60 to 70 feet high and 30 to 45 feet wide, it has a dense, pyramidal form when young, growing into a more

Littleleaf linden *(T. cordata)* in winter

Locust, black *(Robinia pseudoacacia)*

Features: Hardy tree with fragrant spring flowers that's suitable for poor soil
Growth rate: Moderate to fast
Zones: 3 to 8

Description: Adaptable to nearly all soils, black locust is a good choice for a variety of difficult growing conditions. It will tolerate poor, sandy, and infertile soil as well as salt exposure. The fragrant white flowers bloom in spring, giving way to seeds that drop and grow quickly on surrounding soil. It grows from 30 to 50 feet high and up to 30 feet wide. The upright, rounded growth habit showcases the deep blue-green leaves. The fall foliage is yellowish brown, but after it drops, the deeply grooved brown bark is revealed for the winter.

Black locust *(Robinia pseudoacacia)*

Uses: Large landscapes with poor or infertile soil.
Site and care requirements: Will adapt to almost any soil but it should be planted in full sun for best success.
Recommended varieties and related species: **'Frista'** has golden yellow foliage that turns green in the summer heat. **'Umbraculifera'**, or umbrella black locust, has a rounded, globelike form that grows 15 to 20 feet tall.

Lonicera **spp.** (see Honeysuckle)

Maackia, amur *(Maackia amurensis)*

Features: Extremely cold tolerant with attractive peeling bark
Growth rate: Slow
Zones: 4 to 7

Amur maackia *(Maackia amurensis)*

Description: This small tree survives harsh winter temperatures. The orangey brown, peeling bark adds interesting texture to the winter landscape. The foliage has a velvety appearance and may turn yellow in the fall. Creamy white flowers bloom in midsummer, offsetting the dark green foliage. The tree may grow too slowly for some people but the rounded form and attractive bark reward patience. Amur maackia grows 20 to 30 feet high with a spread of 20 to 40 feet.
Uses: Specimen, street tree.
Site and care requirements: Plant the tree in full sun and loamy, moist, well-drained soil. Prune in the winter to maintain its shape.
Recommended varieties and related species: Hard-to-find **Chinese maackia** *(M. chinensis)* has less cold tolerance.

Maclura pomifera (see Osage orange)

Madrone, Pacific *(Arbutus menziesii)*

Features: Showy, peeling bark and small white flowers
Growth rate: Slow
Zones: 8 to 9

Description: Cinnamon-colored bark peels away to reveal the copper-toned bark underneath. This evergreen tree bears glossy, deep green leaves that contrast nicely to the arching

Pacific madrone *(Arbutus menziesii)*

Pacific madrone bark

clusters of fragrant white flowers. The spring flowers give way to orangey red fruit that is appealing to both birds and deer. The fruit matures in autumn and stays on the tree through the winter. While the tree is an evergreen, it sheds its leaves every two years as new foliage emerges. The old leaves turn a brilliant red before they fall, providing a bonus, out-of-season show in the spring. It grows from 20 to 50 feet high and wide in an upright growth habit. The crown becomes more rounded as the tree matures.
Uses: Specimen.
Site and care requirements: Plant in full sun to partial shade in moist, well-drained soil. Add organic matter before planting, and topdress twice a year while the tree is young.
Recommended varieties and related species: The smaller

Strawberry tree *(A. unedo)* fruit

strawberry tree *(A. unedo)* grows 15 to 30 feet tall. It bears unusual bright orange rough-textured berries after flowering from October to December. It needs acid soil and a dry climate.

Mahonia aquifolium (see Grapeholly, Oregon)

Magnolia, bigleaf *(Magnolia macrophylla)*

Features: Large fragrant flowers and large, handsome leaves
Growth rate: Slow
Zones: 5 to 9

Bigleaf magnolia *(Magnolia macrophylla)*

Description: Oversize leaves—12 to 32 inches long—are the hallmark of the bigleaf magnolia. The light green leaves have an underside that is slightly silvery, so the dual color of the foliage creates an eye-catching accent to the landscape. When it blooms in June, the 8- to 10-inch fragrant flowers stand out nicely against the leaves. The rose-color fruit that grows after flowering becomes visible in the early fall. Fruits are large—growing up to 3 inches long—and attracts birds. The upright, rounded habit is somewhat open, and this tree grows 25 to 40 feet high and 15 to 20 feet wide. It is quite a task to find the right space for a large tree with leaves that produce a significant amount of litter, but in wide-open spaces, this is a beauty. Magnolias in general are susceptible to nectaria canker, heart rot, and whiteflies.
Uses: Accent or specimen for large areas.
Site and care requirements: Plant in sun to partial shade and moist, well-drained, acid soil. Incorporate plenty of organic material into the soil when planting. To prevent disease and insect infestation, keep tree well-watered and free from trunk damage.
Recommended varieties and related species: Other large-leafed species are **Fraser magnolia** *(M. fraseri)*, **Ashe magnolia** *(M. ashei)*, and **umbrella tree magnolia** *(M. tripetala)*.

Magnolia, saucer *(Magnolia ×soulangeana)*

Features: Large, magnificent flowers on a smaller tree
Growth rate: Moderate to moderately fast
Zones: 5 to 9

Description: The large, saucer-shape flowers bloom in early spring and bring their pinkish-purple beauty to an emerging spring landscape. The flowers can continue blooming throughout the summer, and even into the winter if mild weather persists. More cold hardy than other magnolias, it is a popular choice for more northern areas through Zone 5. The upright, rounded habit of this tree makes it a lovely accent in

Saucer magnolia *(Magnolia ×soulangeana)*

the landscape, even without the showy flowers. A smaller magnolia, this tree reaches up to 20 to 30 feet high, with a spread of 15 to 25 feet. Frost may kill off the early spring blooms, so it needs to be planted in a protected area—preferably a northern exposure—so that the blooms will have a chance to defrost at a slower rate to lessen the damage.
Uses: Specimen, ornamental, accent.
Site and care requirements: Plant in full sun in a northern exposure and in moist, well-drained soil. It will adapt to many different soil conditions.
Recommended varieties and related species: **'Brozzonii'** boasts large flowers that bloom a bit later in the spring, reducing the chance of frost damage. **'Alexandrina'** flowers early, producing lighter pink-purple blooms. **'Rustica Rubra'** has blooms that are darker and open a bit later in spring, and **'Picture'** features reddish purple flowers with white inside the bloom.

Magnolia, southern *(Magnolia grandiflora)*

Features: Large, fragrant flowers and evergreen foliage
Growth rate: Moderate
Zones: 7 to 10

Southern magnolia *(Magnolia grandiflora)*

Description: The southern magnolia produces the largest flowers of any magnolia tree—5 to 12 inches wide—but they are fleeting, lasting only a few days once they've bloomed. The creamy white flowers are deeply fragrant, providing a lemony scent that fills the air in late May to June. The leaves supply their own interest to the landscape. Their glossy green tops are accented by the downy-looking, reddish-brown color beneath. Some of the leaves will fall during the summer, but are continuously replaced with new ones. Yard litter may be a consideration when choosing a site for this tree. It grows 60 to 80 feet high, with a mature spread of up to 40 feet. The pyramidal, somewhat oval growth habit makes this a good choice as an ornamental or specimen tree for the landscape.

Uses: Ornamental, specimen, or shade.

Site and care requirements: Plant in full sun to partial shade, as a bit of shade may help in reducing stress from drought. It will do well in just about any type of soil, but does best in a moist, well-drained site.

Magnolia, star *(Magnolia stellata)*

Features: Very fragrant, star-shape blooms on a smaller tree
Growth rate: Slow
Zones: 4 to 8

Star magnolia *(Magnolia stellata)*

Description: In March and April the magnificent flowers bloom on this tree, making it look like it's covered with white stars. Carrying a lovely fragrance, these double blooms persist for up to 20 days, providing a lengthy spectacle compared to other magnolias. The blooms are susceptible to frost damage, due to their early-spring blooming. The dark green leaves that replace the blooms give the landscape wonderful color throughout summer, as does the attractive gray bark in winter. This tree grows only 15 to 20 feet tall and has a mature spread of 10 to 15 feet. The low-growing, openly pyramidal shape, along with its smaller size, make this magnolia sometimes resemble a large shrub. It is one of the most cold- and heat-tolerant of all the magnolias.

Uses: Specimen, accent, ornamental.

Site and care requirements: Plant in full sun to partial shade and moist, well-drained soil. Choose a site with northern exposure to reduce the risk of frost damage to the tender blooms.

Recommended varieties and related species: 'Waterlily' has pink buds that bloom into white flowers. 'Royal Star' has a slow, shrubbier growth habit with early spring blooms. 'Centential' is a very cold-hardy variety with large, white blooms.

Magnolia, sweet bay *(Magnolia virginiana)*

Features: Fragrant white late-spring blooms and aromatic dark green leaves
Growth rate: Moderate to fast
Zones: 5 to 9

Sweet bay magnolia *(Magnolia virginiana)*

Description: Creamy white flowers with an almost waxy appearance bloom in May and June, bringing with them a light, lemony scent. The dark green leaves are silvery underneath, and also are fragrant when touched. This magnolia can be deciduous, evergreen, or in-between, depending on the climatic zone—evergreen in warmer climates to fully deciduous in colder climates. It grows 10 to 20 feet high and wide, with a shrubby, vaselike growth habit.

Uses: Specimen, shrub border.

Site and care requirements: Plant in full sun to partial shade and moist, well-drained soil. It will do well in a variety of soils, including wet sites.

Recommended varieties and related species: 'Henry Hicks' is an evergreen tree with larger flowers.

Mahonia, leatherleaf *(Mahonia bealei)*

Features: Yellow flowers in winter and vibrant blue fruit in summer
Growth rate: Moderate
Zones: 7 to 9

Description: This evergreen shrub is a shade-loving favorite of many Southern gardeners, who appreciate the fragrant yellow flower clusters that bloom in winter and the bright blue fruit that attracts birds in summer. The large, glossy, prickly blue-green leaves are very hollylike and grow to a foot long, with up to 15 spiny leaflets. The shrub grows 4 to 8 feet tall and 4 to 6 feet wide. The multistemmed, upright form makes for a striking, shade and drought tolerant addition to the landscape.

Uses: Accent in a shady spot, attacts birds.

Site and care requirements: Plant in shade to partial shade and moist, well-drained, acid soil. Protect from severe winds.

Leatherleaf mahonia *(Mahonia bealei)*

Malus **hybrids** (see Apple)
Malus **spp.** (see Crabapple, flowering)

Maple, amur *(Acer ginnala)*

Features: Early leafing, fragrant flowers, and brilliant red fall foliage

Growth rate: Moderate

Zones: 3 to 8

Amur maple *(Acer tataricum ginnala)*

Description: One of the earliest leafing of the maples, the amur maple begins showing leaves in April and May. The fragrant, white flowers bloom at the same time, giving way to red-winged fruit in late summer to early fall. The fall leaves turn a brilliant red to sometimes yellowish orange, providing a spectacular show. It grows 15 to 20 feet tall and wide, with a rounded, often multistemmed growth habit. It can be grown as a single or multistemmed small tree or multistemmed shrub. This tree withstands winds and drought well.

Uses: Specimen, especially in small landscapes.

Site and care requirements: Plant in full sun to light shade. Amur maple tolerates a variety of soil types, including dry and alkaline soils.

Recommended varieties and related species: 'Flame' is a smaller variety that boasts the classic red fruit and foliage.

Maple, Japanese *(Acer palmatum)*

Features: Colorful foliage and graceful form

Growth rate: Slow

Zones: 5 to 8

Japanese maple *(Acer palmatum)*

Description: Elegantly shaped leaves cover a graceful form that in itself gives the winter landscape appeal. Some Japanese maples have a low-growing, weeping habit, while others are decidedly upright, but all boast a spreading form that makes a statement in the landscape, especially in winter. The fall foliage ranges from yellow to orange and red, and makes a striking

impression. The pointed lobes of the leaves give a delicate look to the foliage, which is complemented by small, reddish-purple flowers that bloom in the spring.

Uses: Accent, container, ornamental, specimen, mixed flower or shrub border.

Site and care requirements: Plant in full sun to part shade, which can boost the color of the foliage. Protect from sun scorch by planting in areas with morning sun and partial afternoon shade. Plant in moist, well-drained, acid soil high in organic matter. Prune to retain shape or to remove some inside branches to allow more light and air.

Recommended varieties and related species: 'Bloodgood' and 'Moonfire' have deep red to purple spring and summer foliage that turns a brilliant red in the fall. 'Sango Kaku' has yellow fall foliage and fiery orange-red stems in winter.

Cutleaf Japanese maple *(A. palmatum dissectum)* is a smaller Japanese maple, growing only to about 6 feet high and 4 to 6 feet wide and is hardy in Zones 5 to 8. The delicate, finger-shape leaves are the trademark of the cutleaf maple, giving this tree an elegant silhouette.

Full moon maple *(A. japonicum)* is hardy in Zones 5 to 7. It grows 20 to 30 feet high and wide, with a rounded, upright growth habit. The bright yellow and red fall foliage, in addition to the attractive gray bark, makes this a good choice for fall and winter interest. 'Aureum' has yellow leaves throughout the season, while 'Vitifolium' boasts yellow to orangey-red to purple fall foliage.

Maple, Norway *(Acer platanoides)*

Features: Yellow flowers in early spring and brilliant fall foliage

Growth rate: Moderate

Zones: 3 to 7

Norway maple *(Acer platanoides)*

Description: Small yellow flowers cover this maple even before the foliage emerges. The dark green leaves turn a vivid yellow to deep red in fall before dropping to reveal the striking, grooved bark that provides winter interest. A shallow root system limits the siting to areas at least 6 feet away from pavement and will compete with grass and other plantings for moisture. Norway maple is tolerant of air pollution and is a good choice for urban areas. It grows 40 to 50 feet high and wide with a rounded growth habit.

Uses: Shade.

Site and care requirements: Plant in virtually any soil and protect from sunscald.

Recommended varieties and related species: 'Crimson King' has purplish summer foliage that fades to a soft maroon red in fall. 'Summershade' has a more upright growth habit and is heat-resistant. 'Deborah' and 'Fairview' reverse the usual foliage color progression from red in summer to a light green in fall.

Maple, paperbark *(Acer griseum)*

Features: Reddish brown, peeling bark and brilliant red fall foliage
Growth rate: Slow
Zones: 4 to 8

Paperbark maple *(Acer griseum)*

Description: Winter landscapes are greatly enhanced by the cinnamon-brown, peeling bark. The blue-green leaves turn a radiant red in autumn with the best color found in the eastern United States. Grows 20 to 30 feet tall and wide with an open, rounded growth habit. This tree is tolerant of either acid or alkaline clay soil so it is appropriate for many different sites. It is not a drought-tolerant tree, however.
Uses: Specimen, shrub border, groupings.
Site and care requirements: Plant in full sun to partial shade in moist, well-drained soil.
Recommended varieties and related species: **Threeflower maple** *(A. triflorum)* also has peeling bark, though less impressive, and can be grown in Zones 5 to 7.

Maple, red *(Acer rubrum)*

Features: Early yellow to red fall foliage
Growth rate: Moderate to fast
Zones: 3 to 9

Red maple *(Acer rubrum)*

Description: The red-tinged, green spring foliage turns a true green in summer then brilliant yellow to fiery red in the fall. Red flowers bloom in early spring, giving way to red fruit in the summer. During the winter the stems turn red, so together with the smooth, gray bark, this tree is a winner in the winter landscape. The upright, rounded growth habit makes this a great choice for a shade tree or as a street tree. It grows 40 to 60 feet high and 20 to 30 feet wide.
Uses: Shade, specimen.
Site and care requirements: Plant in full sun in moist, rich, well-drained soil. It does best in wet sites but will tolerate typical summer (though not extreme) drought conditions. Prune only to maintain shape.
Recommended varieties and related species: **'Indian Summer'** produces the wonderful fall foliage, but is not a heat-resistant variety. **'Red Sunset'** and **'October Glory'** boast the trademark fall color, as does **'Autumn Flame'**, which has a smaller size (up to 35 feet tall) that makes it appealing for the smaller yard.

Maple, silver *(Acer saccharinum)*

Features: Green leaves with silvery-white undersides and a distinctive upright form
Growth rate: Fast
Zones: 3 to 9

Silver maple *(Acer saccharinum)*

Description: This fast-growing maple will reach a height of 50 to 70 feet, with a width of 30 to 45 feet. The distinctly upright branches grow into a vaselike form, making this an attractive addition to the landscape. The silvery-white undersides of the leaves add interest and color to the scenery, especially when in motion in a gentle wind. The red flowers bloom in spring, set amongst the deep green leaves. Summer color gives way to dazzling yellow fall foliage. The vigorous root system can cause problems when planted near sidewalks, driveways and sewer lines. Branches are somewhat weak and are prone to storm damage.
Uses: Quick shade.
Site and care requirements: Plant in full sun to partial shade and deep, moist, well-drained soil, but this tree will also tolerate a variety of soil conditions.
Recommended varieties and related species: **'Silver Queen'** is a fruitless variety, and slightly more rounded, but with all the other attributes of the species.

Maple, sugar *(Acer saccharum)*

Features: Spectacular fall foliage and sap that is used to make maple syrup
Growth rate: Moderate
Zones: 4 to 7

Sugar maple *(Acer saccharum)*

Description: There are few rivals to the sugar maple when it comes to fall foliage. The blazing yellow, orange, or red leaves are almost the definition of autumn color. The oval, upright growth habit lends an elegant shape to the landscape, making this an excellent choice for a shade tree. Sugar maple is not tolerant of road salt and should not be planted near the street. It is not drought tolerant, so plant it in a moist spot or water regularly in drier regions.
Uses: Shade or specimen in a large yard.
Site and care requirements: This tree does not tolerate compacted soil. Plant in full sun to partial shade and moist, deep, well-drained soil. Mulch to retain moisture.
Recommended varieties and related species: **'Commemoration'** and **'Green Mountain'** grow rapidly, have deep green, waxy leaves, and are heat tolerant. **'Bonfire'** has lovely red fall color, and **'Green Column'** has a more upright, columnar form. **'Mill Majesty'** also grows rapidly and had reddish-orange fall foliage.

Mediterranean fan palm (see Palm, Mediterranean fan)
Metasequoia glyptostroboides (see Dawn redwood)

Mexican orange *(Choisya ternata)*

Features: Fragrant
white blooms and
deep green
evergreen foliage
Growth rate: Moderate
Zones: 8 to 10

Mexican orange *(Choisya ternata)*

Description: The
fragrant white flowers
bloom in early spring,
continue for a month or
more, then bloom again
intermittently through
the summer. The shiny,
deep green foliage nicely
complements the showy
white blooms. This
plant grows 6 to 8 feet
tall and wide with a compact, rounded growth habit. Use in
areas where the almondlike aroma of the flowers can be fully
appreciated. This shrub is drought tolerant.
Uses: Shrub border, container.
Site and care requirements: Plant in full sun in coastal
areas with cooler summers, or in partial shade in areas with
hot summers. It will grow thin and bear fewer flowers if
planted in too much shade. Plant in well-drained, acid soil
enriched with plenty of organic material. Prune to maintain
shape or size.
Recommended varieties and related species: 'Sundance'
features golden foliage.

Mimosa (see Silk tree)

Mirror plant *(Coprosma repens)*

Features: Vibrant, shiny oval
leaves
Growth rate: Fast
Zones: 9 to 10

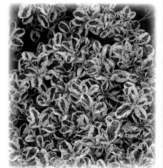

Mirror plant *(Coprosma repens*
'Marble Queen')

Description: Plump, shiny
leaves are the crowning glory
of the mirror plant. It also
produces attractive orange-
red berries in late summer to
fall. The upright, loose form
makes this a good choice for
hedges, screens, or
foundation plantings.
It grows 6 to 10 feet tall and
6 to 8 feet wide but may be
pruned to maintain a smaller size. It is drought and salt
tolerant when it has become established and is susceptible
to root rot if too wet.
Uses: Hedge, foundation planting, screening, espalier, rock
garden planting.
Site and care requirements: Plant in just about any soil as
long as it is well-drained. Plant in full sun in cooler coastal
areas and in partial shade in areas with hot summers. Protect
from frost.
Recommended varieties and related species: A dwarf variety,
'Marble Queen', has white variegated leaves. **'Variegata'** has
grayish green variegated leaves and bears white fruit.

Mockorange, sweet *(Philadelphus coronarius)*

Features: Fragrant white flowers that bloom in late spring
Growth rate: Fast
Zones: 4 to 8

Sweet mockorange *(Philadelphus coronarius)*

Description: Small,
sweetly scented flowers
bloom in late spring to
summer against dark
green foliage. This
shrub is appreciated
most for the aromatic
blooms; when it is not
flowering the foliage
is unremarkable.
So plant where you
can smell the blooms—
near windows,
walkways and
entryways. Sweet
mockorange grows
10 to 12 feet high and
8 to 10 feet wide. The
dense, rounded growth habit can become unkempt looking.
It is drought and wind tolerant.
Uses: Walkways, borders, entryways.
Site and care requirements: Plant in full sun to partial
shade in virtually any type of soil, but does best in moist,
well-drained soil. Prune after flowering or cut to the ground.
Recommended varieties and related species: 'Aureus'
has yellow foliage that turns greener in the summer.
'Variegatus' has variegated, creamy white leaves and the
typical fragrant blooms. **'Galahad'** is a variety that grows
only about 5 feet tall and wide.

Mountain ash, European *(Sorbus aucuparia)*

Features: Vivid orange-red fruit and attractive foliage
Growth rate: Moderate
Zones: 3 to 7

European mountain ash *(Sorbus aucuparia)*

Description:
Also known as the
rowan tree, this
plant has a lot to
offer. Brilliant
orange-red fruit
clusters make a
spectacular early
autumn display
that is its top
attribute. Dark
green leaves
comprised of 7 to
15 leaflets emerge
in spring, just
ahead of the
clusters of creamy
white flowers in
May. Then all is
quiet until the
orange-red berries
ripen in late
summer to early fall, to the delight of birds, which make quick
work of devouring the berries. The leaves turn a yellow to a red-
purple in later autumn before falling to reveal glossy gray bark
in winter. It grows from 20 to 40 feet high and 15 to 30 feet

wide, which makes it useful for shade. This plant starts out as an upright, oval growth tree and then adopts a rounder shape as it matures.

Uses: Specimen, shade.

Site and care requirements: Plant in full sun and moist, slightly acid, well-drained soil. Prune out portions hit by fire blight, to which this shrub is susceptible.

Recommended varieties and related species: '**Pendula**' is a weeping form, while '**Fastigiata**' has a narrower, upright growth habit. Plant '**Edulis**' for larger berries.

Mountain currant (see Currant, alpine)

Mountain laurel (*Kalmia latifolia*)

Features: Beautiful clusters of white, pink, or red flowers that bloom in early summer

Growth rate: Slow

Zones: 4 to 8

Description:
This lovely evergreen shrub boasts glossy green leaves that are an ideal background for the showy flowers. But even before the flowers bloom, the color and shape of the buds add interest. The buds resemble tiny star fruit but are a vibrant pink or red before they

Mountain laurel (*Kalmia latifolia* 'Kaleidoscope')

burst open into the bowl-shape blooms. Flower color ranges from white to pink to red. Mountain laurel grows 7 to 15 feet high and wide and has an upright, rounded habit when grown in full sun. It has a more open growth habit when grown in the shade.

Uses: Specimen, border, grouping, screen.

Site and care requirements: Plant in full sun where summers are cooler, and in part shade in warmer areas. Mountain laurel needs acid, moist, very well-drained soil.

Recommended varieties and related species: There are seemingly countless cultivars, which each produce different color blooms, but otherwise have the same attributes as the species. Try '**Sarah**', '**Richard Jaynes**', or '**Heart of Fire**' for bright red buds and pink blooms. Pink buds with white flowers are found on '**Minuet**' while '**Pristine**' and '**Snowdrift**' have white blooms.

Myrica pensylvanica (see Bayberry, Northern)

Myrtle (*Myrtus communis*)

Features: An evergreen shrub with dainty spring-blooming flowers

Growth rate: Moderate

Zones: 8 to 10

Description: Dark green aromatic foliage sets off the small white or rose-color flowers that bloom in spring. The flowers fleck across the plant like stars in the night sky and then give way to small, blue-black berries that are almost hidden in

the dark foliage. It grows from 5 to 15 feet high and 10 to 12 feet wide in a dense, rounded shape. It can be pruned into a small tree, but is most often used in shrub form and pruned to keep a preferred shape. Myrtle is drought tolerant, but needs a well-drained site.

Uses: Specimen, hedge, or massing.

Site and care requirements: Plant in full sun to partial shade and moist, well-drained soil. Do not overwater or water inadequately, which can cause chlorosis in this plant. Prune in early spring to maintain the shape.

Recommended varieties and related species: '**Compacta**' grows only 2 to 3 feet high and wide. '**Variegata**' is also smaller than the species and has white variegated leaves.

Myrtle (*Myrtle communis*)

Myrtus communis (see Myrtle)
Nandina domestica (see Heavenly bamboo)

Natal plum (*Carissa macrocarpa*)

Features: Year-round flowers and attractive shiny, dark green foliage

Growth rate: Fast

Zones: 9 to 10

Description: Fragrant, year-round white or pink blooms are set against glossy green leaves. After the flowers come the red, plumlike fruit that is good for eating fresh or for preserves. This evergreen shrub has a loose, mounded growth habit that makes it ideal for hedges or barriers— the flowers and fruit are a bonus. It grows from 2 to 7 feet tall (depending on the type) and 7 to 10 feet wide. The stems are covered in thorns, so avoid placing along paths or other places people might brush against it.

Uses: Hedge, barrier, groundcover, foundation planting

Natal plum (*Carissa macrocarpa*)

Site and care requirements: Plant in full sun in well-drained soil. Natal plum can tolerate a variety of soils.

Recommended varieties and related species: Smaller varieties, such as '**Horizontalis**', '**Prostrata**', and '**Green Carpet**', grow only up to 2 feet high and make an effective groundcover in areas where taller plants are inappropriate.

Needle palm (see Palm, needle)
Nerium oleander (see Oleander)
Nyssa sylvatica (see Black gum)

Oak, bur *(Quercus macrocarpa)*

Features: Large noble tree with deeply furrowed bark
Growth rate: Slow to moderate
Zones: 2 to 8

Description: The rough textured bark and large frame give the bur oak winter interest. Named for the bristled caps on its acorns, this large tree needs plenty of room to grow and to showcase its grand size. It reaches 70 to 80 feet

Bur oak (Quercus macrocarpa)

high and wide, producing a massive trunk and large crown when mature. Fall foliage is a yellowish green to yellowish brown.
Uses: Specimen, shade.
Site and care requirements: Plant in a large landscape in full sun. It adapts to many different soils but is notoriously difficult to transplant.

Oak, English *(Quercus robur)*

Features: Large, spreading habit and deeply grooved bark
Growth rate: Slow
Zones: 4 to 8

English oak (Quercus robur)

Description: Featuring an elegant form, a large trunk, and fissured bark, the English oak is a stately presence in the winter landscape. When covered by the dark blue-green leaves the rest of the seasons, it dominates the scene. The leaves may last well into late fall but don't provide bright autumn color. It grows from 40 to 60 feet high and wide. It is susceptible to mildew but is more easily transplanted than bur oak.
Uses: Specimen or shade in a large landscape.
Site and care requirements: Plant in full sun and moist, well-drained soil. Watch for mildew and treat accordingly.
Recommended varieties and related species: These varieties have a more columnar form, which is more familiar in the United States: **'Fastigiata', 'Skyrocket',** and **'Skymaster'.**

Oak, live *(Quercus virginiana)*

Features: Massive spread and trunk, and evergreen leaves
Growth rate: Moderate
Zones: 7 to 10

Live oak (Quercus virginiana)

Description: A favorite of the deep South, the live oak is distinguished by its broad trunk and enormous spread with a canopy that can reach 60 to 80 feet. Also notable for being the only evergreen of the oaks, this oak has leathery green leaves that emerge in midspring followed by clusters of male catkins and female flowers, and, of course, the acorns. The live oak grows 40 to 60 feet tall and can thrive for centuries, especially in Zone 10, where it is happiest.
Uses: Specimen or shade in a large landscape.
Site and care requirements: Plant in full sun and moist, sandy, slightly acid soil. It is vulnerable to limb damage from snow and ice in the northernmost areas that it can survive.

Oak, northern red *(Quercus rubra)*

Features: Handsome fall foliage and rounded habit
Growth rate: Moderate to fast
Zones: 4 to 8

Description: An easy tree to grow, the red oak is a popular choice for its beautiful fall foliage and wide, rounded shape. As the leaves emerge in spring, they start out as a bronzy-red and

Northern red oak (Quercus rubra)

then change to green during the spring and summer. They then turn a brilliant red in the autumn. This oak grows from 60 to 75 feet tall and wide, providing a large canopy for shade. Early acorns are a favorite of a wide range of wildlife.
Uses: Specimen or shade in a large landscape.
Site and care requirements: Plant in full sun in moist, well-drained soil. This tree may be susceptible to oak wilt.
Recommended varieties and related species: **Shumard oak** *(Q. shumardii)* is very similar to Northern red oak, but differs in the size and color of the buds and has a more pyramidal shape.

Oak, pin *(Quercus palustris)*

Features: Red fall foliage and strong pyramidal shape
Growth rate: Moderate to fast
Zones: 4 to 8

Pin oak *(Quercus palustris)*

Description:
Easy to transplant, this is one of the most commonly planted oak trees in the United States. It has a lovely pyramidal shape with lower branches growing downward and upper branches growing straight out or upward, creating a strikingly shaped canopy. Since it also has a beautiful red fall color, it is no wonder this tree is such a favorite. It grows 60 to 70 feet tall with a spread of 20 to 40 feet.
Uses: Shade, specimen.
Site and care requirements: Plant in full sun and acid soil. Alkaline soil makes the pin oak susceptible to iron chlorosis. Oak wilt may also be a problem. Water well and feed in springtime until established. Prune in winter only as needed.

Oak, scarlet *(Quercus coccinea)*

Features: Brilliant scarlet red fall foliage
Growth rate: Fast
Zones: 4 to 9

Description:
Although difficult to transplant, the scarlet oak puts on one fiery red show in the fall, which may last up to four weeks. The round, open habit shows off the foliage to best effect, both when it's a dark, glossy green and when it turns red in fall. It grows 50 to 80 feet high and 40 to 50 feet wide.
Uses: Specimen or shade in a large landscape.
Site and care requirements: Plant in full sun and moist, acid, well-drained soil. This oak can be susceptible to oak wilt, which is mostly spread by

Scarlet oak *(Quercus coccinea)*

beetles. Prune as necessary only in winter to prevent beetles from infesting the pruning wounds.

Oak, white *(Quercus alba)*

Features: A large, stately presence in the landscape
Growth rate: Slow to moderate
Zones: 3 to 8

White oak *(Quercus alba)*

Description: The rounded shape and broad crown of a mature white oak is a striking sight. The light brown, thick trunk has an interesting scaly texture that can be appreciated in the winter landscape. The dark green foliage turns a reddish-wine color in the fall. This tree grows 50 to 80 feet tall and wide at maturity with an attractive rounded shape that is different from the pyramidal shape when the tree is young. This oak is drought tolerant and less susceptible to oak wilt.
Uses: Specimen or shade in a large landscape.
Site and care requirements: Plant in full sun and moist, well-drained soil. White oak needs plenty of space to grow so plant only in larger landscapes.

Olea europaea (see Olive, European)

Oleander *(Nerium oleander)*

Features: Easy evergreen shrub with long-lasting blooms
Growth rate: Fast
Zones: 8 to 10

Oleander *(Nerium oleander 'Petite Pink')*

Description: This shrub thrives with little care in California and the Deep South. Long and thin dark, leathery leaves are an excellent backdrop to the showy blooms, which come in shades of white and pink to red. The flowers appear throughout spring and summer. This drought-tolerant shrub is also tolerant of heat, wind, and air pollution. It grows 12 to 15 feet tall and wide, with an upright, rounded growth habit.
It can be severely pruned to maintain shape and size. This plant is prone to scale, aphids, and mildew. And although it's lovely, all parts of this plant are toxic and ingestion of even a small amount can cause death, so avoid planting it in areas frequented by pets and children.
Uses: Border, hedge, foundation.
Site and care requirements: Plant in full sun to partial shade and well-drained soil. Prune in early spring to remove old wood. Use caution and wear protective gear when pruning since contact with the leaves can cause dermatitis.
Recommended varieties and related species: Plant **'Petite Pink'** for beautiful pink blooms or **'Calypso'** for cherry-red flowers. **'Sister Agnes'** has white flowers.

Olive, European *(Olea europaea)*

Features: Lovely ornamental tree with an interesting shape
Growth rate: Slow
Zones: 9 to 11

European olive *(Olea europaea)*

Description: In Western landscapes (mainly California and Arizona), the olive tree is planted both for its twisting, irregular shape as well as the fruit. The willowlike leaves and white blooms add to its appeal. It grows 25 to 30 feet tall and wide in a rounded, horizontal shape. While the fruit is edible when ripe, it poses a litter problem if not harvested before or immediately after falling. Its pollen may be a health concern and because of that the tree has been banned in some areas.
Uses: Specimen, fruit production.
Site and care requirements: Plant in full sun and well-drained soil. This olive tree requires staking and pruning when young.
Recommended varieties and related species: **'Manzanillo'** is a variety familiar to olive lovers. **'Little Ollie'** grows just up to 12 feet tall. **'Wilsoni'** is a fruitless or almost fruitless variety that grows up to 25 feet tall.

Olive, Russian (see Silverberry, Russian)

Osage orange *(Maclura pomifera)*

Features: A distinctive gnarled shape and dense habit
Growth rate: Fast
Zones: 4 to 9

Osage orange *(Maclura pomifera)*

Description: The knobby, gnarled shape and rounded, uneven crown on the osage orange are a familiar sight in the Midwest. It grows from 20 to 40 feet high and wide with a short trunk and thorny, extended branches. The glossy, thick foliage is a deep green that turns a pleasant yellow in the fall. Once the leaves are gone, the distinctive silhouette decorates the winter landscape. The fruit ripens in the fall, giving off a slight, orangelike fragrance. The fruit grows 4 to 6 inches in diameter and can give you a good knock on the head if you're under the tree when it falls. The fruit grows only on female trees, so choose a male tree to avoid the messy fruit. This tree survives and flourishes in adverse conditions, making it a good choice for sites that will not support any other trees. It is heat and drought tolerant.
Uses: Specimen or in difficult growing conditions.
Site and care requirements: Plant in full sun and a variety of soils—wet, dry, or poor.

Osmanthus fragrans (see Sweet olive)
Oxydendrum arboreum (see Sourwood)
Pacific madrone (see Madrone, pacific)

Pagoda tree, Japanese *(Sophora japonica)*

Features: Fragrant late-summer blooms set against deep green, glossy foliage
Growth rate: Moderate to fast
Zones: 4 to 7

Japanese pagoda tree *(Sophora japonica)*

Description: With its broad, round crown and glossy green leaves, the Japanese pagoda tree is striking. It grows up to 50 to 70 feet tall and wide with an open, extended growth habit. Sweetly fragrant creamy white clusters of hanging flowers bloom in July and August, blanketing the tree's canopy to create a stunning contrast to the other foliage in the summer landscape. Fruit follows the blooms, forming yellow-green strands that hang like strings of beads from the branches. The fruit can create yard litter when it falls, so place it accordingly.
Uses: Specimen, shade.
Site and care requirements: Plant in full sun and well-drained soil, though this tree can adapt to many different types of soil. Don't underestimate the mature size of this tree and allow plenty of room to grow. Blooms do not begin to appear until the tree is at least 10 years old.
Recommended varieties and related species: **'Pendula'** has an attractive weeping habit. **'Regent'** flowers at a younger age and grows more rapidly than the species.

Palm, cabbage *(Sabal palmetto)*

Features: Very salt-tolerant with a loose, natural form
Growth rate:
Moderate
Zones: 8 to 10

Description: Also called the palmetto, this tree has large, fan-shape leaves set on huge trunks, which often cross each other in an attractive manner. Cabbage palm is very salt-tolerant, making it an excellent choice in coastal areas. It also survives flooding and hurricanes well. Its loose, naturalized habit makes it ideal for informal settings. It grows 20 to 60 feet tall and 10 to 15 feet wide with a trunk that often reaches up to 2 feet in diameter.

Cabbage palm (Sabal palmetto)

Uses: Specimen, accent.
Site and care requirements: Plant in full sun to partial shade and sandy soil. However, this palm adapts to different types of soil fairly well. Prune off dead leaves with a saw when they turn yellow.
Recommended varieties and related species: *S. mexicana* and *S. texana* closely resemble *S. palmetto* but these two palms are less cold-hardy.

Palm, California fan *(Washingtonia filifera)*

Features: Massive palm with a large trunk and yellow-green leaves
Growth rate: Fast
Zones: 8 to 10

Description:
The large spiny palmate leaves hang down from the top of this tree, giving it an almost shaggy appearance. This tree can grow up to 100 feet tall in warmer regions, giving it a

California fan palm (Washingtonia filiferia)

commanding presence, especially when planted in groups. It doesn't grow as tall in cooler areas.
Uses: Specimen or grouping in a large landscape.
Site and care requirements: Plant in full sun in just about any well-drained soil. Leaves may discolor because of frost.
Recommended varieties and related species: **Mexican fan palm** *(W. robusta)* has a smaller trunk and is not as cold hardy as California fan palm.

Palm, Canary Island date *(Phoenix canariensis)*

Features: Large palm with a thick trunk and a pineapplelike nut at the top
Growth rate: Very slow
Zones: 8 to 11

Description: This is a stunning, tall, stiff-leafed feather palm that is even more exceptional when planted in rows. This tree can grow up to 60 feet tall, but it will take a long time for it to reach its mature size. It is a bit more cold-hardy than other palms, but does not transplant well. Plant a young specimen and wait

Canary Island date palm (Phoenix canariensis)

it out—the final product will be well worth your patience. This palm is drought tolerant but also tolerant of moist soil.
Uses: Specimen, accent, rows.
Site and care requirements: Plant in full sun and a variety of soils.

Palm, Mediterranean fan *(Chamaerops humilis)*

Features: Drought resistant, cold hardy with lovely fan-shape leaves
Growth rate:
Slow
Zones: 8 to 10

Description:
This is also known as the European fan palm. It is one of the more cold-hardy palms and can grow up to 20 feet tall with a crown reaching up to 15 feet wide. However, it's still considered one of the smaller palms. By the time it has matured, it often has developed multiple trunks with smaller trunks surrounding a larger main trunk. It has a shrubby appearance and survives in climates where other palms can't.

Mediterranean fan palm (Chamaerops humilis)

Uses: Specimen, accent.
Site and care requirements: Plant in full sun to partial shade and well-drained soil. It is excellent in large containers.

Palm, needle *(Rhapidophyllum hystrix)*

Features: Small size and deep green leaves
Growth rate: Slow
Zones: 8 to 10

Needle palm *(Rhapidophyllum hystrix)*

Description: The small size and clumping habit of the needle palm lends itself well to a variety of uses. The long, sharp needles nestled among the leaves make this a great security hedge planting, but you won't want to plant it where there will be much foot traffic. It is cold-hardy for a palm, but can't tolerate extended cold winds. It grows up to 10 feet high and wide in warmer climates, but only to 5 feet tall and wide in cooler climates.
Uses: Specimen, barrier, hedge.
Site and care requirements: Plant in light shade and moist soil. Adaptable to various soil types with adequate moisture.

Palm, pindo *(Butia capitata)*

Features: Long, graceful arching leaves
Growth rate: Slow to moderate
Zones: 8 to 10

Description: With 6- to 8-foot-long leaves gently arching toward the ground, this feather palm is wonderfully elegant.

The trunk has a diameter of more than a foot across and nicely contrasts with the weeping fronds. It grows 12 to 20 feet high. Fairly cold-hardy, this palm needs protection in temperatures reaching below 15°F to avoid damage to the leaves. It tolerates salt spray well.
Uses: Specimen.
Site and care requirements: Plant in full sun. Well-drained soil is preferred.

Pindo palm *(Butia capitata)*

Palm, queen *(Syagrus romanzoffiana)*

Features: Softly drooping leaves and a fast grower
Growth rate: Fast
Zones: 9 to 11

Queen palm *(Syagrus romanzoffiana)*

Description: The gently drooping leaves spread from the top of the tree in a pleasing, fanlike shape. It grows from 25 to 50 feet high and 15 to 25 feet wide at the crown. Avoid trunk damage and do not overprune, as it will damage the tree. Susceptible to palm leaf skeletonizer, scale, and butt rot.
Uses: Specimen, rows, grouping.
Site and care requirements: Plant in full sun in acidic, well-drained soil. Do not plant in alkaline soil as it will stunt leaf growth and can kill the tree.

Palm, sago *(Cycas revoluta)*

Features: A whirl of stiff, whorled leaves
Growth rate: Very slow
Zones: 9 to 11

Sago palm *(Cycas revoluta)*

Description: This extremely slow-growing, long-lived plant isn't a real palm at all—it is a cycad. Native to southern Japan, it can grow up to 20 feet high, but it may take up to 100 years to reach that size. Stiff and shiny, dark green feathery leaves grow 3 to 4 feet long and seem to cover the tree until the trunk shows some height.
Uses: Ornamental, specimen, container.
Site and care requirements: Plant in full sun and sandy, well-drained soil. It requires little care.

Palm, Washington fan *(Washingtonia robusta)*

Features: Very tall with a skirt of dead fronds that hangs from the tree
Growth rate: Fast
Zones: 9 to 11

Description: The "hula skirt in FPO" of dead fronds that hangs from the crown of this palm is its most distinguishing characteristic, besides its immense height, of course. It can grow up to 100 feet tall, so it's quite impressive, especially when planted in rows. Best known for lining streets in Venice, California

Washington fan palm *(Washingtonia robusta)*

and California beaches, these palms can be used in the home landscape, as street trees, or in groupings. They are salt-spray tolerant.
Uses: Ornamental, specimen, container.
Site and care requirements: Plant in full sun to partial shade in well-drained soil. It thrives in sandy soils.

Palm, windmill *(Trachycarpus fortunei)*

Features: Fan-shape leaves on a slim trunk
Growth rate: Moderate
Zones: 8 to 10

Windmill palm *(Trachycarpus fortunei)*

Description: The single trunk, which is often wider at the top than at the base, supports the dark green, fan-shape leaves that are symmetrically arranged around the trunk. It grows 25 to 40 feet high with a crown of about 8 feet wide. It won't tolerate standing water or direct salt spray. Windmill palm prefers slightly cooler climates over extremely warm climates.
Uses: Specimen, grouping.
Site and care requirements: Plant in full sun to partial shade and rich, moist, well-drained soil. Plant in partial shade in warmer climates.

Parrotia, Persian *(Parrotia persica)*

Features: Excellent fall color, multicolored peeling bark, and distinctive maroon flowers
Growth rate: Moderate
Zones: 4 to 8

Persian parrotia *(Parrotia persica)*

Description: The open, spreading growth habit of this tree, also known as Persian ironwood, is one of this tree's many assets. When the small maroon flowers bloom, they make the tree radiant. The simple leaves begin a reddish purple, then turn a glossy deep green. The outstanding fall foliage ranges in colors from yellow-gold to pumpkin orange and deep red. Once the leaves fall, the peeling bark with creamy white, silver, green, and cinnamon brown bark underneath is revealed. The rounded to oval shape mature tree grows from 20 to 40 feet high and 15 to 30 feet wide. It is pest resistant and does best in cooler climates. It is not drought tolerant.
Uses: Specimen, grouping.
Site and care requirements: Plant in full sun to light shade and moist, well-drained soil. This tree can't tolerate wet conditions, so be sure the site isn't soggy.
Recommended varieties and related species: 'Pendula' isn't a true weeping form, but more of a shrublike plant with horizontal branches instead of upright ones.

Paulownia tomentosa (see Empress tree)

Pawpaw *(Asimina triloba)*

Features: Tropical-looking foliage, gorgeous blooms, good fall color, and edible fruit
Growth rate: Moderate
Zones: 5 to 8

Pawpaw *(Asimina triloba)*

Description: Large, deep green, drooping leaves give the pawpaw a tropical look, but the striking purple flowers that bloom in April and May grab attention even before the leaves emerge. The blooms give way to edible fruit that starts out yellowish green, and then turns black when ripe. The fruit is high in vitamins A and C, and has a banana-pear flavor—popular with humans and wildlife. At least two trees need to be planted for pollination to occur and fruit to develop. Once the fruiting is

over, the leaves are back on center stage for the fall, turning a vivid yellow-gold before dropping for the winter. It grows from 15 to 30 feet high and 20 feet wide and has a rounded, upright growth habit. It can grow as a large shrub or may be shaped to form a short-trunked tree.
Uses: Grouping or mass planting.
Site and care requirements: Plant in full sun to partial shade and fertile, loose woodland soil. Allow it to grow without shaping or prune when young to develop a single trunk.

Peach *(Prunus persica)*

Features: Juicy summer fruit and beautiful white, pink, or red flowers
Growth rate: Fast
Zones: 5 to 9

Peach *(Prunus persica)*

Description: The showy flowers bloom in April, even before the leaves emerge. The blossoms range in color from white to pink to red, depending on variety. The dark green leaves provide a nice contrast to the orange-yellow fruit when it develops in mid-to-late summer. The trees will bear fuzzy-skinned fruit the second year but will produce more substantial quantities in the third and subsequent years. They grow 15 to 25 feet high and wide and the upright open growth habit makes them great screen or mass plantings for an incredible spring bloom show.
Uses: Border, screen, grouping, mass planting.
Site and care requirements: Plant in full sun in moist, slight acid, well-drained soil. Mulch well to protect the shallow roots from competition with weeds and grass. Prune in late winter—the tree's dormant period—to encourage the best branches to become stronger. Remove suckers and any branches that overlap. Fruit should be removed when ripe to reduce the weight on the branches. Peach trees can't survive extreme winter temperatures or late frosts. They're susceptible to peach tree borers, peach leaf curl, and brown rot. Two or more trees will need to be planted for pollination, unless the cultivar is self-pollinating.
Recommended varieties and related species: 'Redhaven' is hardy and the most popular cultivar. Cultivars that need a second tree to pollinate include **'Indian Free'** and **'Indian Blood Cling'**. Plant **'Velvet'**, **'Redfree'**, or **'Rio Oso Gem'** for plentiful flowers. **'Dixie Gem'** and **'Sunshine'** are resistant to peach leaf curl, while **'Orange Cling'**, **'Red Bird'**, and **'Sunbeam'** are resistant to brown rot.

Pear, callery *(Pyrus calleryana)*

Features: Showy white blossoms and brilliant fall color
Growth rate: Moderate to fast
Zones: 5 to 8

Callery pear *(Pyrus calleryana)*

Description: Callery pear is an ornamental tree grown for the flowers and fall foliage. Small, slightly odiferous white blossoms cover the bare tree in March before the leaves emerge. The somewhat irregular, open, and upright shape of the tree showcases the profusion of blooms and glossy, dark green leaves. Autumn brings fiery red, yellow, or purple hues to the foliage. Depending on the cultivar, this tree grows 20 to 40 feet high and wide. It is heat and drought tolerant and can grow easily in compacted soils. Fire blight may be devastating to certain cultivars in the South.
Uses: Specimen, grouping.
Site and care requirements: Plant in full sun and a wide range of soil types.
Recommended varieties and related species: **'Aristrocrat'** has glossy, deep green leaves but not as many flowers as other cultivars. The fall foliage is a more muted orange-red. **'Bradford'** is a popular cultivar with an abundance of blooms. The fall foliage is a spectacular sight, but this tree grows weak crotches and can easily lose limbs. **'Chanticleer'** is somewhat more robust than **'Bradford'** and has a more regular growth habit. **'Redspire'** and **'Whitehouse'** are other cultivars that are widely available.

Pear, common *(Pyrus communis)*

Features: Showy blooms and sweet, edible fruit
Growth rate: Moderate
Zones: 4 to 8

Description: Before the leaves emerge, the spring flowers bloom in an incredible display of white blossoms. The clusters of blooms appear just ahead of the glossy green leaves that eventually turn red in autumn. The luscious fruit ripens to a golden yellow with a hint of pink or red. The tree grows 20 to 30 feet tall and 15 to 20 feet wide in an irregular pyramidal shape. When covered in blossoms, the shape of the tree makes the effect all the more striking. Dwarf varieties grow 10 to 15 feet tall and 8 to 10 feet wide and carry the same characteristics as the larger trees. Common pear trees are susceptible to fire blight.
Uses: Specimen, border, grouping.
Site and care requirements: Plant in full sun and slightly acid, fertile soil. Plant in early spring and space full-sized trees 20 to 25 feet apart and dwarf trees 12 to 15 feet apart to

Common pear *(Pyrus communis)*

allow for mature size and spread. Pear trees are not drought tolerant so be sure to provide plenty of water in the summer.
Recommended varieties and related species: Common cultivars include **'Comice'**, **'Bartlett'**, **'Beurre d'Anjou'**, and **'Bosc'**. Disease-resistant varieties include **'Kieffer'**, **'Moonglow'**, or **'Old Home'**.

Pear, Ussurian *(Pyrus ussuriensis)*

Features: A bushy, rounded growth habit, lovely blooms, fall color
Growth rate: Moderate to fast
Zones: 3 to 6

Description: The rounded form of the Ussurian or Harbin pear tree makes this a good addition to the landscape. It resembles a huge shrub, growing 40 to 50 feet high and wide with a short trunk and branches growing at virtually ground level. A profusion of small white flowers covers the tree in April and May, making the tree look almost snow-covered. The dark green

Ussurian pear *(Pyrus ussuriensis)*

leaves turn a subdued reddish-purple in the fall and provide a wonderful show.
Uses: Specimen.
Site and care requirements: Plant in full sun and moist, well-drained soil.
Recommended varieties and related species: **'Mordak'** or **'Prairie Gem'** is smaller and has a more rounded habit. **'Bailfrost'** or **'Mountain Frost'** has a more upright growth habit.

Pearlbush, common *(Exochorda racemosa)*

Features: Pearl-shape flower buds that burst into bloom
Growth rate: Moderate
Zones: 4 to 8

Common pearlbush *(Exochorda racemosa)*

Description: This easy shrub fairly bursts into bloom in springtime. At first, the rangy, open form is covered in pearllike buds. Then, in what seems like an instant, long-lasting, bright white blooms blanket the shrub. The simple, medium green leaves are somewhat nondescript and offer no fall color, but accentuate the loosely rounded shape of the bush. Mature shrubs develop gray, orange-brown peeling bark that adds another dimension to the fall and winter landscape. The upright, irregular growth habit can cause the plant to look untidy as it ages, but it can be severely pruned to bring back a neater shape. It grows 10 to 15 feet high and wide and is heat and drought tolerant. This is a tough shrub that requires minimum maintenance.
Uses: Border.
Site and care requirements: Plant in full sun to partial shade and well-drained, acidic soil. Water regularly during the growing season for the first two years until the plant becomes established. Once established, it is drought tolerant.
Recommended varieties and related species: 'The Bride' is a hybrid of *E. racemosa* and *E. korolkowii.* It grows only 3 to 4 feet tall with a slightly wider spread. **'Northern Pearl'** or *E. serratifolia* is a variety of Korean pearlbush with showy flowers. It is more cold-hardy than common pearlbush.

Peashrub, Siberian *(Caragana arborescens)*

Features: Arching branches that reach toward the ground
Growth rate: Moderate to fast
Zones: 2 to 7

Description: The draping branches of the Siberian peashrub are ideal for holding the elliptical, pea-green leaves. The multistemmed, spreading branches form a loosely rounded shape that shows off the abundance of small yellow flowers in May. While the blooms may tend to get lost in the foliage, up close the flowers are remarkable in their delicate beauty. The long, thin fruit appears green and flat at first, and then turns brown and plump as it matures. The fruit opens with a pop that can startle people nearby. This plant grows 15 to 20 feet high and 12 to 18 feet wide. One of the most important features the Siberian peashrub has is that it is tolerant of extremely cold conditions and dry soil.
Uses: Windbreak, hedge, or screen.

Siberian peashrub *(Caragana arborescens* 'Lobergii')

Site and care requirements: Plant in full sun and a variety of soils, including poor soil.
Recommended varieties and related species: 'Nana' is a dwarf variety that grows only up to 6 feet tall and wide. **'Pendula'** is a weeping variety that is actually grafted onto a standard. **'Lorbergii'** is more graceful with finer textured foliage. **'Walker'** also has a weeping habit and finer leaves.

Pecan *(Carya illinoinensis)*

Features: Edible nuts and a handsome silhouette
Growth rate: Slow to moderate
Zones: 5 to 9

Pecan *(Carya illinoinensis)*

Description: Grown mainly for its famous nuts, the pecan tree can also be an attractive addition to the home landscape. The mature size of the tree limits its home use to large yards, but the effect of this tree planted as a specimen is well worth the space it requires. The spreading upright habit allows for grass to grow underneath, but provides some shade for outdoor comfort. The nuts grow among the deep green leaves and are a favorite for people and squirrels alike. The nuts, twigs, and leaves can cause plenty of yard litter so ongoing cleanup is necessary. The nuts ripen best in warmer climates, but they will ripen in more northern areas, just not as reliably. This tree is very difficult to transplant so it should be positioned carefully with the mature size of the tree in mind. A pecan grows from 70 to 100 feet high and 40 to 75 feet wide. It is susceptible to leaf scab. Late frosts reduce nut production.
Uses: Specimen in large landscapes or for the nuts.
Site and care requirements: Plant in full sun to partial shade and deep, moist, well-drained soil.

Pepper tree *(Schinus molle)*

Features: An elegant, drooping form and eye-catching clusters of red berries
Growth rate: Fast
Zones: 9 to 10

Pepper tree *(Schinus molle)*

Description: A tree for warm climates, the pepper tree provides a dramatic, drooping silhouette. The branches are covered in thin, opposite, light green leaves that add to the gracefully floppy appearance of the tree. The clusters of small red berries hang like bunches of grapes and are sometimes dried and sold as pink pepper. For the home landscape the size of the tree requires careful siting because it grows rapidly to 40 feet high and wide. It produces yard litter from the berries and brittle branches that can break off easily in windy conditions. The surface root system can be invasive, so plant away from sidewalks, driveways, septic systems, and sewer lines. This tree has excellent heat and drought tolerance but is prone to scale, aphids, and Texas root rot.
Uses: Ornamental or shade.
Site and care requirements: Plant in full sun and a variety of soils. Stake new trees until the root system becomes established. Do not overwater once the tree is established.

Persian parrotia (see Parrotia, Persian)

Persimmon, common *(Diospyros virginiana)*

Features: Edible fruit and changing foliage color
Growth rate: Slow
Zone: 4 to 9

Description:
New leaves on the persimmon tree emerge a golden bronze in spring then turn a deep,

Common persimmon *(Diospyros virginiana)*

lustrous green for the summer months. Late spring and early summer bring fragrant white flowers as a prelude to the coming fruit. As autumn nears, the foliage turns an orange-red while the fruit continues to ripen. The leaves fall within a couple of weeks of coloring, but the golden-orange fruit persists well after the leaves are gone. It is usually fully ripe and sweet at the first hard frost. The deeply grooved bark adds winter interest. The shape of the tree changes from a pyramidal shape in youth to more rounded as it matures. It grows 30 to 50 feet high and 20 to 35 feet wide and is extremely adaptable to dry soil conditions. It is susceptible to dry leaf spot.
Uses: Ornamental, fruit production.
Site and care requirements: Plant in full sun to light shade and moist, well-drained soil.
Recommended varieties and related species: Japanese persimmon *(D. kaki)* produces yellow-orange fruit in the later fall. The fragrant white flowers bloom in late spring to early summer, set against the dark green leaves. Hardy in Zones 7 to 9, this tree will grow 10 to 25 feet high and wide. Varieties include **'Chocolate', 'Fuyu',** and **'Hachiya'.**

Japanese persimmon *(Diospyros kaki)*

Phellodendron amurense (see Cork tree, amur)
Philadelphus coronaries (see Mockorange, sweet)
Phoenix canariensis (see Palm, Canary Island date)

Photinia, redtip *(Photinia ×fraseri)*

Features: Red foliage, red berries, and white flowers
Growth rate: Moderate to fast
Zones: 7 to 10

Description: The red-tipped leaves emerge in spring, turning a dark green as they mature. The clusters of white

Redtip photinia *(Photinia ×fraseri)*

flowers bloom in spring, emitting an unpleasant odor until they die off. Fortunately, the foliage makes up for the smell, as the coppery red leaves look lovely against the blooms. Clusters of small red berries follow the flowering and stay with the plant through winter. The dense, upright, somewhat rounded growth habit makes this a nice shrub for screens or hedges. It grows 10 to 15 feet high and 5 to 10 feet wide. This is a heat-resistant plant but is susceptible to fire blight.
Uses: Hedge, screen.
Site and care requirements: Plant in full sun to partial shade and moist, well-drained soil amended with plenty of organic matter. Water the roots of the shrub only, and avoid getting the leaves wet. If fire blight occurs, prune out diseased branches. Remove fallen leaves and twig debris so that disease spores do not overwinter near the plant. Prune in spring only as necessary to keep the plant tidy.
Recommended varieties and related species: Chinese photinia *(P. serratifolia)* is a larger shrub, growing up to 30 feet tall with a spread up to 20 feet. The evergreen leaves emerge a purplish-burgundy, turning a deep, dark green rather quickly. The white blooms also have an unpleasant odor, blooming in late spring. Hardy in Zones 7 to 9, the Chinese photinia makes a good hedge planting or it can also be grown as a privacy screen.

Picea **spp.** (see Spruce)
Pieris japonica (see Andromeda, Japanese)
Pindo palm (see Palm, pindo)

Pine, Austrian *(Pinus nigra)*

Features: A hardy tree with thick, deep green needles
Growth rate: Moderate
Zones: 4 to 7

Austrian pine *(Pinus nigra)*

Description: The deep green needles and pyramidal growth habit makes this one of the most popular landscape pines. It tolerates heat, drought, and salt, and can be planted in a wide range of soils. It grows 30 to 60 feet high with a spread of 20 to 40 feet. It is susceptible to pine nematode, tip blight, needle blight, and pine moths.
Uses: Screen, windbreak.
Site and care requirements: Plant in full sun and a variety of soil conditions.
Recommended varieties and related species: Varieties available include **'Arnold Sentinel'** and **'Globosa'.**

Pine, bristlecone *(Pinus aristata)*

Features: Dark green needles and a striking outline
Growth rate: Very slow
Zones: 4 to 7

Bristlecone pine *(Pinus aristata)*

Description: This ancient, dwarf, shrubby tree has an interesting look that serves it well as an accent in the landscape. The open, irregular growth habit accentuates the blue-green color of the needles, which are often speckled with white resin. The branches point distinctly upward, and the unusual cones for which it is named appear at the tips. It grows 8 to 20 feet high and 10 to 15 feet wide. It is not tolerant of air pollution or drying winds, but will survive in dry, infertile soil.
Uses: Accent, specimen.
Site and care requirements: Plant in full sun and a variety of soils, including dry, poor soil.

Pine, eastern white *(Pinus strobus)*

Features: Horizontal, spreading branches and fine, blue-green needles
Growth rate: Fast
Zones: 3 to 8

Eastern white pine *(Pinus strobus)*

Description: Soft needles cover spreading, horizontal branches that arrange themselves in an open growth habit. The pyramidal shape and rapid growth rate make this a good choice for a fast screen. It grows 50 to 80 feet high and 20 to 40 feet wide. Six- to eight-inch brown cones decorate the deep green tree. It is not tolerant of air pollution, constant wind, or salt. It self-mulches with its fallen needles.
Uses: Specimen, screen.
Site and care requirements: Plant in full sun to light shade and moist, fertile, well-drained soil.
Recommended varieties and related species: **'Pendula'** has an elegant slightly weeping form. **'Fastigiata'** has a more narrow growth habit than the species.

Pine, Himalayan *(Pinus wallichiana)*

Features: Long, soft, blue-green needles on an elegant form
Growth rate: Slow to moderate
Zones: 5 to 7

Himalayan pine *(Pinus wallichiana)*

Description: The softly pyramidal shape and lovely upright habit showcase the 5- to 8-inch needles that drape gracefully over the branches. It grows 30 to 50 feet high and 20 to 30 feet wide so the overall look is a standout in the landscape. It does not tolerate damaging winds.
Uses: Specimen.
Site and care requirements: Plant in full sun to partial shade and moist, well-drained soil.
Recommended varieties and related species: ‘Zebrinus’ has lighter, almost cream-colored needles.

Pine, Japanese black *(Pinus thunbergii)*

Features: Long, thin white buds and a picturesque shape
Growth rate: Fast
Zones: 5 to 8

Description: Well-suited for coastal areas, the Japanese black pine is very tolerant of salt spray, as well as heat and drought. The shape is irregularly pyramidal, and while many appreciate its shrubby, natural form, it can be pruned into a neater shape without difficulty. The distinctive long white buds resemble candles sitting on the ends of the branches. It grows 15 to 25 feet high and up to 25 feet wide.
Uses: Specimen, border, grouping.
Site and care requirements: Plant in full sun and a variety of soil, but it does best in well-drained soil.
Recommended varieties and related species: ‘Monina’ (Majestic Beauty) has a more compact growth habit and ‘Thunderhead’ has a dwarf, broader habit.

Japanese black pine *(Pinus thunbergii)*

Pine, Japanese red *(Pinus densiflora)*

Features: Peeling, orange-red bark and a spreading, open growth habit
Growth rate: Slow to moderate
Zones: 3 to 7

Description: The colorful, peeling bark shows through the open, upward-tilted branches of bright green needles to provide year-round interest in the landscape. It's not tolerant to high winds and should be sited in a place where it is protected. It grows 40 to 60 feet high and wide. When mature, this tree has an airy, open crookedness to its form that is quite appealing.
Uses: Specimen.
Site and care requirements: Plant in full sun in well-drained soil. Leave the fallen needles under the tree as natural mulch.
Recommended varieties and related species: ‘Umbraculifera’ has an umbrella shaped form. ‘Pendula’ is a weeping variety, and ‘Oculus-draconis’ (dragon's eye pine) is a slow-growing tree with yellow-banded needles.

Japanese red pine *(Pinus densiflora)*

Pine, Japanese white *(Pinus parviflora)*

Features: Spreading branches and blue-green needles.
Growth rate: Slow
Zones: 4 to 7

Description:
Wide spreading branches form a densely shaped tree when young. As the tree matures, it becomes more open as the top levels out and becomes flatter. The bluish green needles have a silvery-colored underside. The cones grow to 4 inches long and have waxy scales that turn brown-red as they mature. This tree makes a lovely specimen or accent in the home landscape.
Uses: Specimen, accent.
Site and care requirements: Plant in full sun in moist, well-drained soil.
Recommended varieties and related species: Some varieties that are available are **'Glauca'**, **'Kokonoe'**, and **'Aoba Jo'**.

Japanese white pine *(Pinus parviflora)*

Pine, red *(Pinus resinosa)*

Features: Reddish-brown, scaly bark and tufted foliage
Growth rate:
Moderate
Zones: 2 to 5

Description:
Dark green needles are tufted around the branches of this informal, irregularly shaped tree, giving it an almost fluffy appearance. The effect is enhanced by the oval shape of the tree that becomes less dense as the tree matures. The bark of this tree when young is reddish brown and gets scaly with age.
This tree grows from 50 to 80 feet tall with a variable width.
Uses: Grouping, windbreak.
Site and care requirements: Red pine can be planted in a wide range of poor soils—sandy, acid, rocky, or dry.

Red pine *(Pinus resinosa)*

Pine, Scotch *(Pinus sylvestris)*

Features: Orange-brown bark that shows through an open form
Growth rate: Moderate
Zones: 3 to 8

Description:
The young tree has an irregular pyramid shape that becomes more open, from the bottom up, making it take on an umbrella-like shape as it matures. The twisting, gnarled branches add character and draw attention to the colorful, textured bark. It adapts well to a variety of different soils and makes a good loose screen or mass planting. It grows from 30 to 60 feet high and 30 to 40 feet wide. This tree makes a lovely specimen or accent in the home landscape.
Uses: Screen, specimen, accent, or mass planting.
Site and care requirements: Plant in full sun in well-drained soil. Scotch pine will tolerate poor, dry soils, but it is also highly susceptible to pine wilt nematode.
Recommended varieties and related species: **'Watereri'** grows only to about 10 feet high and boasts steel blue foliage. **'French Blue'** has blue-green needles and also grows smaller than the species.

Scotch pine *(Pinus sylvestris)*

Pine, Swiss stone *(Pinus cembra)*

Features: Dense, dependably columnar shape
Growth rate: Slow
Zones: 4 to 7

Description: This pine has a uniformly dense, columnar shape and is narrower than other pines, making it a good choice for smaller landscapes. It grows 30 to 40 feet high and 15 to 25 feet wide. The dark green foliage may turn a yellowish green in winter, but the colors add interest. Groupings of this tree are particularly attractive and can create a formal effect.
Uses: Specimen, screen, grouping.
Site and care requirements: Plant in full sun and moist, slightly acid, well-drained soil.

Swiss stone pine *(Pinus cembra)*

Pinus spp. (see Pine)
Pistacia chinensis (see Pistachio, Chinese)

Pistachio, Chinese *(Pistacia chinensis)*

Features: Appealing yellow to red fall foliage and a lovely, rounded shape
Growth rate: Moderate to fast
Zones: 6 to 9

Chinese pistachio *(Pistacia chinensis)*

Description: The Chinese pistachio is a moderate-size tree that offers pleasantly dappled shade in spring and summer and vivid red foliage in autumn. The rounded to oval shape of the canopy becomes more open as the tree matures and the lower branches tend to arch toward the ground. This interesting shape and gently shedding bark only add to the splendor of the tree once the leaves fall. Small greenish flowers bloom in spring, but are hardly noticeable in the deep green foliage. Female trees have small bluish-red fruit that develops in summer, while the male trees are fruitless. The berries may create yard litter when they drop—if the birds don't eat them all. It grows 25 to 40 feet tall and 25 to 35 feet wide. This is a good tree for city planting because it can withstand poor conditions. Its fall color adds a nice spark to smaller landscapes. It is drought tolerant and easy to transplant.
Uses: Specimen, light shade tree, street tree.
Site and care requirements: Plant in full sun in moist, well-drained soil. This tree will tolerate poor or dry soil, as long as adequate drainage is available. Stake young trees to develop a straight trunk and good crown.

Pittosporum, Japanese *(Pittosporum tobira)*

Features: Leathery, dark green leaves and fragrant white blooms
Growth rate: Slow
Zones: 8 to 10

Japanese pittosporum *(Pittosporum tobira)*

Description: This spreading, densely mounded shrub is popular in Southern landscapes. The glossy, deep green leaves grow 2 to 4 inches long. Clusters of fragrant, creamy white to light yellow flowers bloom in the late spring. This shrub grows from 8 to 12 feet high and 12 to 15 feet wide, making it a good hedge planting as well as a suitable screen shrub. It is drought tolerant when established and is heat and salt spray tolerant as well, making it a good choice for coastal areas. It is a hardy shrub that requires little maintenance other than pruning, if you desire, for tidiness.
Uses: Hedge, screen, foundation planting.
Site and care requirements: Plant in full sun to partial shade, though it can survive in deep shade. This plant can tolerate sandy or clay soil as long as it is well-drained. Prune frequently when young to maintain shape. It will require less pruning as it matures.
Recommended varieties and related species: **'Wheeler's Dwarf'** grows only up to 2 feet tall. **'Nana'** is also a smaller variety, growing up to 3 feet tall. **'Variegatum'** has white variegated leaves that can grow up to 5 feet tall, while **'Karo'** *(P. crassifolium)* grows up to 25 feet high.

Japanese pittosporum 'Wheeler's Dwarf'

Platanus ×acerifolia (see Plane tree, London)
Platanus occidentalis (see Sycamore, American)

Plane tree, London *(Platanus ×acerifolia)*

Features: Peeling bark exposes white, smooth bark below
Growth rate: Moderate to fast
Zones: 5 to 8

London plane tree *(Platanus ×acerifolia)*

Description: This tree's peeling bark and narrow, spreading growth habit make this a classic choice for a shade or street tree. It grows from 70 to 100 feet tall and 65 to 80 feet wide when mature. The large, dark green leaves are wonderful but don't turn color in autumn. The peeling bark may leave yard litter and this tree needs plenty of room to grow, making it a good choice only in larger spaces.
Uses: Shade, specimen, street tree.
Site and care requirements: Plant in full sun to partial shade and virtually any type of soil, though it does best in moist to wet soil. This tree can be pruned heavily for more formal shaping. It is prone to anthracnose and powdery mildew, so remove dropped leaves and twigs to eliminate opportunity for spores to overwinter.
Recommended varieties and related species: 'Bloodgood', 'Liberty', and 'Columbia' are all cultivars that are disease resistant.

Plum, cherry *(Prunus cerasifera)*

Features: Reddish-purple leaves of the cultivars and fragrant spring flowers
Growth rate: Moderate
Zones: 5 to 8

Cherry plum *(Prunus cerasifera 'Vesuvius')*

Description: The real beauty of this tree is in the color of the foliage, which is found in the hybrids and cultivars, not the species. Leaves are red-purple throughout the growing season, providing a reliable accent color. The fragrant white or pink flowers bloom in the spring, often before the leaves emerge. The rounded, spreading growth habit makes the tree look a bit shrubby, but it is useful as a patio tree or the focal point in a shrub border. It grows to 20 feet tall and wide. It is susceptible to aphids, cankers, caterpillars, and leaf spots.
Uses: Specimen, accent, large containers, shrub border.
Site and care requirements: Plant in full sun and moist, well-drained soil. Check it often for pests and disease and treat accordingly.
Recommended varieties and related species: 'Atropurea' has reddish-purple leaves and pink flowers. It grows up to 25 feet high. 'Thundercloud' has deep purple leaves with flowers that bloom before the leaves emerge. The leaves of 'Newport' emerge a bronze-purple, turning a deep purple as they mature. The light pink to white flowers bloom before the leaves emerge.

Plum, Natal (see Natal plum)
Podocarpus macrophyllus (see Yew pine)
Poplar, Eastern (see Cottonwood)

Poplar, Lombardy *(Populus nigra 'Italica')*

Features: Tall, narrow columnar shape
Growth rate: Fast
Zones: 3 to 9

Lombardy poplar *(Populus nigra 'Italica')*

Description: The upright, narrow habit of the Lombardy poplar makes a striking statement in the landscape, particularly when planted in rows. Unfortunately, this fast-growing tree is short-lived, but is good for a fast screen. It grows 70 to 90 feet high and only 10 to 12 feet wide. Highly susceptible to fungal disease, canker, and borers, it often dies back as a result and becomes unsightly.
Uses: Screen.
Site and care requirements: Plant in full sun and a variety of soil conditions.

Poplar, white *(Populus alba)*

Features: Fast-growing screen, interesting bark, shimmery foliage
Growth rate: Fast
Zones: 2 to 6

White poplar *(Populus alba)*

Description: Somewhat narrower than its cousin, the cottonwood, and not quite so long-lived, the white poplar grows quickly to provide a screen, windbreak, or shade. The creamy white bark develops an interesting, almost distressed patina as it matures. The leaves, which are dark green on top and light on the underside, seem to shimmer as they flutter in the wind. Interestingly, the leaves are covered with a cottony white fuzz when they first appear. They turn a pale yellow in fall. Pyramidal in shape, this tree grows 75 feet tall and 40 feet wide, providing quick gratification when planted among more slow-growing trees.

White poplar fuzz

Uses: Screen, windbreak, shade.
Site and care requirements: Plant in moist, well-drained soil and full sun. It is susceptible to a variety of pests, including canker. Prune out deadwood and remove suckers that can become a weed problem in wet areas.
Recommended varieties and related species: *P. alba* **'Pyramidalis'** or **Bolleana poplar** is more columnar in shape, and grows up to 70 feet tall and 20 feet wide. It is also more disease resistant and robust.

Privet, California *(Ligustrum ovalifolium)*

Features: Lovely, dark green semievergreen foliage
Growth rate: Fast
Zones: 6 to 9

California privet *(Ligustrum ovalifolium)*

Description: California privet makes a good hedge plant because it can easily be pruned into a desired shape. Its lustrous, dark green leaves are especially attractive. The foliage is evergreen in warmer climates and semievergreen in cooler climates. The heavily scented white flowers are not particularly showy but contrast nicely with the foliage when they bloom in early to midsummer. When allowed to develop into its natural form, the shrub's oval to round growth habit makes it useful as a screen or barrier for a larger space. A plant can be pruned to fit a smaller space, although the fast-growing shrub will require frequent trimming. Hot, wet weather tends to speed up the growing process. California privet grows 10 to 15 feet high and wide with plants growing at the larger end of the spectrum in the warmer climates. Seedlings are a problem that can make hedges look unkempt if they're not removed when small.
Uses: Hedge, screen, barrier.
Site and care requirements: California privet survives in most conditions. Prune it frequently to maintain a desired form.
Recommended varieties and related species: 'Argenteum' has white-edged leaves; the leaves of 'Aureum' are bordered in yellow.

Privet, common *(Ligustrum vulgare)*

Features: Dense, quick-growing shrub for screening
Growth rate: Fast
Zones: 4 to 7

Common privet *(Ligustrum vulgare)*

Description: Common privet is an ideal hedge plant with its natural denseness and ability to tolerate shearing. The plant develops an upright, irregular, and spreading form when it is not shaped. It features unpleasant-smelling yet pretty white flowers in spring, followed by glossy black berries. Trimming the flowers early in the summer keeps the odor to a minimum. This privet grows to 15 feet high and wide.
Uses: Hedge, screen, barrier.
Site and care requirements: Plant in full sun to part shade in almost any kind of soil. Site away from foot traffic if you intend to keep the blooms. Prune as necessary to maintain the desired shape.
Recommended varieties and related species: 'Lodense' is compact and grows to 3 feet high and wide. Cold tolerant 'Cheyenne' grows to 6 feet tall and wide.

Common privet goes bushy without shaping.

Privet, golden vicary *(Ligustrum ×vicaryi)*

Features: Golden yellow foliage
Growth rate: Moderate
Zones: 5 to 8

Golden vicary privet *(Ligustrum ×vicaryi)*

Description: The yellow foliage is the outstanding feature of the golden vicary privet. It remains a golden yellow throughout the season but may become more yellow-green if planted in shade. The panicles of creamy white flowers bloom in late spring but bring with them a disagreeable odor that makes this plant inappropriate for areas with foot traffic. The vaselike shape is slightly oval to round and may be pruned to a desired shape. It is useful as a hedge planting or a screen when left to grow naturally. It may also be used as a specimen to highlight the wonderful foliage color. It grows 10 to 12 feet high and wide and is adaptable to a variety of soil conditions. It is drought tolerant.
Uses: Specimen, hedge, screen.
Site and care requirements: Plant in full sun to partial shade. Exposure to full sun will ensure lasting yellow leaf color, while it may be hard to develop and sustain the yellow color if it is planted in shade.

Privet, Japanese *(Ligustrum japonicum)*

Features: Evergreen shrub with glossy, green leaves
Growth rate: Moderate
Zones: 7 to 10

Japanese privet *(Ligustrum japonicum)*

Description: The compact growth of the Japanese privet makes it versatile in the home landscape. It can be used as a hedge or screen or even shaped into topiary. The leathery green leaves maintain their color throughout the year. They serve as a nice background for the panicles of white flowers that bloom in May. The blossoms have a strong fragrance that some might find unpleasant, so site the plant accordingly. The flowers give way to berries that turn bluish black when they ripen in fall. There may be yard litter when the berries fall because birds do not seem to favor them. Japanese privet requires little care other than occassional pruning to shape it. The shrub survives in a wide variety of soil conditions. This tough plant is drought, heat, and salt tolerant, making it a great choice for urban planting. If grown in the shade, it is susceptible to whiteflies and sooty mold but these can be controlled with proper treatments.
Uses: Hedge, screen, topiary.
Site and care requirements: Plant in full sun to develop the most maintenance-free plant. It can be pruned any time during the year to maintain the desired shape. It will survive in almost any soil except in soil that is constantly wet.

Privet lends itself to formal hedge shaping and topiary.

Prunus cerasifera (see Plum, Japanese flowering)
Prunus laurocerasus (see Cherry laurel)
Prunus maackii (see Chokecherry, amur)
Prunus persica (see Peach)
Prunus spp. (see Cherry, flowering)
Prunus triloba (see Almond, flowering)
Pseudotsuga menziesii (see Fir, douglas)
Pyracantha spp. (see Firethorn)
Pyrus spp. (see Pear)

Quaking aspen (Populus tremuloides)

Features: Golden yellow fall foliage that shakes in the breeze
Growth rate: Fast
Zones: 2 to 6

Quaking aspen (*Populus tremuloides*)

Description:
This is a tree in motion, with leaves that shimmer and quake at the slightest breeze. An extremely cold-hardy tree, the quaking aspen is a favorite in higher elevations and cooler climates of the North and West. It is not heat tolerant, however. When the leaves fall, the striking silhouette of a bare, pale trunk and branches is revealed. Aspen has a gently pyramidal shape

Quaking aspen in fall color

and grows 40 to 50 feet tall and about 20 to 30 feet wide. It is useful in naturalized landscapes, as it is particularly attractive when planted in groups. The quaking aspen tree is short-lived and is susceptible to canker and borers.
Uses: Grouping in a larger landscape.
Site and care requirements: This tree tolerates a variety of soils, including rocky, clay, or shallow.

Queen palm (see Palm, queen)
***Quercus* spp.** (see Oak)

Quince, common flowering (Chaenomeles speciosa)

Features: Lovely spring blooms in a vibrant variety of colors
Growth rate: Moderate
Zones: 4 to 8

Common flowering quince (*Chaenomeles speciosa*)

Description: The brilliant blooms of the common flowering quince, a Southern favorite, are nothing short of fantastic. In spring the shrub lights up with single or double blooms in rich shades of scarlet, pink, or pure white. The flowers may bloom again during the fall.

Flowering quince 'Pink Lady'

Bare stems are often brought inside and forced in winter. The blooms give way to yellow-pink fruit that ripens in October and is used in jellies and preserves. The shrub has an unusual growth habit, with branches reaching this way and that in a dense tangle. Sharp spines cover the branches, making this an effective plant for a barrier or privacy screen. Flowering quince grows 6 to 10 feet tall and wide and can be pruned into a more manageable shape. It tolerates drought and air pollution.
Uses: Specimen, screen, hedge.
Site and care requirements: Plant this shrub in full sun for best flowering and fruit production. It tolerates some shade but will produce fewer blooms. It adapts to many different soil conditions, but high pH soils make it prone to chlorosis. Prune after flowering to maintain its shape or cut it back severely to rejuvenate it.
Recommended varieties and related species: **'Orange Delight'** has bright orange flowers on a plant that grows to 3 feet tall. Red-flowered varieties include **'Old Red'**, **'Texas Scarlet'**, and **'Scarff's Red'**. The latter two varieties are nearly thornless. **'Jet Trail'** has pure white flowers. **'Cameo'** boasts double, peachy-pink blooms, while **'Pink Lady'** offers true pink blooms.

Rhaphiolepis indica (see Indian hawthorn)

Redbud, eastern *(Cercis canadensis)*

Features: Rosy pink-purple spring blooms and heart-shape leaves
Growth rate: Moderate
Zones: 4 to 9

Eastern redbud *(Cercis canadensis)*

Description: Deep reddish purple buds open up to rosy pink-purple blooms in April. Since blooms appear before leaves, the tree looks as if it's frosted in pink, especially when planted in rows

Eastern redbud 'Forest Pansy'

or groups. It makes a nice focal point in a shrub garden. The heart-shape green leaves turn yellow-green in fall and when they drop, the layered, horizontal branches are showcased in the winter landscape. The tree grows 20 to 30 feet tall and 25 to 35 feet wide, with a spreading habit.
Uses: Accent, specimen, grouping.
Site and care requirements: Plant in full sun to partial shade and moist, well-drained soil. It will tolerate a variety of soil conditions, including high pH or acid soil. Protect from wind to prevent storm damage. A damaged trunk may make the tree susceptible to canker.
Recommended varieties and related species: 'Forest Pansy' features purple heart-shaped leaves, though it requires some shade to keep the leaf color vibrant. 'Royal White' and 'Alba' are white-flowered varieties. 'Pinkbud' and 'Wither's Pink' both have bright pink blossoms.

Red cedar, eastern *(Juniperus virginiana)*

Features: A tough tree for screens and windbreaks
Growth rate: Moderate
Zones: 2 to 9

Description: This broadly shaped, pyramidal tree with rich, soft green foliage makes an excellent screen planting due to its dense growth habit and foliage. The tree is tough, often known for taking well to areas where few other plants can grow.

It tolerates a wide variety of soil conditions as well as drought and heat. It grows 40 to 50 feet high and 10 to 20 feet wide. It is susceptible to mites, bagworms, and cedar apple rust.
Uses: Screen, windbreak.
Site and care requirements: Plant the tree in full sun and well-drained soil.
Recommended varieties and related species: 'Canaertii' has a

Eastern red cedar *(Juniperus virginiana)*

dense, pyramidal form when pruned. When left to grow naturally, it becomes more open. 'Manhattan Blue' has blue-green foliage, while 'Silver Spreader' has silvery gray foliage. 'Glauca' has a more narrow growth habit.

Redwood, coast *(Sequoia sempervirens)*

Features: Notably large West Coast tree
Growth rate: Fast at the start, slowing with age
Zones: 7 to 9

Description: This native Northern California tree is a common site in western coastal areas where it grows very large—75 to 100 feet. Although it can be planted on the East Coast, this redwood won't reach its full potential for height there. Branches and foliage often fail to appear on the mature tree until almost 75 to 80 feet up the trunk. The young tree is pyramidal in shape and has branches all along the trunk. The reddish brown bark is vertically fissured, giving it another dimension of interest in

Coast redwood *(Sequoia sempervirens)*

the landscape. These trees require plenty of room to grow and are appropriate in large landscapes and woodland areas. While not drought tolerant, it withstands flood conditions.
Uses: Specimen.
Site and care requirements: Plant in full sun and deep, moist, acid, well-drained soil. It requires planting in areas with ample atmospheric moisture.
Recommended varieties and related species: Giant sequoia *(Sequoiadendron giganteum)* is the largest tree on earth, reaching heights of up to 300 feet in the Pacific Northwest.

Rhapidophyllum hystrix (see Palm, needle)

Rhododendron *(Rhododendron spp.)*

Features: Abundant, showy spring blooms
Growth rate: Slow
Zones: 4 to 10

Catawba rhododendron *(R. catawbiense* 'English Roseum')

Description: Rhododendrons and azaleas are planted almost exclusively for their profuse, colorful spring blooms. Both fall under the genus *Rhododendron* and are distinguished by their leaf and flower types. Rhododendrons are generally evergreen and feature large bell-shape flowers, while azaleas are generally deciduous and have funnelshape blooms. Both shrubs range from low-growing groundcovers to sprawling forms 20 feet high and wide. They make excellent specimens in a shrub border or mass plantings in a larger landscape. Evergreen rhododendrons tend to have more attractive foliage that may be a consideration when the plants aren't in bloom. Evergreen azaleas can be planted to make use of the postflower foliage as well. They prove especially useful in foundation plantings or as a background to shrubs or perennials that bloom later in spring or summer.

Uses: Specimen, shrub border, informal hedge or screen, groundcover.

Site and care requirements: Evergreen types need some shade while deciduous types that grow in colder climates need full sun. All require some shade in the South. Plant in well-drained, acid soil. Feed in spring and mulch to keep soil consistently moist throughout the growing season. Prune only as necessary after flowering. Watch for canker and leaf spot, Japanese beetles, and spider mites, as well as powdery mildew in humid climates. Treat conditions accordingly.

Recommended varieties and related species: First consider basic categories of rhododendrons and azaleas—evergreen rhododendrons, deciduous azaleas, and evergreen azaleas—and then delve into a sampling of recommended choices among the 900 species available.

Some basic species of **evergreen rhododendrons** include **Carolina rhododendron** *(R. carolinianum),* which is a smaller, gently rounded shrub with white or pink flowers and dark green leaves. It grows from 3 to 6 feet high and wide in Zones 5 to 8.

Rosebay rhododendron *(R. maximum)*

Catawba rhododendron *(R. catawbiense)* is a large, broad shrub featuring a profusion of bluish purple blooms and dark green foliage. It grows 6 to 10 feet high and wide in Zones 4 to 7.

Rosebay rhododendron *(R. maximum)* has a loosely open habit and blooms of white or pinkish purple, along

Rhododendron 'Dido'

with interesting thin-leafed foliage. It's somewhat more cold hardy than others but requires part shade. It grows up to 15 feet high and wide in Zones 4 to 7.

'Golden Torch' hybrid evergreen

Yakushima rhododendron *(R. yakushimanum)* is compact and rounded, and features a density of beautiful large flowers that bud in pink and rosy red before going white in full bloom. It grows only to 3 feet tall and wide in Zones 5 to 7.

Yakushima rhododendron *(R. yakushimanum)*

P.J.M. hybrids have late-blooming lavender flowers and dark green foliage that turns purple in autumn. They are rounded in form and grow from 3 to 6 feet tall and wide in Zones 4 to 7.

Kurume hybrid 'Ayaginu'

Evergreen azalea hybrids include **torch azaleas** *(R. kaempferi)*, which have blooms ranging in color from white to salmon to red on an oversize shrub. They grow to 10 feet tall in Zones 6 to 8.

Kurume hybrids are home landscape favorites, with their manageable scale and dense and profuse blooms. They grow to about 6 feet tall in Zones 6 to 9.

Gable hybrids feature blooms of all shades of reds and purples, with foliage that reddens in fall in the cooler areas where they grow. A moderate-size shrub, it grows in Zones 6 to 8.

Girard hybrids feature oversized flowers in red, pinks, purples, and white on an attractive 4- to 6-foot shrub that grows in Zones 6 to 9.

Gable hybrid 'Herbert'

Glenn Dale hybrids offer long-blooming flowers of pink, orange, red, and white, with occasional flecks or stripes of contrasting color.

Robin Hill hybrids are somewhat cold hardy and feature late blooms of white, pink, salmon, red, and lavender.

Glenn Dale hybrid 'Glamour'

Kurume hybrid

Knapp Hill-Exbury hybrid 'Iora'

shrub with bright green foliage and fragrant pink to white blooms that appear in April or May. Unlike other rhododendrons this plant prefers full sun.

Royal azalea (*R. schlippenbachii*) has an upright, rounded form and features fragrant pink to white flowers in May. Foliage is dark green during the growing season and changes to a variety of classic colors in autumn. It grows 6 to 8 feet tall and wide in Zones 5 to 8.

Knap Hill-Exbury hybrid 'Harvest Moon' rhododendron

Some **deciduous azalea hybrids** include the popular **Knapp Hill-Exbury hybrids,** which feature large blooms in a vast selection of colors and foliage that turns yellow, orange, and red in autumn. These grow 4 to 8 feet tall and wide in Zones 6 to 8.

Knapp Hill hybrid

Flame azalea (*R. calendulaceum*) grows from 6 to 8 feet tall and features blooms of yellow, orange, and red, as well as fine yellow to copper fall foliage. It is hardy in Zones 5 to 7.

Korean azalea (*R. mucronulatum*) features an abundance of small, cheerful, rosy purple blooms in early spring. This shrub has an open, spreading, natural form and grows from 4 to 8 feet high and wide in Zones 4 to 7.

Pinxterbloom azalea (*R. periclymenoides*) is a tidy, smaller

Flame azalea (*R. calendulaceum*)

Rhus **spp.** (see Sumac)
Ribes alpinum (see Currant, alpine)
Robinia pseudoacacia (see Locust, black)

Rock rose *(Cistus spp.)*

Features: Fragrant evergreen foliage and bright, cheerful blooms
Growth rate: Moderate
Zones: 8 to 10

Rock rose *(Cistus spp.)*

Description: The handsome grayish-green foliage on this low-growing evergreen shrub is almost as winning as the colorful five-petaled blooms of white, pink, red, or purple that appear in summer. Rock rose makes a nice specimen planting or grouping, especially at the front of a shrub border. It grows in an irregular mounded shape 3 to 6 feet tall and 4 to 8 feet wide.
Uses: Accent, specimen, shrub border, grouping, slope.
Site and care requirements: Plant in full sun and well-drained soil. Once established it's drought resistant as well as salt and wind tolerant. Pinch back young plants to encourage vigorous growth.
Recommended varieties and related species: 'Sunset' rock rose (*C. ×pulverulentus*) is a spreading groundcover with sea green leaves and bright pink flowers. It grows no more than 1 foot tall and about 5 feet wide. **Pink rock rose** (*C. incanus*) is a hearty bloomer and has a vigorous spread. **Sage leaf rock rose** (*C. salvifolius*) is an upright shrub with sagelike leaves and white blooms that grows to 3 feet tall and wide.

Rosa **spp.** (see Rose)

Rosemary *(Rosmarinus officinalis)*

Features:
Aromatic, edible leaves and tiny purple blooms
Growth rate: Fast
Zones: 7 to 9

Description:
Generally known as an herb garden standard, rosemary also makes an excellent aromatic shrub in hot, dry climates. Its bushy, irregular

Rosemary *(Rosmarinus officinalis)*

habit gives a rough or informal impression, but the unmistakable scent of the needlelike gray-green foliage and purple blooms is a delightful component of a shrub border, rock garden, or container planting. When well-established, rosemary withstands shearing and makes a delightful choice for a hedge. It grows 2 to 4 feet tall and 3 to 5 feet wide.
Uses: Container, shrub border, rock garden.
Site and care requirements: Plant in full sun and well-drained soil. Rosemary can tolerate heat, poor soil, and drought but not soggy soil. Plant in containers in northern locations and overwinter in a sunny spot indoors.

Rosemary 'Arp'

Recommended varieties and related species: 'Tuscan Blue' has bright blue flowers and an upright habit. **'Lockwood de Forest'** is a low-growing spreader with blue flowers. **'Arp'** is an upright variety with purple blooms.

Rose of Sharon *(Hibiscus syriacus)*

Features: Lovely summer blooms in a variety of colors
Growth rate: Moderate
Zones: 5 to 9

Rose of Sharon *(Hibiscus syriacus)*

Description: Its large cheerful blooms, in colors ranging from white to pink, red, or purple, are a welcome midsummer sight. This open, rounded shrub is a valuable component in a shrub border and groupings, and even in a loose, informal screen, as it grows 8 to 12 feet high and 6 to 10 feet wide. It needs supplemental watering during dry spells, so site accordingly.
Uses: Border, grouping, screen.
Site and care requirements: Plant in full sun and moist, well-drained soil. Feed only in the springtime and protect from wind in winter. Mulch to keep the soil moist during the growing season. Prune back aggressively in late winter to encourage vigorous flowering.
Recommended varieties and related species: 'Diana' is a dwarf variety with white, ruffled flowers. **'Minerva'** has lavender blooms tinged with pink and a distinct red center. **'Blue Bird'** bears lavender-blue flowers.

Rose (Rosa spp.)

Features: Beauty, elegance, fragrance
Growth rate: Fast
Zones: 2 to 10, depending on the species

'Henry Fonda' hybrid tea

Description: For their unique beauty and seemingly infinite variety, roses appeal to the amateur as well as the connoisseur. They proudly stand alone, they form elegant groups, they climb, they hedge, and they do much more. In every case they make plants nearby rise to the elegant occasion. With so many types, colors, and forms to choose from, selecting roses for the home landscape is less about gardening than it is about discovering your particular affinity.

Uses: Specimen, border, informal hedge, climber, groundcover, container.

Site and care requirements: Plant in full sun and moist, fertile, slightly acid, well-drained soil. Feed throughout spring and summer for abundant blooms. Prune according to the requirements of each type of rose; generally hybrid teas, floribundas, miniatures, and grandifloras take pruning in early spring, while climbers and shrub roses are pruned after flowering. Depending on the zone, some roses require protection from winter conditions. Avoid wetting foliage when watering to reduce the chance for black spot to develop. Watch for aphids, spider mites, and Japanese beetles and treat an infestation accordingly.

Recommended varieties and related species: Consider the following general categories of roses and a sampling of recommended choices among hundreds of species and thousands of hybrids.

Hybrid tea roses produce large flowers on single stems, and they bloom repeatedly. As the most popular type of rose, it offers a wealth of bloom colors on generally upright plants that grow up to 5 feet high and 3 feet wide. Hybrid teas make nice specimen plants.

'Queen Elizabeth' hybrid tea

They require regular feeding, pruning, and attention to pests and disease. Recommended choices include **'Double Delight'**, **'First Prize'**, **'Miss All-American Beauty'**, **'Rio Samba'**, **'Whisper'**, and **'Queen Elizabeth'**.

'Rio Samba' hybrid tea

'Double Delight' hybrid tea

'Diana' hybrid tea

'Glowing Peace' grandiflora

Grandifloras are in most ways similar to hybrid teas, but feature a greater abundance of blooms that are often clustered. Excellent choices include **'Cherry Parfait'**, **'Fame!'**, **'Glowing Peace'**, **'Strike It Rich'**, **'Mount Hood'**, and **'Candelabra'**.

Climbers grow from long, flexible canes that can be affixed to an arbor, fence, trellis, or wall. Without training they form somewhat gangly, arching shrubs or sprawling mounds. Recommended choices include **'Altissimo'**, **'Paul's Scarlet Climber'**, **'Iceberg'**, **'White Dawn'**, and **'Austrian Copper'**.

'Austrian Copper' climber

'Cherry Parfait' grandiflora

'Candelabra' grandiflora

Floribundas are shorter and broader shrubs than hybrid teas, growing 3 feet high and 4 feet wide, with profuse clustered blooms of smaller flowers on shorter stems. These plants have a bushier habit and are somewhat hardier and more disease resistant than hybrid teas. Floribundas lend themselves to massing as well as informal hedges. Recommended choices include **'Betty Boop'**, **'Gingersnap'**, **'Hot Cocoa'**, **'Livin' Easy'**, and **'Rainbow Sorbet'**.

'Iceberg' climber

'Hot Cocoa' floribunda

'Baby Love' miniature

Miniatures, as diminuatives of mostly hybrid tea roses, have smaller leaves, stems, and flowers. They grow to about 2 feet tall and wide, making them good choices for containers, groundcovers, and low hedges. Recommended choices include **'Baby Grand'**, **'Baby Love'**, **'Black Jade'**, **'Child's Play'**, **'Gourmet Popcorn'**, and **'Party Girl'**.

'Betty Boop' floribunda

'Gourmet Popcorn' miniature

Shrub roses include the classic varieties with an abundance of blooms; bushy, spreading habits; and a reputation for general hardiness. You'll find shrub roses come in various sizes—generally growing to 4 feet tall and 6 feet wide. Popular choices include **'Pearl Meidiland'**, **'Carefree Wonder'**, **'DayDream'**, and **Simplicity**.

'Carefree Wonder' classic shrub

'Scarlet Meidiland' classic shrub

'Simplicity' classic shrub

'Graham Thomas' modern shrub

Modern shrub roses feature the repeat blooms of hybrids combined with the old-fashioned form, colors, and scents of old garden roses. They are compact, bushy shrubs that are often hardy to Zone 4. Recommended choices include **'Ballerina'**, **'Gertrude Jekyll'**, **'Graham Thomas'**, and **'William Baffin'**.

'Ballerina' modern shrub

Species roses are wild roses that feature fragrant, open, five-petaled flowers that bloom for several weeks in early summer, and rose hips that are lovely in winter and of great interest to birds. These roses can be upright or low-spreading and are notoriously thorny. They are hardy and quite adaptable in many soils, and tend to be more disease and pest resistant than the hybrid roses. **Red-leaf roses** (*R. glauca*) are grown for their foliage, which is somewhat tinged with purple, and for the attractive rose-pink blooms. **Rugosa roses** (*R. rugosa*) feature red, pink, or white flowers and crinkled foliage that turns orange in autumn.

Red-leaf species rose (*Rosa glauca*)

Rosmarinus officinalis (see Rosemary)
Rowan tree (see Mountain ash, European)
Russian silverberry (see Silverberry, Russian)

Sabal palmetto (see Palm, cabbage)
Sago palm (see Palm, sago)
Salix spp. (see Willow)
Sambucus spp. (see Elder)
Sapium sebiferum (see Tallow tree, Chinese)

Sassafras *(Sassafras albidum)*

Features: Fragrant foliage and wood, lovely spring blooms, and fine fall color
Growth rate: Moderate to fast
Zones: 5 to 9

Sassafras *(Sassafras albidum)*

Description: Sassafras is a wonderful native tree with distinctive, aromatic, mitten-shape leaves that are bright green during the growing season and turn excellent shades of yellow, orange, and red in autumn. Delightful clusters of yellow flowers appear in early spring, ahead of the leaves and purple

Sassafras blooms

berries beloved by birds and other wildlife. The tree has an irregular, somewhat pyramidal form, with branches that grow out horizontally and zigzag a bit, to offer an interesting layered effect similar to that of the eastern redbud. It grows 30 to 60 feet tall and 25 to 40 feet wide. It works well as a shade tree or planted in a group to form a naturalized grove.
Uses: Specimen, shade, shrub border, grouping.
Site and care requirements: Plant in full sun to part shade and slightly acid, well-drained soil. It is prone to chlorosis in soil with high pH. The plant does not transplant well, so site

it carefully. Male and female trees must be planted together for fruit to be produced. Feed once in springtime and prune in winter, as necessary, to maintain the overall shape.

Schinus molle (see Pepper tree)
Sciadopitys verticillata (See Umbrella pine, Japanese)

Sea buckthorn *(Hippophae rhamnoides)*

Features: Striking orange fruit clusters and distinctive gray-green and silver leaves
Growth rate: Fast
Zones: 3 to 7

Sea buckthorn *(Hippophae rhamnoides)*

Description: The sea buckthorn is a terrific feature in a seaside landscape with distinctive orange berries that appear in September and stay with the plant through the fall and winter. The silvery green foliage is similar to that of an olive tree. It is thorny and therefore best planted in a spot away from foot traffic. Though hard to transplant, this shrub is hardy in most soils, even salty or wet soil.
Uses: Mass planting, border, specimen.
Site and care requirements: It needs full sun and thrives in poor soil. Prune as necessary in late summer, before fruiting.

Serviceberry, downy (Amelanchier arborea)

Features: Cheerful spring blooms, sweet purple berries, and fall color
Growth rate: Moderate
Zones: 4 to 9

Downy serviceberry (*Amelanchier arborea*)

Description: The downy serviceberry offers something for every season in the home landscape. The multistemmed shrub can be pruned when young to form a lovely specimen tree. Clusters of delicately fragrant, pure white flowers bloom at the ends of the branches as early as March and last as late as June. Not long after first bloom, bright green leaves appear that turn stunning orange and red in autumn. Sweet, edible, dark purple berries appear in June and last until August—or until harvested by man or beast. The berries are often used to make jams, jellies, and wine. The downy serviceberry has a naturally rounded shape and can grow from 15 to 25 feet high and 15 to 20 feet wide. It makes a fine informal hedge or screen if left to grow as a shrub.
Uses: Specimen, shrub border, hedge, screen, grouping.

Downy serviceberry blooms

Allegheny serviceberry

Site and care requirements: Plant in full sun or part shade and moist, well-drained soil. It is tolerant of a variety of soils as well as drought. Prune root suckers that appear in spring.
Recommended varieties and related species: See below.

Allegheny serviceberry (*A. laevis*) is similar to the downy serviceberry in size and general presentation, but it is more upright than rounded, and has leaves that are tinged purple, as well as sweeter berries. It is also less drought and heat tolerant and does best in Zones 4 to 8.

Apple serviceberry (*A. ×grandiflora*) is a hybrid of the downy and Allegheny serviceberries and features the best qualities of both—and then some. It has a slightly more graceful form than its parents, and larger, more profuse blooms that appear pink to white in May. It has an irregular rounded form and grows 20 to 25 feet high and wide in Zones 3 to 8. It adapts to a wide range of soils and is drought tolerant.

Sequoia sempervirens (see Redwood, coast)

Seven-son flower (Heptacodium miconioides)

Features: Creamy white late-summer blooms and interesting peeling bark and fruit
Growth rate: Moderate
Zones: 5 to 8

Seven-son flower (*Heptacodium miconioides*)

Description: This wonderful shrub or small tree offers all its gifts late in the growing season, making it a fine complement to early blooming and fruiting trees and shrubs. Its upright, spreading form features arching dark green foliage that turns purple-green before it drops in late autumn, revealing a lovely, peeling, cinnamon-colored bark. Fragrant, creamy white panicled clusters of seven flowers (hence the name) appear in late summer, followed by small round berries. Each berry is topped with an extraordinary red flowerlike calyx. This plant makes a good specimen or an outstanding feature in a shrub border. It grows to 20 feet high and up to 15 feet wide.
Uses: Specimen, shrub border, grouping.
Site and care requirements: Plant in full sun to moderate shade and moist, well-drained soil. Mulch to keep soil consistently moist throughout the growing season. Feed in spring and prune as necessary in winter to remove damaged or crossed branches and to shape the plant. Does not tolerate drought, so supplemental watering is necessary during dry spells.

Shepherdia argentea (see Buffaloberry, silver)
Siberian peashrub (see Peashrub, Siberian)

Silk tree *(Albizia julibrissin)*

Features: Fernlike foliage and unusual pincushion blooms
Growth rate: Moderate to fast
Zones: 6 to 9

Silk tree *(Albizia julibrissin)*

Silk tree bloom

Description: This tropical-looking tree doesn't grow in the tropics. Also known as the mimosa tree, its fernlike foliage and exotic-looking blooms set it apart from other plants in the home landscape. On a wide, spreading, vase-shape form, distinctive leaves appear later in springtime than those of other trees. Flowering follows in mid- to late summer. The extraordinary blooms are fragrant and round, resembling silky pink bristles. Hummingbirds and bees favor the flowers. Silk tree makes a nice specimen if you don't mind the litter of the leaves, blooms, and seedpods that follow the blooms. This unusual tree complements most settings, whether used as a specimen, a strong mass, or a group planted at the edge of the landscape. It grows to 20 to 35 feet high and wide.
Uses: Specimen, grouping, massing.
Site and care requirements: Plant in full sun and well-drained soil. Adaptable to most types of soil, this tree is wind, drought, and salt tolerant. Prune sparingly only to remove damaged branches. Silk tree is susceptible to webworm, leaf spot, and rust but especially to vascular wilt disease and freezing injuries, leading to dieback.
Recommended varieties and related species: **'Rosea'** is somewhat smaller and has deeper pink flowers. **'Ernest Wilson'** is more cold tolerant.

Silverbell, Carolina *(Halesia tetraptera)*

Features: Lovely clusters of white late-spring flowers and attractive fruit
Growth rate: Moderate
Zones: 5 to 8

Carolina silverbell *(Halesia tetraptera)*

Description: This lovely ornamental tree is a great choice for planting among other trees or shrubs that bloom before or after it. Glossy, yellow-green leaves appear in April or May, just as the clusters of bell-shape flowers begin to pop out. These blooms are exceptional beauties, comparable to those found on crabapple or dogwood. Winged fruit appears in early autumn and can remain on the tree through winter. This tree has a loosely pyramidal form and grows up to 35 feet high and 25 feet wide. Enjoy Carolina silverbell as a specimen or grouped for a naturalized effect.
Uses: Specimen, border, grouping.
Site and care requirements: Plant in full sun to part shade in moist, well-drained, nutrient-rich soil. Mulch to keep soil consistently moist throughout the growing season. Feed in early spring and prune, as necessary, after flowering. Does not tolerate drought or heat, or poor or alkaline soils.
Recommended varieties and related species: **'Rosea'** has lovely pink flowers. **'Meehanii'** is smaller with a shrubbier form. **'Silver Splash'** and **'Variegata'** have leaves of green and white or yellow.

Silverberry, Russian *(Elaeagnus angustifolia)*

Features: Rustic, gray-green foliage
Growth rate: Moderate to fast
Zones: 2 to 7

Russian silverberry *(Elaeagnus angustifolia)*

Description: Often called Russian olive, this handsome small tree has a loosely rounded form and fine silvery gray-green foliage. Fragrant flowers appear in the spring, though they're too small to see among the leaves. Silvery green berries appear in late summer and are relished by birds. Plant the tree as an accent in a shrub border or to form a loose hedge or screen. This tree does best in dry climates and is salt and drought tolerant once established. It grows to 15 feet tall and wide.
Uses: Shrub border, hedge, screen, grouping.
Site and care requirements: Plant the tree in full sun and loamy, sandy soil. Prune to desired shape. Russian olive does not do well in extreme heat where leaf spot, canker, rust, wilt, aphids, and scale may become a problem.
Recommended varieties and related species: Silverberry *(E. commutata)* grows to a dense 6 to 12 feet high and is hardy in Zones 4 to 6. **Thorny silverberry** *(E. pungens)* is hardy in warmer climates—Zones 6 to 10—and forms a good natural barrier due to the spiny leaves and occasional thorns found on the twigs.

Smoketree *(Cotinus coggygria)*

Features: Abundant feathery fruit clusters and fine foliage
Growth rate: Moderate
Zones: 4 to 8

Smoketree *(Cotinus coggygria)*

Description: Cottony feathery plumes flower in June, distinguishing the tree and creating an illusion of smoke around it—suggesting its name. The tiny hairs on these panicled blooms turn from salmony pink to purple over time. The foliage is blue-green in spring and summer but typically turns orange to red in autumn. It grows 10 to 15 feet tall and wide and can be pruned to the shape of a small tree or left in its naturally shrubby state.
Uses: Accent in a shrub border, grouping, slope.

Smoketree foliage

Site and care requirements: Plant in full sun and well-drained soil of just about any type. Maintain consistently moist soil during the growing season, but avoid areas where soil remains wet. Feed in springtime and prune out older branches in early spring to encourage vigorous growth. Winter dieback is common in colder zones; prune out deadwood after the plants leaf out in spring.
Recommended varieties and related species: 'Royal Purple' and 'Nordine' feature lovely purple foliage. 'Daydream' offers dense, dark buff-colored blooms.

Snowbell, Japanese *(Styrax japonicum)*

Features: Showy bell-shape flowers, handsome bark, and horizontal form
Growth rate: Moderate
Zones: 5 to 8

Description: This is a prized tree in any landscape, with its striking horizontal habit and delightful spring blooms. Slightly drooping branches are the host to lightly fragrant, pendulous, white bell-shape flowers that hang below the foliage on the branch, as if protected by little green parasols. The branching pattern of this tree is exceptionally handsome, as is the smooth, gray-brown bark, and

Japanese snowbell *(Styrax japonicum)*

offers fine winter interest. It grows 20 to 30 feet high and wide. Plant as a specimen or for gentle shade.
Uses: Specimen, shade.
Site and care requirements: Plant in moist, well-drained acid soil in full sun to part shade. Does not tolerate dry or alkaline soil and should be protected from harsh wind. Mulch to keep soil consistently moist throughout the growing season. Feed in spring and prune lightly in winter, only to maintain the tree's shape.
Recommended varieties and related species: 'Emerald Pagoda' has larger, darker leaves and flowers and is more heat-tolerant. **'Pendula'** has a weeping habit, and **'Pink Chimes'** has pink flowers.

Fragrant snowbell *(S. obassia)* is a narrower, more upright tree, with large green leaves that lend texture. It features large clusters of fragrant white flowers and is hardy in Zone 6.

Snowberry *(Symphoricarpos albus)*

Features: Attractive white autumn fruit on a shade-loving shrub
Growth rate: Moderate
Zones: 3 to 7

Description: This is an excellent late-blooming shrub for shady areas of the landscape. The foliage stays blue-green throughout the growing season, and small slightly pink blooms appear in late summer. The real payoff is the abundant white berrylike fruit that follows the blooms, staying on the plant from September through the winter. This plant, which grows 3 to 6 feet high and wide, tends to form a thicket, so it's a good choice for edges of the landscape or slopes. Hummingbirds like the flowers, and a range of wildlife finds refuge in the dense shrub.
Uses: Shady areas, grouping, slope.
Site and care requirements: Plant in full sun to deep shade and moist, well-drained soil of just about any type. Keep soil

consistently moist throughout the growing season. Prune to shape in early spring and feed in springtime. It's susceptible to anthracnose, blight, and powdery mildew, so watch for signs and treat accordingly.
Recommended varieties and related species:
Indian currant

Snowberry *(Symphoricarpos albus)*

coralberry *(S. orbiculatus)* has an arching, lower-growing, and wider-spreading habit, and the fruit is an ordinary red, compared to the remarkable white of the snowberry.

Sophora japonica (see Pagoda tree, Japanese)
Sorbus aucuparia (Mountain ash, European)
Sorrel tree (see Sourwood)
Sour gum (see Black gum)

Sourwood *(Oxydendrum arboreum)*

Features: Fine foliage for three seasons, and fragrant, drooping flowers
Growth rate: Slow
Zones: 5 to 9

Description: This tree makes a fine specimen with its nearly weeping, pyramidal form and top-notch foliage. The lustrous dark green leaves are at their best deep

Sourwood *(Oxydendrum arboreum)*

into the summer, when fragrant flowers appear on 10-inch-long drooping racemes that extend from the tips of the branches. The long-lasting blooms turn to yellow fruit that hangs on to the tree into winter. Come autumn the leaves turn a spectacular range of colors, from yellow, orange, and red to purple, often all at once on the same tree. It grows 25 to 30 feet tall and 20 feet wide. Plant it close enough to your house that you can appreciate its features year-round.
Uses: Specimen, accent in a shrub border.
Site and care requirements: Plant in full sun to part shade and acid, moist, well-drained soil. It does not transplant well, so site carefully. Mulch to keep soil consistently moist during the growing season. Feed in spring and avoid cultivating the soil beneath the tree, so as to protect the shallow roots.
Recommended varieties and related species:
'Chameleon' is more upright and has a wonderful changing color palette when the leaves turn in autumn. **'Mt. Charm'** features early fall color.

Spirea, vanhoutte *(Spiraea ×vanhouttei)*

Features: Showy blooms on arching branches
Growth rate: Fast
Zones: 4 to 8

Vanhoutte spirea *(Spiraea ×vanhouttei)*

Japanese spirea *(S. japonica)*

Recommended varieties and related species: Japanese spirea *(S. japonica)* is a smaller shrub that features showy rosy pink to red flowers and lime green summer foliage. Flower clusters appear in late spring through early summer. It works nicely planted in groups or to form an informal low-growing hedge. It grows 4 to 5 feet tall and wide in Zones 4 to 8 and prefers full sun.

Japanese white spirea *(S. albiflora)* is a dense, low-growing mounded shrub that's a useful complement to the mixed shrub border. It features attractive blue-green foliage and large clusters of white flowers that look like little bouquets from a distance. It grows 2 to 3 feet high and wide in Zones 5 to 8.

Bumald spirea *(S. ×bumalda* 'Goldflame')

Description: This tough, dependable shrub is covered with charming clusters of small white flowers in mid to late spring. Before and after the flowers bloom, the foliage is pleasant but unremarkable, though the broad, arching habit of the shrub has year-round appeal and is useful in a mixed shrub border or foundation planting. It grows 6 to 8 feet high and 10 to 12 feet wide.

Uses: Specimen, shrub border, foundation planting, grouping.

Site and care requirements: Plant in full sun to part shade and well-drained soil. It's prone to chlorosis in overly alkaline soils. Keep soil consistently moist throughout the growing season. Feed sparingly in springtime and prune out a few older stems each spring to encourage vigorous growth and flowering for the upcoming season. Prune to shape after flowering.

Bumald spirea *(S. ×bumalda)* has many fans of its pink to rosy red blooms, bright green foliage, and open, spreading habit. It typically grows 3 feet high and up to 5 feet wide in Zones 4 to 8. Longtime favorite **'Goldflame'** bears pink blooms and lime green spring and summer foliage that can turn red in autumn. **'Crispa'** has fringed foliage, and **'Anthony Waterer'** has large pink blooms.

Spruce *(Picea* spp.)

Features: Large adaptable needled group of evergreens
Growth rate: Slow to moderate
Zones: 2 to 7, depending on the species

Bird's nest Norway spruce (*P. abies* 'Nidiformis')

Description: Spruces are evergreen favorites, with their large pyramidal forms and appealing variety of foliage color, cones, and branching habits. Some are more formal and commanding, while others are friendly and more versatile in the home landscape. They are fine as specimen trees or planted in groups to form a windscreen or barrier in a larger landscape. Each has its particular appeal, but all are a welcome sight in a bleak winter landscape, especially when frosted with snow. Spruces tend to grow at a slow to moderate pace, and are generally adaptable in a variety of soils and environmental conditions.
Uses: Specimen, grouping, screen.
Site and care requirements: Plant in full sun to light shade and well-drained, slightly acid soil. Keep evenly moist as it becomes established. Prune only lightly at the tips, after new growth is finished, to maintain shape.

Recommended varieties and related species: Norway spruce *(P. abies)* is commonly planted in the home landscape. Among the largest of the spruces, it grows to 100 feet tall, although it usually reaches about 40 to 60 feet tall and 25 to 30 feet wide. This spruce features a classic pyramidal shape with branches that become softly drooping as the tree matures. The stiff, dark green needles replace themselves every eight years. New cones are soft and purple or green. They turn dry and brown over the course of a season. This tree is a wildlife favorite for its cones as well as its dense, nest-friendly habit. It is hardy in Zones 2 to 7. Bird's nest spruce, or *P. abies* **'Nidiformis',** is a slow-growing dwarf that makes a fine specimen in a shrub border or rock garden. It grows only to 3 feet high and wide.

White spruce (*P. glauca* 'Arneson's Blue')

White spruce *(P. glauca),* also known as Alberta spruce, is a hardy, dependable evergreen with a dense, narrower pyramidal form and neatly spreading habit. The foliage is a silvery blue-green, and tight light green cones appear on the tree in early spring and turn brown over the course of the summer, often hanging on until winter. The cones are wildlife favorites. It grows to 40 to 60 feet high and 10 to 20 feet wide, and while a slow grower, it is long-lived, often lasting in the landscape for hundreds of years. It's hardy in Zones 2 to 7. **'Conica'** is a dwarf white spruce that grows only to 10 or 12 feet and features light green needles that circle around the stem like a bottlebrush. **'Arneson's Blue'** is a dwarf with bluish needles.

Serbian spruce *(P. omorika)*

Oriental spruce *(P. orientalis* 'Connecticut Turnpike')

Colorado blue spruce *(P. pungens* var. *glauca)*

Serbian spruce *(P. omorika)* is a fine spruce to plant as a specimen, with its more open form and elegantly feathered branches. The dark green foliage is flat like that of a hemlock or fir. Cones appear in May or June, turning purple and hanging down from the branches through early winter. As with other spruces, its cones are popular with squirrels and other creatures, and the tree is a welcome nesting place for birds. It grows 50 to 60 feet tall and 20 to 25 feet wide in Zones 4 to 7.

Oriental spruce *(P. orientalis)* has a graceful, narrowly pyramidal form, denser than the Serbian spruce but with the same upward-tilted, feathery-branched appeal. It has glossy, dark green foliage and features red to reddish purple cones in springtime, which turn brown over the course of the season. It makes a fine specimen tree or screen, growing slowly but to an impressive height of up to 60 feet and 15 feet wide. It is hardy in Zones 6 to 8. **'Aurea'** features delightful visual appeal with its bright gold new-growth foliage. **'Gowdy'** grows only to 10 feet, with a narrow, columnar form.

Colorado spruce *(P. pungens)* is a cool winter climate standard, with its dense branches and gray to blue-green foliage. **Colorado blue spruce** *(P. pungens* var. *glauca)* is a hands-down favorite, flaunting stiff blue needles and a handsome pyramidal form. Growing from 30 to 60 feet high and 10 to 20 feet wide, it's suitable even for a moderate-size landscape as a specimen. It also makes an impressive grouping in a larger landscape. It's hardy in Zones 3 to 7. Popular cultivars include **'Hoopsii',** which has a dense pyramidal form and **'Thompsonii',** which has silver-blue foliage and somewhat horizontal branching on a very regular, pyramidal form. **'Moerheimii'** has a more open habit and deep blue needles.

Stewartia, Japanese *(Stewartia pseudocamellia)*

Features: Elegant summer flowers, deep fall color, fine peeling bark
Growth rate: Slow
Zones: 5 to 7

Japanese stewartia *(Stewartia pseudocamellia)*

Description: Stewartia aims to please in every season. In winter the peeling reddish brown bark reveals patches of gray, green, and orange beneath, providing one of the most distinctive sights of the season. Spring brings handsome medium to dark green foliage, followed by exquisite white camellialike blooms in July, long after most trees have finished their flowery show. In autumn the leaves turn a deep reddish purple before falling. Stewartia grows 30 to 40 feet tall and 25 to 30 feet wide in a pyramidal to oval shape. Due to its multiseason appeal, stewartia makes a fine specimen tree, especially when planted within easy view from the house, or as a focal point in a shrub border.
Uses: Specimen, shrub border.
Site and care requirements: Plant in moist, acid, well-drained soil and part shade to full sun, although the tree prefers some shade during the hottest part of the day. Mulch to keep the soil moist throughout the growing season. Provide supplemental water during periods of extreme heat or drought.
Recommended varieties and related species: 'Ballet' features 4-inch flowers and a spreading habit. **'Milk and Honey'** bears an abundance of larger blooms and brighter bark. **'Cascade'** has a somewhat weeping form.

Korean stewartia *(S. koreana)* is very similar to Japanese stewartia but somewhat smaller, growing only to 20 or 30 feet

Japanese stewartia blooms

tall and 15 to 20 feet wide, making it a suitable choice for a smaller landscape. The blooms are long-lasting and the fall foliage is more red than purple. It's also hardy in Zones 5 to 7.

Tall stewartia *(S. monadelpha)* is shorter than Japanese stewartia although somewhat wider than Korean stewartia, growing 20 to 30 feet tall and 20 to 30 feet wide. It distinguishes itself with slightly smaller blooms that have purple centers. It is also more heat tolerant, making it a good prospect for Southern gardens. It is hardy in Zones 5 to 8.

Tall stewartia *(S. monadelpha)* in fall color

Styrax japonicus (see Snowbell, Japanese)

St. johnswort, shrubby *(Hypericum prolificum)*

Features: Easy to grow, sweet yellow blooms, and ornamental fruit
Growth rate: Slow
Zones: 4 to 8

Description: This dense, low-growing rounded shrub is a treat tucked in pockets of a shrub border. It has attractive dark green foliage, bright yellow blooms that last from June to August, and dark red berrylike fruit that lasts into the winter. Cut winter stems are a favorite for dried arrangements. This plant is agreeable and easy to grow in a variety of soil conditions. St. Johnswort grows from 1 to 4 feet tall and wide.
Uses: Border, massing, rock garden.

Shrubby st. johnswort *(Hypericum prolificum)*

St. johnswort blooms

Site and care requirements: Plant in full sun to light shade and well-drained soil. Water well until established and it becomes drought tolerant. Prune in late spring, after new growth is finished.
Recommended varieties and related species: Golden st. johnswort *(H. frondosum* 'Sunburst') has smart-looking blue-green foliage. **Kalm st. johnswort** *(H. kalmianum)* is a 3-foot shrub that blooms heartily and is most suited to Zone 4.

Sumac, fragrant *(Rhus aromatica)*

Features: Fuzzy red fruits and fine fall foliage
Growth rate: Slow to moderate
Zones: 3 to 9

Fragrant sumac *(Rhus aromatica)*

Description: This shrub takes on a densely mounded, spreading, and slightly tangled appearance that lends itself to effective massing as a groundcover, especially on a slope. It has glossy green foliage and fuzzy berrylike fruit that ripens on female plants in August or September. The leaves turn orange-red or red-purple before falling in autumn. Sumac grows 2 to 6 feet high and 6 to 10 feet wide.
Uses: Groundcover, massing, barrier, slope.
Site and care requirements: Plant in full sun to part shade and well-drained, slightly acid soil. Sumac will tolerate a variety of soil types, including poor or gravelly soil. Mulch to keep consistently moist through the growing season, especially in the first two years.
Recommended varieties and related species: 'Grow-Low' has a lower-growing, spreading form and foliage that is a warm orange-red in autumn.

Sumac, staghorn *(Rhus typhina)*

Features: Brilliant fall color and fernlike leaves
Growth rate: Fast at first, then slow as it matures
Zones: 4 to 8

Staghorn sumac *(Rhus typhina)*

Description: The fernlike foliage on this shrubby tree gives it an exotic appearance. The deep green leaves have 11 to 31 leaflets and turn a glorious golden orange to red in autumn. The unusual upright, red panicled fruits appear in summer and stay with the tree through fall, enhancing the seasonal display. Staghorn sumac grows 15 to 25 feet high and twice as wide, with an aggressively spreading habit. It works well grouped at the edge of the landscape or on a slope.
Uses: Specimen if trained to a neat tree, massed as a shrub, groundcover on a slope.
Site and care requirements: Plant in full sun to part shade and any well-drained soil. Prune to form a tree, and remove suckers to keep the plant from overtaking the area.
Recommended varieties and related species:
For a large staghorn sumac, 'Laciniata' is the best; for a dwarf, try 'Tiger Eyes'.

Chinese sumac *(R. chinensis)* features bright green, smaller leaves and large white panicled blooms that appear in late summer. It grows to 20 or 25 feet high, spreads vigorously, and tolerates dry, poor soil. It's hardy in Zones 5 to 7.

Staghorn sumac fruit

Summersweet *(Clethra alnifolia)*

Features: Fragrant late-summer flowers and yellow fall foliage
Growth rate: Slow to moderate
Zones: 4 to 9

Summersweet *(Clethra alnifolia)*

Description: Fragrant spikes of white to light pink flowers bloom in July and August, nestled against lustrous, dark green leaves. The flowers themselves are small, but they bloom in clusters that spike outward from the shrub. Butterflies are drawn to the blossoms; birds savor the small berrylike fruits that follow. While the summer color and aroma are fine assets, the colorful fall foliage is the real treat. The leaves turn a distinctive golden yellow, making this a good choice for a shrub border. Summersweet grows 3 to 8 feet tall and wide and has a densely rounded to oval form. The suckering habit of this shrub makes it useful where erosion is a problem because the suckers help keep soil in place. This shrub is adaptable to many different soil types, including wet and saline types.
Uses: Shrub border, grouping, wet areas, slope.
Site and care requirements: Best when planted in moist, acid, well-drained soil. Plant in part shade for best results, but it can also be planted in full sun to heavy shade. Mulch to keep soil consistently moist throughout the growing season. Supplemental watering may be necessary in periods of drought. The shrub tolerates wet soil after it has become well established. Feed the shrub in spring and prune only established plants after flowering to maintain their shape and remove old wood.
Recommended varieties and related species: 'Ruby Spice' has rose-colored blooms, while **'Pink Spires'** and **'Rosea'** have light pink flowers. **'Hummingbird'** and **'Compacta'** are dwarf varieties that grow 2 to 3 feet high and wide.

Sweet gum *(Liquidambar styraciflua)*

Features: Star-shape leaves and beautiful fall color
Growth rate: Moderate to fast
Zones: 5 to 9

Sweet gum *(Liquidambar styraciflua)*

Description: The highlight of this tree is its attractive, dark green, star-shaped foliage. The leaves turn shades of crimson, purple, and orange in the fall. This tree produces spiny, golf-ball-size fruit that drop in the winter, creating

Sweet gum foliage in fall

litter. Therefore take care when considering a site for this tree. The growth habit begins with the young tree forming a pyramidal shape; it becomes more rounded as the tree matures. It grows 60 to 75 feet high and 40 to 50 feet wide. Sweet gum needs plenty of room to grow and does not tolerate air pollution. It may suffer damage in the winter in the coldest areas of Zone 5. Yellow-bellied sapsuckers flock to the sweet gum tree. Chlorosis may become a problem in alkaline soils.
Uses: Specimen, shade.
Site and care requirements: Plant in full sun to partial shade and moist, well-drained soil, although it can tolerate dry soil. Plant the tree in an area with plenty of room for it to grow and in consideration of the yard litter.
Recommended varieties and related species: 'Burgundy' has deep red to purple fall foliage, as do **'Moraine'** and **'Rotundiloba',** which has no fruit. **'Variegata'** has yellow variegated leaves. For peachy-orange fall color, plant **'Festival'.**

Sweet olive *(Osmanthus fragrans)*

Features: Fragrant flowers and evergreen foliage
Growth rate: Moderate
Zones: 8 to 10

Sweet olive *(Osmanthus fragrans)*

Description: Also known as the tea olive, this plant has fragrant white flowers bloom almost year-round in warmer climates. The flowers may be small, but the scent is powerful, as the blooms grow in clusters at the end of the branches. The dark green leaves also tend to grow at the end of the branches as the plant matures, giving it a leggy—but still pleasing—appearance. This shrub grows up to 20 feet high and 6 to 8 feet wide, but it is usually kept to about 8 to 10 feet high in home landscapes with pruning. It has an upright growth habit that can be shaped into a more oval to rounded form when pruned. Plant near the house to enjoy its fragrance.
Uses: Hedge, screen, espalier, container.
Site and care requirements: Plant in sun to part shade. It is adaptable to many different types of soil. Prune at any time to shape. Pinch back tips to encourage dense growth.
Recommended varieties and related species: **'Variegatus'** has creamy white variegated leaves. The orange flowers of **'Aurantiacus'** bloom in the fall. **Holly osmanthus** *(O. heterophyllus)* also blooms in the fall and has dark green leaves that resemble holly foliage.

Sweet pepperbush (see Summersweet)
Syagrus romanzoffiana (see Palm, queen)

Sycamore *(Platanus occidentalis)*

Features: A strong rounded form and peeling bark
Growth rate: Fast
Zones: 4 to 9

Sycamore *(Platanus occidentalis)*

Description: The peeling bark is probably the best known attribute of the American sycamore. The outer gray-brown bark peels away to reveal a mixture of colors from creamy white to olive green and tan. The gnarled branches are enhanced by the colored bark, providing a striking silhouette that brings a lot of character to the winter landscape. Insignificant flowers bloom on the tree in late spring to early summer, followed by round fruit that matures in late fall and hangs on

Sycamore bark

through much of the winter. The dark green leaves are the largest leaves found on any native North American tree, often growing to 8 inches long and wide. The tree itself grows 75 to 100 feet tall and wide, with a rounded growth habit. The sycamore is a classic American tree.
Uses: Specimen, shade.
Site and care requirements: Plant in moist, well-drained soil. It will adapt to many different soil types as long as it's well drained. Plant in full sun or part shade in moist to wet sites. Sycamore is susceptible to anthracnose.

Symphoricarpos albus (see Snowberry)
Syringa **spp.** (see Lilac)

Tallow tree, Chinese *(Sapium sebiferum)*

Features: Brilliant fall foliage
Growth rate: Fast
Zones: 8 to 10

Chinese tallow tree *(Sapium sebiferum)*

Description:
Scarlet red, maroon, orange, and yellow are the colors of the tallow tree's fall foliage. The delicate diamond-shape leaves are dark green in spring and summer, and flitter gracefully in a gentle breeze, creating a moving show in the spring

Chinese tallow tree blooms

through autumn landscape. Small yellow flowers grow in long clusters at the ends of the branches, hanging around as a temptation to the honeybees from March through May. The summer fruit of the tree is brown and lobed, opening to reveal popcornlike seeds, which attract birds that then spread the seeds into surrounding areas. It grows up to 40 feet high and 20 feet wide, with a rounded growth habit.
Uses: Fast shade, screen, ornamental.
Site and care requirements: Plant in full sun to partial shade and moist, well-drained soil. It will need plenty of water when young as it is not very drought tolerant. Fruit and flower litter can be a nuisance, so consider this when choosing a site.

Tamarack *(Larix laricina)*

Features: A lovely, open pyramidal shape and golden yellow fall foliage
Growth rate: Moderate to fast
Zones: 1 to 4

Tamarack *(Larix laricina)*

Description: The blue-green needles emerge in spring, and as the tree matures, at about 15 years old, small flowers bloom. These produce reddish purple female cones and smaller yellow male cones. The needles turn golden yellow in the fall, dropping to reveal a distinctive winter silhouette. Tamarack grows 30 to 50 feet high and up to 20 feet wide, with an open, pyramidal shape. It does best in cold climates and cannot tolerate extreme heat. It is susceptible to larch casebearer infestation, which browns the needles until they drop in fall.
Uses: Specimen, grouping.
Site and care requirements: Plant in full sun to partial shade and wet, boggy soil for best results. Growth can become stunted if planted in areas with warmer summers.

Taxodium distichum (see Bald cypress)
Taxus **spp.** (see Yew)

Tea tree, New Zealand (*Leptospermum scoparium*)

Features: Evergreen shrub with aromatic foliage
Growth rate: Moderate
Zones: 9 to 10

New Zealand tea tree (*Leptospermum scoparium*)

Description: Fragrant leaves densely cover this warm-weather shrub with green year-round. Then, small white, pink, or red flowers blanket the tea tree from late winter to summer, nearly masking the light green leaves. The tree grows up to 10 feet tall and wide and has a somewhat open, vaselike growth habit but diligent pruning keeps it shapely and compact. It is drought tolerant when mature but can be susceptible to chlorosis in alkaline soil. It thrives in coastal Western regions.
Uses: Specimen, accent in a shrub border.
Site and care requirements: Plant in full sun in a site with good drainage. Do not prune all the way back to the old wood, as the mature wood does not have live buds. Prune lightly after the tree flowers.
Recommended varieties and related species: '**Snow White**' has white flowers, while '**Gaiety Girl**' blooms pink. '**Helene Strybing**' also has pink flowers, while '**Red Damask**' produces red blossoms and grows 6 to 8 feet tall.

Thuja **spp.** (see Arborvitae, American)
Tilia americana (see Linden, American)
Trachycarpus fortunei (see Palm, windmill)
Tsuga canadensis (see Hemlock, Canadian)

Tulip tree (*Liriodendron tulipifera*)

Features: Tulip-shape flowers and yellow fall foliage
Growth rate: Moderate to fast
Zones: 4 to 9

Tulip tree (*Liriodendron tulipifera*)

Description: Distinctive tulip-shape flowers bloom in late spring to early summer. The yellow-orange blossoms are often hard to see, as the tree is quite large and the blooms grow close to the top of the tree. As the tree matures, the flowers become more abundant and prominent, making a unique spectacle. The lustrous, dark green leaves surround the flowers, providing a handsome contrast. The leaves turn a bright golden yellow in the fall, when the size of the tree in fall color makes a striking feature in the landscape. The tulip tree is the tallest deciduous tree native to North America, growing from 70 to 100 feet high. The large, oval to rounded shape spreads out from 35 to 50 feet wide. The tulip tree is not drought tolerant and the soft wood is susceptible to storm damage.

Tulip tree bloom

Uses: Specimen, grouping in a large landscape.
Site and care requirements: Plant in full sun and deep, rich, moist soil. Water young trees regularly and provide supplemental water during periods of drought. Aphids may be a problem in summer, and dry conditions may make the tree prematurely lose its leaves in late summer.
Recommended varieties and related species: '**Aureomarginatum**' has yellow variegated leaves, which add another dimension of color to the landscape. '**Fastigiatum**' has a smaller and narrower growth habit—up to 50 feet tall and 10 feet wide.

Ulmus americana (see Elm, American)

Umbrella pine, Japanese *(Sciadopitys verticillata)*

Features: Unusual texture and shape
Growth rate: Slow
Zones: 5 to 8

Japanese umbrella pine *(Sciadopitys verticillata)*

Description: The whorled needles on the Japanese umbrella pine open out from the ends of the branches—resembling the spine of an umbrella—and give this tree a distinctive appeal. The young tree branches grow out horizontally from the trunk, but as the tree matures, it takes on a more open, pyramidal shape. The dense growth habit of this tree, paired with the unusual configuration of the needles, make this an interesting evergreen planting for the home landscape. It grows 20 to 30 feet high and 15 to 20 feet wide, so it can be planted in smaller yards and provides the effect of large evergreens in a more compact space. The peeling reddish brown bark is quite attractive but is most often hidden behind the dense foliage. This tree is best planted in an area where it can be seen up close to get the full effect of the extraordinary foliage.
Uses: Specimen, border, rock garden.
Site and care requirements: Plant in moist, acid, well-drained soil. It does best in areas with afternoon shade.
Recommended varieties and related species: 'Aurea' and 'Ossorio Gold' have golden yellow foliage, and 'Variegata' has yellow and green variegated needles. 'Wintergreen' has a more narrow growth habit, while 'Pendula' has a weeping habit.

Vanhoutte spirea (see Spirea, vanhoutte)
Vaccinium corymbosum (see Blueberry, highbush)

Veronica, shrubby *(Hebe* spp.)

Features: Abundant, long-lasting flowers and evergreen foliage
Growth rate: Moderate to fast
Zones: 8 to 10

Shrubby veronica *(Hebe* spp.)

Description: With more than 90 cultivars and hybrids available, the choice is almost unlimited as to flower color and size, plant size, and growth habit. In general this species of shrub has evergreen foliage and lovely flowers. The blooms are tubular shape and grouped in short racemes among the branches. They range in color from white, pink, purple, or red and bloom from early summer to late fall. They can grow as shrubs up to 6 feet high or as groundcover, reaching only up to 1 foot high. They can grow in a variety of areas, from alpine regions to coastal zones. Some cultivars are more cold hardy than others, so check with your local nursery for varieties that will do well in your particular climate.
Uses: Specimen, border, groundcover, hedge, rock garden.
Site and care requirements: Plant in full sun and well-drained soil. It adapts better to drier soil than wet soils. Prune after flowering to maintain desired shape.
Recommended varieties and related species: 'Turkish Delight' has wonderful, purple-colored foliage with small, bluish-pink flowers. It grows quickly and reaches up to 3 feet high and wide. 'Beverly Hills' is also a compact variety that grows up to 3 feet tall and wide and has dark blue to purple blooms set against deep green leaves. 'Pagei' has bluish green foliage with similarly colored flowers, and 'Sutherlandii' has white flowers set against blue-gray foliage.

Viburnum *(Viburnum* spp.)

Features: Versatile, multifaceted shrub
Growth rate: Moderate
Zones: 3 to 9, depending on the species

Viburnum *(Viburnum* spp.)

Description: There's a viburnum for almost every preference in the home landscape—gorgeous blooms, brilliant fruit, stunning fall foliage, and habits ranging from round and compact to open and expansive. Viburnums are attractive and useful, providing volume when grouped or massed, focal interest as a specimen, or food for wildlife. Viburnum is among the most useful, versatile, and adaptable plants around.

Viburnum fall foliage

Uses: Specimen, shrub border, grouping, massing.
Site and care requirements:
Plant in full sun to part shade and moist, slightly acid, well-drained soil. Keep consistently moist throughout the growing season, especially the first two or three. Feed in spring and prune as desired after flowering.
Recommended varieties and related species: Arrowwood

American cranberrybush *(V. trilobum)*

Arrowwood viburnum *(V. dentatum)*

viburnum *(V. dentatum)* is a large multistemmed shrub with a dense habit, glossy green leaves, and showy white blooms that appear in late spring. Bluish black berries follow but are soon gone because they're a favorite of birds. This adaptable shrub grows 6 to 15 feet high and wide. It is tolerant of harsh conditions in Zones 2 to 8. Arrowwood viburnum makes a good hedge or screen barrier.

Burkwood viburnum *(V. ×burkwoodii)*

Burkwood viburnum *(V. ×burkwoodii)* is an upright shrub with an open, informal way about it. It is prized for the fragrant, round, white to pink blooms that appear first on the plant in springtime. Flowers are followed by glossy green leaves that turn a smoky red in fall. It makes a good feature in a shrub border or massed as a hedge or a screen. It grows 6 to 15 feet high and wide in Zones 3 to 8.

Doublefile viburnum (*V. plicatum* var. *tomentosum* 'Shasta')

Doublefile viburnum (*V. plicatum* var. *tomentosum*) is a thing of beauty, with graceful horizontal branches; dark green foliage that turns burgundy in fall; broad, lacy white blooms in May; and bright red summer berries that are coveted by the birds. It's a fine specimen planting in a shrub border, adding color, shape, and contrast. **'Mariesii'** and **'Shasta'** feature the biggest bloom and berry clusters. They grow 8 to 10 feet tall and 10 to 12 feet wide in Zones 5 to 8.

Fragrant snowball viburnum (*V. ×carlcephalum*)

Fragrant snowball viburnum (*V. ×carlcephalum*) has a relaxed, open habit and sweet-smelling, white, ball-shape blooms that appear in April and May. It is appreciable as a single specimen or grouped in a shrub border. It grows 6 to 10 feet high and wide in Zones 6 to 9.

Korean spice viburnum (*V. carlesii*) is a densely rounded shrub, highly favored for the spicy fragrant pink to white blooms that appear in April or May. The otherwise unremarkable foliage turns a warm red in autumn. The shrub grows 4 to 8 feet high and wide in Zones 5 to 7 and works well as a foundation planting, grouped elsewhere in the landscape, or featured in a shrub border.

Korean spice viburnum (*V. carlesii*)

Linden viburnum (*V. dilatatum*) has an upright, stiff but somewhat open habit and is known for the profusion of bright red berries that ripen in September and October and often remain on the plant until winter. Deep green foliage turns a range of reds in fall, depending on the plant and conditions, from

Linden viburnum (*V. dilatatum*)

bright, true crimson to deep burgundy. Excellent for grouping, linden viburnum grows 8 to 10 feet high and 5 to 8 feet wide in Zones 5 to 8.

Tea viburnum (*V. setigerum*) also features showy red fruit, but the form of this shrub is distinctly upright, with a certain fountainlike arch to the branches. The flowers are less notable than with others, but the glossy green leaves turn a handsome maroon in fall, while the bright red berries steal the show from September until long after the leaves drop in late autumn. The shape of this shrub gives it a unique appeal in the winter landscape, and suits a spot in the back of a border, where shorter shrubs can skirt the stemmy lower half of the bare plant. It grows 10 to 12 feet tall and 8 feet wide in Zones 5 to 7.

Tea viburnum (*V. setigerum*)

Virgilia (see Yellowwood)
Vitex agnus-castus (see Chaste tree)

Walnut, black *(Juglans nigra)*

Features: Beautiful shape; handsome, dark bark; and edible nuts
Growth rate: Slow to moderate
Zones: 4 to 9

Black walnut *(Juglans nigra)*

Description: The large, rounded canopy of the black walnut provides welcome shade from the summer sun. The edible nuts are about 2 inches in diameter, starting green and maturing into the more familiar black-husked nuts. The nuts ripen and fall in late summer and autumn, much to the delight of squirrels and other wildlife as well as people. The dark, yellowish green leaves fall periodically during the season, before turning a muted yellow and dropping entirely in the autumn. The winter silhouette of the tree highlights the spreading habit of the branches and the dark, massive trunk that measures from 2 to 4 feet in diameter. The tree reaches 50 to 75 feet tall and wide at maturity and is best used in large landscapes.
Uses: Shade for the large landscape, edible nuts.
Site and care requirements: Plant in full sun and deep, moist, well-drained soil. Many plants are highly susceptible to poison from the toxic chemical juglone, which is found in the roots of the black walnut, so take care to cultivate only plants not affected nearby.

Walnut, English *(Juglans regia)*

Features: Excellent shade; soft-shelled, edible nuts
Growth rate: Slow to moderate
Zones: 6 to 9

Description: Frequently grown for commercial nut production, the English walnut has softer-shelled nuts that are beloved by both people and other creatures. A smaller tree, this walnut grows from 40 to 60 feet high and wide, making it more suitable for an average home landscape. Dark green leaves are the background to the catkins of small flowers that bloom in spring, which lead to the nuts in late summer and fall.

English walnut *(Juglans regia)*

Fall foliage is an understated yellow, but the tree's mottled bark and open, rounded habit provide winter interest after the leaves have fallen. The tree can self-pollinate, but for best nut production, plant two or more.
Uses: Shade, edible nuts.
Site and care requirements: Plant in full sun and deep, loamy, and well-drained soil. Feed in spring and prune only in summer or fall to prevent bleeding sap. Nuts can be a nuisance on the lawn unless harvested.

Washington fan palm (see Palm)
Washingtonia filifera (see Palm, California fan)
Washingtonia robusta (see Palm, Washington fan)

Weigela *(Weigela florida)*

Features: Lovely irregular, rounded shape and plentiful flowers
Growth rate: Moderate
Zones: 5 to 9

Weigela *(Weigela florida)*

Description: Late spring and early summer bring a profusion of blooms to this versatile shrub. Small and trumpet-shaped, the flowers take over the plant, sometimes obscuring the deep green foliage. The rounded, spreading growth habit makes this a great choice for shrub borders and mass planting, or as an ornamental specimen to show off the blooms. It grows 6 to 9 feet high and 9 to 12 feet wide. The branches gently arch toward the ground, giving this shrub an appealingly delicate shape.
Uses: Specimen, shrub border, mass planting.
Site and care requirements: Plant in full sun and well-drained soil. It is adaptable to different soil types as long as it's well drained. Prune after flowering to maintain shape.
Recommended varieties and related species: Red-flowered cultivars include **'Red Prince'**, **'Minuet'**, **'Newport Red'**, and **'Bristol Ruby'**. **'Pink Princess'** has lavender-pink blooms, while **'Polka'** has blooms that are pink on the outside and yellow on the inside. **'Wine and Roses'** has red foliage.

Willow, Babylon weeping *(Salix babylonica)*

Features: Long, weeping branches and leaves
Growth rate: Fast
Zones: 6 to 8

Description:
The dramatically weeping habit of this willow is its distinctive feature. The sweeping canopy flows gracefully toward the ground. The tree grows from 35 to 50 feet high with a comparable spread. The short trunk is covered with deeply grooved gray bark that is hidden by the foliage in the spring and summer but is revealed when the leaves drop, adding interest to the winter landscape. This is one of the first trees to leaf out in spring and the last to drop its leaves in fall.

Weeping Babylon willow *(Salix babylonica)*

Uses: Specimen.
Site and care requirements: Plant in full sun and moist to wet soil conditions. Avoid planting near water or sewer lines because the root system is invasive. This tree is susceptible to canker and has brittle wood.
Recommended varieties and related species: 'Crispa' has extraordinary curled leaves.

Willow, Hankow *(Salix matsudana 'Tortuosa')*

Features: Golden fall foliage and fascinating bent and twisted branches
Growth rate: Fast
Zones: 4 to 8

Description:
Curled and contorted branches are the signature feature of the corkscrew hankow willow. It grows 30 to 40 feet high and 15 to 25 feet wide in an upright, rounded shape. The green leaves turn a lovely golden yellow in the autumn, before falling to reveal the uniquely bent branches of the tree for the winter landscape. The more vigorous the growth of this tree, the more curled and contorted the branches become. This is a short-lived tree that is useful as a fast-growing specimen featuring the distinctive branches.

Hankow willow *(Salix matsudana 'Tortuosa')*

Uses: Specimen.
Site and care requirements: Plant in full sun and moist soil. It may be cut back a great deal to promote vigorous growth.
Recommended varieties and related species: 'Scarlet Curls' has reddish, curled branches and leaves.

Willow, golden weeping *(Salix alba 'Tristis')*

Features: Golden-colored bark and graceful, weeping habit
Growth rate: Fast
Zones: 3 to 8

Description:
The golden bark on the drooping branches characterizes the golden weeping willow. The long, deep green leaves turn a gleaming, golden yellow in the fall, making it resemble something out of a fairy tale. It grows 50 to 70 feet high and wide, with an upright, rounded growth habit. The drooping branches arch gracefully toward the ground, with the long, light green foliage filling out the shape.

Golden weeping willow *(Salix alba 'Tristis')*

Uses: Specimen in large landscapes.
Site and care requirements: Plant in full sun and moist soil. It can be planted along streams or other bodies of fresh water. This tree is susceptible to canker and can produce lots of yard litter from broken branches and twigs. It also has an invasive root system that can break through water and sewer lines.

Willow, pussy *(Salix discolor)*

Features: Strong, upright stems and characteristic gray-brown, fuzzy catkins
Growth rate: Fast
Zones: 4 to 8

Description:
Early spring brings the beloved fuzzy catkins of the pussy willow to the winter-weary landscape. The fluffy, male catkins are as much a touchable attraction of this shrub as they are

Pussy willow *(Salix discolor)*

appealing to look at. The upright, catkin-covered branches are often cut and used in flower arrangements, but they provide as much visual pleasure when they are enjoyed on the full shrub itself. The plant grows 15 to 25 feet high and 12 to 15 feet wide in an upright, oval shape.
Uses: Specimen, shrub border.
Site and care requirements: Plant pussy willow in full sun and moist to wet soil.
Recommended varieties and related species: 'Pendula' is a weeping variety. *S. gracilistyla* var. 'Melanostachys' has catkins that open almost black, then turn yellow as the season progresses.

Windmill palm (see Palm)

Winterberry *(Ilex verticillata)*

Features: Excellent bright red berries
Growth rate: Slow
Zones: 3 to 9

Winterberry *(Ilex verticillata)*

Description: A profusion of bright red berries appears on this shrub from late fall through winter, providing a distinctive seasonal display. Winterberry features small dark green foliage during the rest of the year and grows in a dense and twiggy oval form 6 to 10 feet tall and wide. Plant in groups for a dramatic effect or as a specimen in a small landscape.

Winterberry 'Sparkleberry'

Uses: Specimen, shrub border, group, massing.
Site and care requirements: Plant in full sun to light shade and fertile, acid, well-drained soil. It is prone to chlorosis in alkaline soil. Berries appear only on female plants, so plant one male plant for every three to five female plants for pollination and fruit.
Recommended varieties and related species: **'Jim Dandy'** is a slow-growing dwarf male that makes an excellent pollinator. **'Winter Red'** features abundant bright red fruit. **'Sparkleberry'** grows to 12 feet tall with persistent fruit.

Wintergreen *(Gaultheria procumbens)*

Features: White flowers, red berries, and fragrant foliage
Growth rate: Moderate
Zones: 3 to 10

Description: This low-growing shrub has it all—spring flowers, autumn berries, and aromatic leaves. The small white flowers bloom in spring and summer, set against the deep green, glossy leaves. The edible red berries mature in fall, attracting birds and other wildlife. The aromatic foliage releases a wintergreen fragrance when crushed, and may be chewed for a wintergreen flavor as well. It grows 4 to 6 inches tall and up to 5 feet wide in a low, spreading growth habit, which makes it a wonderfully fragrant groundcover. The dark green leaves turn reddish purple in fall, adding another dimension of color to the autumn landscape.
Uses: Shrubby groundcover.
Site and care requirements:

Wintergreen *(Gaultheria procumbens)*

Plant in shade and acid, moist, well-drained soil.
Recommended varieties and related species: **Creeping snowberry** *(G. hispidula)* grows even smaller—2 to 3 inches high—and has white berries.

Winter hazel, buttercup *(Corylopsis pauciflora)*

Features: Fragrant yellow flowers and yellow fall foliage
Growth rate: Moderate
Zones: 6 to 8
Description: Yellow characterizes the buttercup winter hazel. It features aromatic yellow flowers that bloom in spring, and dark green foliage that turns to golden yellow in the autumn landscape. Zigzag twigs fill out the frame of this shrub, which grows 4 to 6 feet high and 6 to 8 feet wide. Popular in the home landscape due to its small size and neatly spreading habit, it makes a great addition to the shrub border or in a woodland garden setting. The leaf edges may burn when it is planted in full sun or in a windy site, so give it a protected spot.
Uses: Shrub border, woodland garden, against a dark background for contrast.
Site and care requirements: Plant in part shade in moist, well-drained, acid soil in an area protected from wind. Mulch to keep the soil consistently moist throughout the growing season. Feed in spring and prune after blooming.
Recommended varieties and related species: *C. spicata,* or **spike winter hazel,** has fragrant yellow blooms that hang in small, draping clusters. It is hardy to Zone 5 and makes a good shrub border or is particularly attractive in mass plantings. It has a similar size and shape to buttercup winter hazel.

Buttercup winter hazel *(Corylopsis pauciflora)*

Witch hazel, hybrid *(Hamamelis ×intermedia)*

Features: Interesting yellow to red late-winter flowers and colorful fall foliage
Growth rate: Slow to moderate
Zones: 5 to 8

Hybrid witch hazel *(Hamamelis ×intermedia* 'Arnold Promise')

Description: Clusters of yellow to red flowers bloom in late winter to offer one of the first signs of spring. The delicate, twisted petals resemble threads of saffron hanging from the empty branches. These fragrant blooms can last up to a month

Witch hazel 'Ruby Glow'

and are resistant to cold winter weather. The rough dark green leaves emerge after the flowers and turn a yellow gold to orange-red in autumn. The plant grows 10 to 20 feet high and 8 to 10 feet wide in an upright, loosely spreading habit.
Uses: Specimen, woodland shrub.
Site and care requirements: Plant in full sun for best flowering, but it can tolerate part shade. Plant in moist, well-drained soil and provide additional water during times of drought. Prune to remove dead branches.
Recommended varieties and related species: 'Diane' is a variety that has deep red flowers, as does **'Ruby Glow'**. **'Jelena'** bears yellow to copper-colored blooms and orangey red fall foliage color. **'Arnold Promise'** has bright yellow flowers and yellow-orange fall leaf color.

Xanthorhiza simplicissima (see Yellowroot)

Yellowroot *(Xanthorhiza simplicissima)*

Features: Good shrubby groundcover
Growth rate: Fast
Zones: 3 to 9

Yellowroot *(Xanthorhiza simplicissima)*

Description: This hardy, dense, low-growing shrub is easy to grow and survives in shady areas where other plants would struggle. The bright green foliage turns a lovely orange-yellow in fall. Small star-shape purple flowers bloom in early spring before the leaves emerge. While less than showy, they provide welcome color to the early spring landscape. This low-maintenance plant grows 2 to 3 feet high and wide and tolerates heat and wind. It spreads by suckering, quickly filling in a given area.
Uses: Groundcover, slope, difficult planting area.
Site and care requirements: Plant in full sun for best results, although partial shade will work too. Plant yellowroot in moist, well-drained soil, but it tolerates wet conditions.

Yellowwood *(Cladrastis kentukea)*

Features: Fragrant, hanging white blooms and yellow fall foliage, silvery bark
Growth rate: Slow to moderate
Zones: 4 to 8

Yellowwood *(Cladrastis kentukea)*

Description: Hanging clusters of fragrant white flowers envelop the yellowwood in late spring and early summer. The pendulous, wisterialike blooms are a spectacle for their beauty and heavy fragrance. The flowers give way to small, brown seedpods that mature in the summer. The bright green foliage of summer turns yellow or golden orange in autumn. The zigzag, low-hanging branches, fine gray bark, and seedpods

Yellowwood bloom

offer interest in winter. It grows 30 to 50 feet high and 40 to 50 feet wide. This tree makes an outstanding specimen tree for the average-size yard.
Uses: Specimen, shade.
Site and care requirements: Plant in full sun to part shade and moist, well-drained soil of any kind. Water well and feed in spring for the first few seasons. Prune weak branch forks in summer when the tree is young to prevent later storm damage. Protect young trees in winter from sunscald.
Recommended varieties and related species: 'Rosea' features fragrant pink flowers along with all the other characteristics common to the yellowwood.

Yew, English *(Taxus baccata)*

Features: Evergreen that takes well to shaping
Growth rate: Slow
Zones: 6 to 7

English yew *(Taxus baccata* 'Dovastonii Aurea')

Description: Excellent for hedges the English yew can be trimmed to a particular shape, and then it usually remains at the desired height without further extreme pruning. The shiny, dark green needles generally keep their color year-round but may discolor somewhat in colder climates. Red berrylike seeds grow on female plants, adding a burst of color to the foliage. The reddish brown, flaky bark is hidden beneath the foliage but is colorful and interesting in its own right. The English yew grows from 30 to 50 feet high and 15 to 25 feet wide when left to grow in its natural state. It has a naturally broad, pyramidal shape, but it can be pruned into almost any desired shape. Most parts of this tree are toxic and can be deadly if they are ingested.
Uses: Hedge, foundation planting, screen, mass, accent.
Site and care requirements: Plant in sun to partial shade and soil with excellent drainage. Trim to shape and then to remove errant branches to maintain the shape. Site it to protect from extensive winds and to maintain foliage color.
Recommended varieties and related species: 'Adpressa Fowle' and 'Aurea' grow only up to 8 feet tall, with 'Aurea' sporting foliage that emerges yellow, eventually turning light green. 'Amersfort' grows up to 10 feet tall, with shorter, flatter foliage. 'Fastigiata', also known as Irish yew, has a columnar growth habit and grows from 15 to 30 feet high, with a spread that reaches 4 to 8 feet. 'Standishii' is a slow-growing tree with yellow foliage that reaches 6 feet high. 'Repandens' grows only 2 to 3 feet high but 12 to 15 feet wide, giving the tree a very different shape than most other yews. 'Cheshuntensis' has a narrower, columnar form that bears silver-green foliage.

Yew, Japanese *(Taxus cuspidata)*

Features: Cold-hardy shapable evergreen
Growth rate: Slow
Zones: 4 to 7
Description: The many cultivars available are much more cold hardy than English yew. The size varies, depending on variety, as does the overall shape of the tree. All have green foliage and small red fruit. Tolerant of urban conditions and drought, they do not like wet soil.
Uses: Specimen, hedge, screen, foundation and

mass planting. **Site and care requirements:** Plant the tree in full sun to partial shade and well-drained soil of almost any type. **Recommended varieties and related species:** **'Aurescens'** is a dwarf variety with needles that emerge yellow, then turn green. **'Capitata'** has a

English yew (*T. baccata* 'Fastigiata')

pyramidal shape and grows 40 to 50 feet high when left to mature. It can also be trimmed in hedges and screens. **'Densa'**

Japanese yew (*Taxus cuspidata* 'Capitata')

grows only 3 to 4 feet high and up to 8 feet wide, with very dark green needles. **'Nana'** is also small, growing up to 3 feet high and 6 feet wide. In hybrid medium-size varieties (*T. ×media*), **'Densiformis'** and **'Hicksii'** will tolerate shady locations.

Japanese yew 'Green Wave'

Yew pine *(Podocarpus macrophyllus)*

Features: Dark green foliage and an upright, columnar shape
Growth rate: Slow
Zones: 8 to 10

Yew pine (*Podocarpus macrophyllus*)

Description: This evergreen tree is valued for its columnar shape, which is ideal for screens and wherever a tall, slender planting is needed. The long, needlelike foliage is flat and deep green and particularly attractive against a lighter background. Small blue fruits grow amongst the needles, providing a lovely color contrast. These fruits are somewhat toxic and should never be eaten. Yew pine grows 30 to 40 feet high with a spread up to 10 feet wide. The tree tolerates trimming to shape it into square columns, rounder forms, or into a cone. Cuttings from this tree are often used in flower arrangements. The tree can be planted in part shade, making it a useful courtyard specimen.
Uses: Hedge, foundation planting, screen.
Site and care requirements: Plant in full sun to partial shade and fertile, well-drained soil. It can tolerate heat and salt.
Recommended varieties and related species: **'Maki'** is a smaller form, growing only up to 10 feet tall.

Zelkova, Japanese *(Zelkova serrata)*

Features: Attractive vase shape, colorful fall foliage
Growth rate: Moderate
Zones: 5 to 8

Japanese zelkova *(Zelkova serrata)*

Description: A good shade tree, the Japanese zelkova is prized for its vaselike shape that is reminiscent of an elm tree. The dark green, serrated leaves turn a yellow-orange to reddish purple in the fall, adding a distinctive color to the autumn landscape. It grows 50 to 80 feet high and 40 to 50 feet wide, with an early low-branched habit that becomes more upright in maturity. Young trees have smooth brown bark that develops into peeling gray bark when the tree matures. This adds an interesting sculptural element to the winter landscape. If you want the shape of an elm tree without the problems of an elm tree, try Japanese zelkova. It is resistant to Dutch elm disease and elm leaf beetle.

Uses: Shade.

Site and care requirements: Plant in full sun to partial shade and moist, well-drained soil. When choosing plants select young trees with good branch structure from the start. Prune to maintain shape. It is wind and drought tolerant.

Recommended varieties and related species: **'Green Vase'** is an upright, vase-shape tree with dark green leaves that turn orange-bronze in the fall. **'Village Green'** also has dark green foliage, but it turns a deeper red in the fall. **'Halka'** has a vaselike form and grows fast, which makes it a good choice for a quick shade tree.

Zenobia, dusty *(Zenobia pulverulenta)*

Features: Anise-scented flowers and gray-green foliage
Growth rate: Fast
Zones: 5 to 9

Dusty zenobia *(Zenobia pulverulenta)*

Description: White blooms with a faint scent of licorice fill the air around this shrub in late spring and early summer. The small bell-shape flowers hang in clusters from pale, green-blue stems, providing a delicate color contrast. The gray-green leaves have an almost dusty look to them—a lovely muted color that can appear almost silvery blue in the summer sun. The foliage turns a pleasing yellowish orange tinged with a purple-red in fall. It grows 3 to 6 feet high and wide, in a nicely rounded mound shape with open, arching branches.

Uses: Shrub border, massing.

Site and care requirements: Plant in full sun to light shade and moist, acid, well-drained soil. The foliage will achieve its best color when planted in full sun. It is adaptable to many different soil conditions.

Recommended varieties and related species: **'Woodlander's Blue'** grows 6 to 8 feet high and wide and boasts powder blue foliage.

Resources for plants and supplies

Bovees Nursery
1737 S.W. Coronado St.
Portland, OR 97219
866/652-3219
bovees.com

Camellia Forest Nursery
9701 Carrie Rd.
Chapel Hill, NC 27516
919/968-0504
camforest.com

Carroll Gardens, Inc.
444 E. Main Street
Westminster, MD 21157
800/638-6334
carrollgardens.com

Eastern Plant Specialties
P.O. Box 5692
Clark, NJ 07066
732/382-2508
easternplant.com

Forestfarm
990 Tetherow Rd.
Williams, OR 97544
541/846-7269
forestfarm.com

Gossler Farms Nursery
1200 Weaver Rd.
Springfield, OR 97478
541/746-3922
gosslerfarms.com

Greenwood Nursery
P.O. Box 686
McMinnville, TN 37111
800/426-0958
www.greenwoodnursery.com

Greer Gardens, Inc.
1280 Goodpasture Island Rd.
Eugene, OR 97401
800/548-0111
greergardens.com

Heirloom Roses, Inc.
24062 N.E. Riverside Dr.
St. Paul, OR 97137
503/538-1576
heirloomroses.com

High Country Gardens
2902 Rufina St.
Santa Fe, NM 87507
800/925-9387
highcountrygardens.com

Hydrangeas Plus
P.O. Box 389
Aurora, OR 97002
866/433-7896
hydrangeasplus.com

Jackson & Perkins
84 Rose Ln.
Medford, OR 97501
877/322-2300
jacksonandperkins.com

Louisiana Nursery
5853 Hwy. 182
Opelousas, LA 70570
337/948-3696
www.durionursery.com

Mellinger's
2310 W. South Range Rd.
North Lima, OH 44452-9731
800/321-7444
www.mellingers.com

Monrovia Nursery
sells wholesale only;
for retail sources in
your area,
www.monrovia.com

Morse Nursery
12300 Betz Rd.
Battle Creek, MI 49015
800/338-2105
www.morsenursery.com

Musser Forests Inc.
1880 Rte. 119 N.
Indiana, PA 15701
800/643-8319
musserforests.com

Plants of the Southwest
3095 Agua Fria Rd.
Santa Fe, NM 87507
505/438-8888
plantsofthesouthwest.com

Richard Owen Nursery, Inc.
2300 E. Lincoln St.
Bloomington, IL 61701
309/663-9553
excitinggardens.com

Siskiyou Rare Plant Nursery
2115 Talent Ave.
Talent, OR 97540
541/535-7103
siskiyourareplantnursery.com

Vintage Gardens
4130 Gravenstein Hwy. North
Sebastopol, CA 95472
707/829-2035
vintagegardens.com

Wayside Gardens
1 Garden Ln.
Hodges, SC 29695
800/213-0379
waysidegardens.com

White Flower Farm
P.O. Box 50, Rte. 63
Litchfield, CT 06759
800/503-9624
whiteflowerfarm.com

Wilkerson Mill Gardens
9595 Wilkerson Mill Rd.
Palmetto, GA 30268
770/463-2400
hydrangea.com

Woodlanders, Inc.
1128 Colleton Ave.
Aiken, SC 29801
803/648-7522
woodlanders.net

Yucca Do Nursery, Inc.
P.O. Box 907
Hempstead, TX 77445
979/826-4580
yuccado.com

Index

METRIC CONVERSIONS

U.S. UNITS TO METRIC EQUIVALENTS			METRIC EQUIVALENTS TO U.S. UNITS		
To convert from	Multiply by	To get	To convert from	Multiply by	To get
Inches	25.4	Millimeters	Millimeters	0.0394	Inches
Inches	2.54	Centimeters	Centimeters	0.3937	Inches
Feet	30.48	Centimeters	Centimeters	0.0328	Feet
Feet	0.3048	Meters	Meters	3.2808	Feet
Yards	0.9144	Meters	Meters	1.0936	Yards
Square inches	6.4516	Square centimeters	Square centimeters	0.1550	Square inches
Square feet	0.0929	Square meters	Square meters	10.764	Square feet
Square yards	0.8361	Square meters	Square meters	1.1960	Square yards
Acres	0.4047	Hectares	Hectares	2.4711	Acres
Cubic inches	16.387	Cubic centimeters	Cubic centimeters	0.0610	Cubic inches
Cubic feet	0.0283	Cubic meters	Cubic meters	35.315	Cubic feet
Cubic feet	28.316	Liters	Liters	0.0353	Cubic feet
Cubic yards	0.7646	Cubic meters	Cubic meters	1.308	Cubic yards
Cubic yards	764.55	Liters	Liters	0.0013	Cubic yards

To convert from degrees Fahrenheit (F) to degrees Celsius (C), first subtract 32, then multiply by 5/9.

To convert from degrees Celsius (C) to degrees Fahrenheit (F), multiply by 9/5, then add 32.

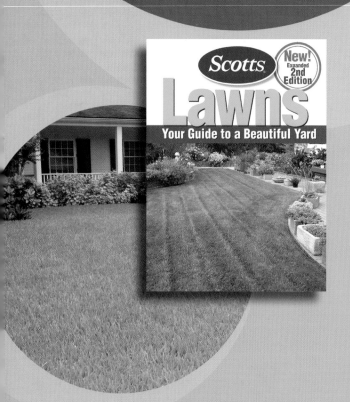